M000288978

NEXT GENERATION ADAPTATION

NEXT GENERATION
ADAPTATION
—— **Spectatorship and Process** ——

Edited by Allen H. Redmon

University Press of Mississippi
Jackson

The University Press of Mississippi is the scholarly publishing agency of
the Mississippi Institutions of Higher Learning: Alcorn State University,
Delta State University, Jackson State University, Mississippi State University,
Mississippi University for Women, Mississippi Valley State University,
University of Mississippi, and University of Southern Mississippi.

www.upress.state.ms.us

Designed by Peter D. Halverson

The University Press of Mississippi is a member
of the Association of University Presses.

Copyright © 2021 by University Press of Mississippi
All rights reserved

First printing 2021
∞

"I, Too" from THE COLLECTED POEMS OF LANGSTON HUGHES by Langston Hughes, edited by Arnold Rampersad with David
Roessel, Associate Editor, copyright © 1994 by the Estate of Langston Hughes. Used by permission of Alfred A. Knopf, an
imprint of the Knopf Doubleday Publishing Group, a division of Penguin Random House LLC. All rights reserved. // Reprinted
by permission of Harold Ober Associates.

Library of Congress Cataloging-in-Publication Data

Names: Redmon, Allen H., 1972– editor.
Title: Next generation adaptation: spectatorship and process / edited by
Allen H. Redmon.
Description: Jackson: University Press of Mississippi, 2021. | Includes
bibliographical references and index.
Identifiers: LCCN 2020051282 (print) | LCCN 2020051283 (ebook) | ISBN
978-1-4968-3260-3 (hardback) | ISBN 978-1-4968-3261-0 (trade paperback) | ISBN
978-1-4968-3262-7 (epub) | ISBN 978-1-4968-3259-7 (epub) | ISBN 978-1-4968-3263-4
(pdf) | ISBN 978-1-4968-3264-1 (pdf)
Subjects: LCSH: Film adaptations. | Cultural fusion in popular culture. |
Stereotypes (Social psychology) in motion pictures.
Classification: LCC PN1997.85 .N49 2021 (print) | LCC PN1997.85 (ebook) |
DDC 791.43/6--dc23
LC record available at https://lccn.loc.gov/2020051282
LC ebook record available at https://lccn.loc.gov/2020051283

British Library Cataloging-in-Publication Data available

CONTENTS

INTRODUCTION

Introducing the Next Generation of Adaptation

ALLEN H. REDMON

INVARIABLY, THE STUDENTS IN MY ADAPTATION CLASSES REACH A POINT, USUALLY AFTER WE have read Robert Stam's (2005) discussion of the move within adaptation studies from matters of fidelity to an interest in intertextuality, where they decide "everything is an adaptation." I am always delighted when we reach this point. The most rewarding benefits of seeing a text as an adaptation emerge just after one realizes that most every text can be seen as an adaption of something. Such awareness disrupts the idea of a closed set of texts where one text is taken to be an original, some other text is understood as an off-spring of that source, and the discussion of either relies on the presence of the other. An initial pairing of texts provides plenty of rewards, to be sure. Those who know both texts can experience the "repetition without replication" that Linda Hutcheon (2013) marks as one of the primary appeals of experiencing a text as an adaptation (7). Still, as Hutcheon notes, every retelling can "create a manifestly different interpretation," one that reaches toward new texts and contexts (8). The adaptor's supposed dependence on the original necessarily weakens each time a text can be shown to be reaching toward something other than the admitted source. Those experiencing the adaptation as a more broadly conceived adaptation have the opportunity to explore these other texts and contexts. One sees an example of this opportunity in Kenneth Branagh's *Henry V* (1989). Branagh clearly intends to present Shakespeare's play, but he does so through sustained allusions to George Lucas's (1977) *Star Wars*. Deborah Cartmell (2000) explains Branagh's reliance on Lucas's film on two levels: "Henry begins the film as Darth Vader and is gradually transformed into Luke Skywalker [. . .] and, like *Star Wars*, this nationalistic 'authentic' Shakespeare belongs to a world of make-believe" (108). Branagh's characters and the world they inhabit rely both on an admitted relationship to Shakespeare's play and on an unannounced relationship to the *Star Wars* universe. Cartmell's comment does more than account for an unexpected echo or presence in Branagh's film; it commemorates the ways in which even seemingly straightforward adaptations can be found to be adapting more than one text. Such a possibility changes what it means to read a text as an adaptation. The closed circuit between a source and an original gives way to the presence of a text that can be shown to be adapting any number of texts. An adaptation becomes complex rather than simple, extending toward whatever texts or contexts, questions and interests audiences recognize within its expression.

The role of the audience, scholars included, obviously changes when confronted by a complex rather than a simple adaptation. The audience no longer simply experiences the complex adaptation; rather, it helps produce it, which is to say that it participates in the adaptation's ongoing creation. Following Thomas Leitch (2006), who uses Mikhail Bakhtin's (1981) idea of the readerly and writerly texts to explain the role the audience can play in the ongoing creation of an adaptation, "texts remain alive only to the extent that they can be rewritten and that to experience a text in all its power requires each reader to rewrite it" (12–13). Leitch argues that cinematic adaptations, especially "pro-creational adaptations," to use, as Leitch does, Lindiwe Dovey's (2002) terminology, serve as an example of writerly texts "by incessantly raising rather than settling questions of motive, agency, and interpretation" (19). In this way, pro-creational cinematic adaptations leave themselves open to the audience, to multifaceted and multidirectional readings. These complex adaptations invite audiences to rewrite them, to complete their expression, and to do so in whatever way they are prepared to do so. Stated another way, complex adaptations encourage adaptations to enter a process of adaptation rather than to accept one specific expression. The adaptation comes to life. Those who experience it no longer need to uncover anything. They can explore everything, reaching specific conclusions while always knowing that some other exploration will produce some other conclusion. Every reading, individual interpretation, can always be rewritten. Every experience can lead to some new experience. Such is the promise of the complex adaptation.

One could argue that the complex adaptation solicits acts of reading or, in the case of cinematic texts, spectatorship, that keep a text alive by exploring aspects of the text that are at once complex, nuanced, and temporary. Leitch (2017) addresses this last quality in the conclusion to *The Oxford Handbook of Adaptation Studies*, which is, ironically, titled "Against Conclusions." Leitch calls for adaptation studies to move toward what he labels "petit theory," which "operates not as a series of dogmas or organizing principles, still less as a set of solutions to consensual problems, but as a series of working hypotheses" (703). Petit theory, Leitch continues, focuses on questions "not as a necessary means toward the end of generating answers, but as a desirable end in themselves" (704). The purpose of the questions we ask, Leitch explains, should be to articulate better questions. From this view, the real worth of a text, and any response to a text for that matter, lives more in the questions that a text or a response generates than in its ability to capture some permanent, discoverable truth. Neither complex adaptations nor complex spectatorship mean to resolve the uncertainties of the moment they capture. These acts simply mark some moment as *having been*. This having been will give way to other ways of being should the text remain alive, which is to say should the text continue to be written. The next adaptation of a familiar text, or a subsequent moment of reception or scholarship, will mark some other *having been*. The process of adaptation will continue to isolate these moments, and to do so with a looseness that ensures that every moment can always be reopened, reexperienced, and reset.

The contributors in this volume embrace the qualities of Leitch's petit theory. They write not to uncover some truth about their text but to see the questions their adaptation or set of adaptations helps one articulate. Admittedly, the authors herein are particularly interested in the political and ethical questions their texts raise. Each writer writes the chapter they do to demonstrate the way in which the process of adaptation isolates and produces the political and ethical questions a particular moment wants to ask. Julie Sanders (2016) justifies such a belief when she writes that "it has become abundantly clear in the discussion of adaptation and appropriation that these processes are frequently, if not inevitably, political acts [especially when] the appropriation extends beyond fragmentary allusion to a more sustained reworking and revision" (123). As Sanders explain, "revisionary texts or reworkings [do not need to] merely accept or cite their precursor texts without question or debate"; rather, such texts will often "respond to, and [. . .] write back to, an informing original from a new and revised perspective" (126). Sanders offers Charlotte Brontë's (1847) *Jane Eyre* as an example. She contends that no twenty-first-century reader can read Brontë's story the same way after encountering the insights of Sandra Gilbert and Susan Gubar's (1979) *The Madwoman in the Attic* or Jean Rhys's (1969) *Wide Sargasso Sea*. These intermedial works alter the earlier expression in specific ways. They encourage those who experience Brontë's text to do so with new political and ethical questions in mind. They provide readers a chance to encounter Brontë's text anew. This is what good scholarship and intriguing adaptations do: they offer readers and spectators the chance to reexperience a text. For the authors in this anthology, this opportunity means to continue the process of adaptation that the adaptations they explore initiated, and to do so with a keen interest in the political and ethical questions their exploration emboldens.

Adaptation scholars involved in investigating the process of adaptation an intertextually minded examination animates have been documenting the political and ethical interests of adaptations throughout this century. Both matters inform, for instance, Darlene J. Sadlier's (2000) discussion of *How Tasty Was My Little Frenchman* (*Como era gostoso o meu francês*, 1971). Sadlier writes that "the study of adaptation becomes more interesting when it takes into account historical, cultural, and political concerns" (190). She offers the films of Nelson Pereira dos Santos, whom she deems "one of Brazil's most admired directors," as an example: "All of his films have liberal or left-wing sources and are largely proletarian in theme [. . . ;] his adaptations can be seen [. . .] as an indirect way of speaking about contemporary social problems" (190). Sadlier presents *How Tasty Was My Little Frenchman* as Pereira dos Santos's "most interesting" example (191). As Sadlier recounts, Pereira dos Santos bases the film on the chronicles of a sixteenth-century German explorer, Hans Staden, who details his capture by an indigenous group. Pereira dos Santos combines this historical narrative with the then-contemporary newspaper coverage "of the plight of an indigenous community in the northeast with which [Pereira dos Santos] had had contact when making *Vidas Secas* [Barren Lives, 1963]" (191). Sadlier argues that Pereira dos Santos juxtaposes these two realities, and a series of other historical narratives, to "treat a whole tradition of colonial discourse and ethnographic representation as if it were present-day news [. . . ,] offering a political satire about global capitalism and the Brazilian economic 'miracle' of the 1960s and 1970s" (192). The mixture results in a film that pushes audiences to consider again the historical narratives and contemporary debates that shape them.

Such a push fits the interest Bazin brings to cinema when writing about film in the middle part of the nineteenth century. In his essay "In Defense of Mixed Cinema" (1952/1967), an essay that is as much about a very broad notion of cinematic adaptation as it is a defense of the cinema, Bazin boasts that "the first filmmakers effectively extracted what was of use to them [. . . as they . . .] gave new life to the conditions out of which came an authentic and great popular art" (57–58). Bazin offers as one example the resurgence of sixteenth-century dramatic farce in the form of the Mack Sennett comedies produced "between 1910 and 1914 at the Pathé and Gaumont Studios" (58). The comedic form virtually vanishes before Sennett brings it to the screen. When it reappears, it does so with a slightly different expression. Bazin argues that a similar kind of revitalization occurs when a filmmaker adapts a novel, and even when the adaptor brings the elements the novel provides onto the screen with the utmost care. Even a well-curated film provides audiences a "new way of seeing things [. . .] seeing things in close-up or by way of story-telling forms such as montage," which should "refurbish" those elements in the novel (61). For Bazin, cinema revitalizes literary forms brought to the screen. Bazin also finds the process of renovation he describes working beyond the literary sources to include the reality within that text and the resulting film. Bazin explains that while lens-based photographic cinema does adopt "a mode of expression" that depends on "realistic representation," the lens has "a thousand ways of acting on the appearance [of that world] so as to eliminate any equivocation and to make of [its] sign one and only one inner reality" (62). Every inner reality recognized on the screen will differ from the external reality found before the camera. Each representation will go beyond merely re-presenting reality; each act will showcase some specific, temporary picture of that reality. The task of the scholar, then, is to capture that reality in the way the filmmaker has captured a text.

Adaptation scholars have an especially clear opportunity to capture the political and ethical reality of the adaptations they discuss. An adaptation will always exist in at least two places, in the current moment in which it finds itself, and in the moment where the admitted source once existed. This dual existence reveals the arbitrary nature of the cultural and historical influences associated with a text. No detail can be deemed intrinsic. Every representation extends from some choice. For this reason, one can refer to adaptations as Guerric DeBona (2010) refers to them, as "cultural text[s]" capable of performing a "politics of redeployment," a concept openly drawn from Bazin's notion of "mixed cinema" (2). DeBona's approach shifts focus from a texts-for-text's-sake to a study of how a text is put to use and what political or ethical questions such uses raise. In some cases the political or ethical questions center on whether or not an adaptation should be celebrated. Jennifer Jeffers's *Britain Colonized: Hollywood's Appropriation of British Literature* (2006) pursues this line of thought. Jeffers contends that some uses of a text might more rightly be labeled as misuses, which is to say abuses of a text. Jeffers cautions that adaptations most generally and Hollywood's use of British literary texts more specifically always promote a particular point of view, a certain ideology. An American filmmaker like Stephen Frears, for instance, turns a British novel like Nick Hornby's *High Fidelity* (1995) into an American film with the same name (2000). The main character from the novel becomes for the film, "a male thirty-something record store owner in the throes of a life crisis" (14). Jeffers argues that the presumably minor shift reimagines and reperforms the original story in significant ways. Jeffers reasons that the change "radically reiterates the literary text," which results in a kind of "deterritorialization" (5). The text begins to serve some universal rather than local observation.

At the same time, Jeffers continues, the story on screen satiates a desire to repeat that which is already known by making the original story into "a recognizable [Hollywood] product" (5). The story that once played according to one local tradition begins to conform to some other convention. This second turn reterritorializes the artificially deterritorialized story. The Hollywood machine takes a story from one place and uses it to buttress the ideologies of its place. Jeffers presents Neil LaBute's *Possession* (2002), an adaptation of A. S. Byatt's novel *Possession: A Romance* (1990), as an example of this second turn. The film sets Byatt's novel within the attributes of the western genre. Jeffers insists that the placement "radically deterritorializes [. . .] the text into a different context of meaning [. . . while also . . .] reterritorializing the film into a *recognizable* and predictable product for American audiences" (106). Following Jeffers, LaBute's film ultimately appropriates a British text so that a particular view of "England" emerges that can reassert the cultural ideals contained in the western genre as it is widely circulated and recognized by Hollywood. The process Jeffers describes suggests an active denial of the original, so that the new product replaces the old one. In this case the American product appropriates the British one. Such a move stages "the politics of redeployment" DeBona mentions, and the kinds of cultural negotiations an adapted text can perform.

For Jeffers, the films from Frears and LaBute offer a (re)telling that is blatantly political and that raises a series of ethical questions. The above parenthetical satisfies more than a desire to be economical. It plays with the criticism Jeffers levels in an effort to create some space for something more than Jeffers admits, at least explicitly. In an important sense, a retelling is also always a telling, which is also always already a tell. At the root of every retelling, in other words, is a clue about the people, places, and political and ethical concerns that produce it. In some cases, especially those that follow the tradition of translation from one medium to another that George Bluestone (1957) establishes, a retelling means to look like a telling. It tries to preserve the original. When working in the tradition of performance the auteur theorists advocate, a retelling means to re-tell, which is to say to tell again, to tell anew, to refurbish, to return to Bazin's word. Such an act provides audiences an opportunity to see some of the social, cultural, or political concerns at play in the text. These concerns were, of course, always present in a text. The retelling just brings them to some surface that might not have otherwise existed.

This idea of a new surface is especially useful to anyone wanting to adopt Leitch's petit theory. Michael Ryan and Douglas Kellner (1988) show one of the reasons why in their monograph *Camera Politica: The Politics and Ideology of Contemporary Hollywood Film*. The authors insist that every film becomes political the moment the filmmaker adopts their "concrete representational strategies" (2). They are made political again when audience members bring those strategies to the political discussions of their epoch. The contributors in this volume agree, and even go one step further, claiming that adaptations are even more specifically political, even more attuned to particular ethical concerns, and for all of the reasons above described. An adaptation should have an easier time showing its stitching, those beliefs, those ideologies that hold together the narrative, the characters, the actions, and the attitudes on display. Every adaptation is, after all, always already a ready-made. The text has been previously shaped and formed in preferential ways. An adaptation reveals this quality, especially when it alters some detail. To return to the discussion of *High Fidelity*, there is no inherent reason why Rob, the main character of Hornby's novel and Frears's film, exists in London or Chicago. Rob could be in London, Chicago, or in any other city in the world. Frears's adaptation, which moves Rob from one city to another, reminds spectators of his film and readers of Hornby's story of this point. Rob's place is, in some ways, arbitrary. Still, the choice of locale can raise interesting questions. The site of a story can, after all, extend into political and even ethical considerations. An adaptation, to return to the earlier analogy, provides audiences an opportunity to pull the threading from the textual quilt a text forms and to accept, adjust, or dismiss the surrounding squares that once seemed so neatly to fit together. The adaptation serves as a site of negotiation rather than simply a return to some familiar place. It invites spectators to participate in the ongoing negotiation its seemingly new surface permits.

Astrid van Weyenberg (2013) explores this opportunity in her intriguing monograph *The Politics of Adaptation: Contemporary African Drama and Greek Tragedy*. Van Weyenberg examines six dramatic texts written in South Africa and Nigeria over the last quarter of the twentieth century and the first part of the twenty-first century. Each adapts classical Greek tragedies. Her study contends that these playwrights turn to the ancient texts they do to "engage with and perform politics" (xii). For van Weyenberg, their engagement occurs as they use ancient texts as a way to negotiate the political realities of their contemporary moment. Their performance emerges to the extent that audiences keep the contemporary text in relationship with the adapted text and its tradition. Van Weyenberg argues that the contemporary adaptations in her study never mean to erase the classical text in the way Jeffers sees Hollywood erasing the British texts it appropriates; instead, the South African and Nigerian writers attempt to "undermine eurocentric claims of ownership and authority [. . .] by performing, through adaptation, a cultural politics directed at the Europe or West that has traditionally considered Greece as its property" (xii). Such a performance depends on the adapted text and the adaptation remaining in a reciprocal relationship. Only through reciprocity can the "plurality of traditions [that] includes the rewriting of existing traditions and the invention of new ones" that van Weyenberg champions, through the ideas of Lorna Hardwick (2007), truly emerge (xix).

The kind of interchange van Weyenberg imagines depends on active readers and spectators who experience an adaptation as an adaptation. Van Weyenberg admits as much when she explains the concept of performative she wants to advance: "reading a text is, much like viewing a play, a performative practice that takes place in the present *act* of reading" (xiii, emphasis in original). The idea is that every conclusion is temporary. The meaning that extends from any one way of seeing exists in the moment it is realized, and maybe only in that moment. Such a view might remain in a later moment, but it need not do so. Either way, a reading is always a progressive act that occurs in a specific time and space, within a particular history and geography. When any of these coordinates change, so too might the meaning. All of this brings one back to the mode of engagement van Weyenberg encourages, a mode of engagement Linda Hutcheon describes when she writes about how an adaptation "is fitted to a given environment" (31). Hutcheon's point is that "stories [like other biological processes] also evolve by adaptation and are not immutable over time [. . . ;] stories adapt just as they are adapted [. . . ; they . . .] get retold in different ways in new material and cultural environments" (31–32). As stories shift, new qualities appear both in the exchange between texts the process of adaptation initiates and in the environments that support those texts. In the words of Pascal Niklas and Oliver Lindner (2012), a "new cultural capital" arises, one that isolates a new series of ethical and political assumptions and that raises a new set of questions (6). The authors in this anthology strive to illustrate this point by isolating the assumptions their texts carry and addressing the questions they raise, albeit always in a speculative rather than conclusive manner.

In this way the authors present their chapters as but "the next generation" of the adaptation they consider. The basis for this generational understanding of adaptation actually extends from the words of Niklas and Lindner, on the one hand, and van Weyenberg, on the other. One finds this idea in Niklas and Lindner's phrase "new cultural capital," which is employed to mark the differences between two distinct moments of cultural capital. The idea of a new cultural capital conceals, at least momentarily, the commonalities that assuredly remain between the two instances of cultural capital being juxtaposed. Every new cultural capital is at the same time borrowing something from the old. Certain commonalities remain even if the pairing of new and old means to highlight the differences between the two. It is something like what happens when children begin to focus on what distinguishes them from a parent. More times than not, more commonalities remain than differences. The emphasis on the differences arises so that the new generation can see itself as new even though there is always the chance to arrange the generations along one family line. One sees the same kind of arbitrary parsing of groups of people each time a generation is broken into distinct epochs. The differences between Baby Boomers, Gen Xers, Gen Yers, Millennials, and the like might not overwhelm the similarities these groups share in specific places, but they are drawn to highlight differences, so that is what they do. Given enough time, some other organizing strategy will emerge, one that might very well bring these now distinct generations under one heading. This is what van Weyenberg sees happening in South Africa and Nigeria. The playwrights she discusses use Greek tragedy to erase differences between perceived African and non-African realities rather than to insist on them. The adaptors van Weyenberg introduces adapt what they do to mark certain ancient writers as part of their family tree. They assert the privilege one enjoys having these foundational authors as their ancestors. They do so to reclaim some authority and ethical imperative in their political moment. They mark themselves as the next generation in the extended record of generations found to be adapting their story to the story of human existence.

There is, perhaps, a sense in which every adaptation performs this same work. An adaptation marks the adaptor's place in a particular moment, as well as some place on the string of such moments that holds all moments on it. Adaptation scholarship can do the same thing. Scholarship is, at least when stripped of dogma and demagogy, to echo Leitch, a kind of ongoing construction of a text, a kind of adaptation. The chapters in this anthology are offered in this spirit. Each chapter begins with the kind of traditional pairing of some source text and some adaptation in the conventional sense of such things. For some, the source will be a specific literary period or historical moment. For others, it will be a particular novel, epic tradition, or literary perspective. For still others, the source will be more terministic. In every case, these initial sources give way to broader concerns. Each source becomes a first influence, or an early influence, rather than the only influence. Contributors treat their adapted work as complex adaptations that go beyond any strict pairing of adapted text and source text. They actively participate in the ongoing construction of the texts they present, keenly aware of the political or ethical questions their approach isolates. Above all, each author writes knowing that they are exploring some aspect of a text this moment, this generation, is especially able to see, and to see in a specific way. They write knowing that still other experiences of this text also await. Some next generation will follow our contributors if the texts they consider remain alive, and that generation will reopen, reexperience, and rewrite that text just as our contributors have done here.

The chapters that follow can be read on their own or in conversation with one another. Each chapter means to stand on its own, but, interestingly, readers will see some shared concerns across the chapters. While never writing to each other, the individual contributors do sustain a discussion of agency, gender, place, ethnicity, history, and confession. Two factors might account for these shared interests. First, despite rather obvious demographic differences, each contributor does exist within a broadly conceived political and ethical moment. The lines that would mark any differences between the contributors may not be as pronounced as the shared concerns that brought them together. At the same time, the authors did agree to write according to a kind of poetics of adaptation that means to set the process of adaptation above the product. The first two chapters present this poetics, although neither was assigned this task. Jack Ryan begins the collection with a chapter on poetry, place, and cinematic form in Jim Jarmusch's *Paterson* (2016). As Ryan notes, Jarmusch's film is not a strict adaptation of the 1946 William Carlos Williams epic poem by the same name. One might more appropriately bill it as a cinematic homage to observational poetry, as Ryan does. Jarmusch does, after all, as Ryan notes, shape his films around the tenets of such poetry. Jarmusch structures the film around what is a taken to be a typical workweek of its hero, Paterson (Adam Driver). That hero builds a deep sense of place into the poems he writes. Ryan offers that these qualities form the center of Jarmusch's adaptation, which finds a way to allow a daily routine to protect the creative consciousness from the crush of modernity. The film ultimately favors the process of poetry over the content of any singular poem, a point Ryan claims Jarmusch returns to each time Paterson meets another poet. The cumulative effect of these encounters, encapsulated in the final encounter with the Japanese poet, who inspires Paterson to start writing again, insists that all poetry requires is observation and practice. The student of life can create poetry by observing and making connections that would otherwise appear meaningless. Ryan's chapter is an excellent way to begin the anthology, in part because this willingness to make connections imbues each of the chapters that follow.

The second chapter, which finds Emine Akkülah Doğan investigating a series of filmic adaptations of Oscar Wilde's *The Picture of Dorian Gray* (1890), also reveals the attitude of carnival at play exhibited throughout the anthology. Akkülah Doğan's interest is in how the cinematic adaptations of Wilde's work perform the task assigned the picture in Wilde's story. Akkülah Doğan settles on this view of the picture after breaking each of the adaptations she discusses from the normal view brought to adaptations of Wilde's book. Rather than fixating on perceived homosexuality in Wilde's novel, Akkülah Doğan sees the adaptations that follow as instances of Mikhail Bakhtin's idea of the carnivalesque. Akkülah Doğan justifies this shift through a sustained interest in the use of The Picture, which she assigns an unmistakable agency, across three adaptations: Albert Lewin's *The Picture of Dorian Gray* (1945), Oliver Parker's *Dorian Gray* (2009), and John Logan's *Penny Dreadful* (2014–16). Akkülah Doğan maintains that each of these adaptations treats The Picture as an agentic force that means to subvert cultural authority and challenge self-denying ethical positions that might otherwise be privileged in the worlds brought to the screen. In this way Akkülah Doğan finds each of these adaptations to use The Picture as a means to degrade the human characters, in the Bakhtinian sense, so that some new birth to some higher ethic can occur. This chapter makes a great contribution in its own right, but it also captures some part of the spirit motivating each of the chapters.

Each of the next three chapters reconsiders some earlier established perception to reveal their adaptations as a site of negotiation over important ethical or political questions. Together, the three chapters offer an extended discussion of gender. Larry T. Shillock's chapter, "Into the Future from *Out of the Past*," for instance, brings attention to the ways mid-twentieth-century film forms limit the role of place for women. Shillock tests standard assessments of the femme fatale before detailing the ways in which noir stories change when approached through the women. Following Shillock's argument, these women often occupy the center of the stories, anyway. Shillock uses one of the quintessential noir narratives, *Out of the Past* (1947), and its heroine, Kathie Moffat (Jane Greer), to support his proposal. Shillock describes the adjustments Jacques Tourneur makes to Daniel Mainwaring's novel *Build My Gallows High* (1946) to show the care taken to ensure that Moffat appears as something other than a dame, a moll, or an object of male affection. Shillock maintains that Tourneur's Moffat proves herself no less than an equal to the men she encounters. By the end of the film, she is their better if only because she recognizes the abiding constraints her world places on her as a woman. Moffat's understanding, Shillock argues, pushes her toward a higher, more forgiving ethic than the one the noir world assigns her.

Noelle Hedgcock offers a similar discussion of the cultural attitudes that entangle women in her chapter, "'Acting Victorian': Marketing Stars and Reimagining the Victorian in Classical Hollywood." Hedgcock examines the tension the studios create when they market the stars of their prestige pictures—think Bette Davis, Joan Crawford, Evelyn Venable, and Joan Fontaine—as "authentically Victorian" even as the women themselves are demonstrating characteristics of an emerging class of modern women. Hedgcock shows how the studio's marketing strategies result in a strain between ideologies that underscores the mediated nature of the "New Woman" in mid-twentieth-century Hollywood and the United States. Images of the New Woman could circulate, but only when set in very specific conditions. Following Hedgcock's insightful analysis, the studios would allow the New Woman to appear as a rich young woman in an urban setting, for instance, but not in more customary small-town, middle-class, conservative America. In this way, Hedgcock suggests, the studios were willing to appeal to the aspirations and anxieties of womanhood found in their audiences, but only if they also left space for their stars to fit the less sophisticated notions of womanhood. Hedgcock ultimately concludes that the contest between identities actually reveals how the mid-twentieth-century concept of the New Woman competes with residual gender constructs given to more conservative, even Victorian, notions of the "true woman."

Rashmila Maiti finds a similar contest between residual and emerging constructs of womanhood and femininity in her chapter, "Ruthless Ram and Sexual Sita." Maiti focuses on three recent adaptations of India's *Ramayana* to show how each update provides Sita freedoms more normally denied her in retellings of this epic. Maiti moves through *Raavan* (2010), *Main Hoon Na* (2004), and *Sita Sings the Blues* (2008) to show that those shaping these films reject standard perceptions not only of Sita but of her husband, Ram, and the villain of the story, Raavan. Each shift provides Sita with more mobility. Raavan is rarely as villainous. Ram is more approachable. Sita is far less constrained. Maiti proposes that these updates mirror contemporary shifts in more-progressive notions of gender in India, while also establishing a more nuanced understanding of good and evil. Taken together, Maiti estimates, these two updates cooperate to turn traditional exemplars of virtue or vice into sites of contemporary debate about the ethical justifications of the choices the characters make. These shifts return the *Ramayana* to contemporary audiences, Maiti reasons, as a site of negotiation over a range of issues confronting contemporary women.

The four chapters that follow turn the discussion from issues of gender to matters of ethnicity and, more generally, place. Zoe Bursztajn-Illingworth creates a contest of place and tradition through her close interpretation of the opening montage of Spike Lee's *He's Got Game* (1998). Bursztajn-Illingworth treats Lee's montage as an example and critique of the Whitmanic montage tradition Sergei Eisenstein describes. Bursztajn-Illingworth reaches this perspective after tracing the line of criticism against Whitman's view of America to consider the ways that poem might silence rather than celebrate Black experience. Bursztajn-Illingworth turns to the response Langston Hughes's poem "I, Too" gives to Whitman, a poem that is as much a protest as it is a declaration. Bursztajn-Illingworth regards Hughes's poem as a precursor to Lee's opening montage. She relates Lee's recurring use of direct-facing photographs of Black subjects that constitute something of a formal portrait to Hughes's moves. Bursztajn-Illingworth's discussion illustrates the ways in which Lee gives voice to those in America who may not otherwise have one. Bursztajn-Illingworth ultimately shows how Lee sets his portraits against an American landscape that refuses to give way to one experience. The land belongs to each of those Lee places in the center of his frame. In this way Bursztajn-Illingworth sees Lee providing his audiences a sense of Black presence in America, even if that presence stands outside the main narrative of the larger film.

Caroline Eades casts Jean-Jacques Annaud's *Wolf Totem* (2015) as a similar site of cultural negotiation. Eades focuses on Annaud's adaptational dialogue with Jiang Rong's (2004) novel by the same name to show the ways in which the famed director turns a deeply local story into a transnational film. Eades contends that Annaud achieves a more general perspective than a local story could by refusing to make any claims to historical accuracy or documentary objectivity. Eades demonstrates the ways that this transformation matches Annaud's larger oeuvre, which often permits his audience to follow his lead in confronting each reality from an independent, informed, and critical position. Eades argues that Annaud sets aside his own political agenda to celebrate cinema's independence from any political or material constraint. The story Annaud tells subsumes every element in the film. The result, Eades offers, is an experience that dedicates itself to exposing the shortcomings of any representation of an unknown culture that depends on stereotypes and prejudice.

Geoffrey Wilson provides an additional example of the shortcomings of representational strategies in his chapter, "Adaptation, Authenticity, and

Ethics in Carl Davis's score to *The Thief of Bagdad*." Wilson notes Davis's self-proclaimed practice of reviving the score the films might have had in their original release, but he faults the leading composer in the silent film revival movement for failing to realize his aim. Wilson cautions that a number of contemporary practices mark Davis's scores, including his use of leitmotivs to denote characters, a willingness to allow those leitmotivs to shape the overall narrative, and his readiness to adopt a unified musical style for the film. Each of these practices belongs to a more contemporary period of film scoring. Wilson contends that one of the only aspects of silent scoring Davis keeps is a willingness to create musical cues that present non-Western characters and settings in essentialist if not outright racist ways. Wilson concludes that Davis's claim to authenticity is misleading. While Davis's scores may make a historical film more accessible to a modern audience, they do so by promoting reductive stereotypical constructs.

Richard Vela provides a third study of the dangers associated with reductive projections of ethnic stereotypes in "*Sicarios* and the Latin American Assassin on Film." Vela discusses a range of *sicario* films before comparing the focus of that tradition to Taylor Sheridan's two recent screenplays, *Sicario* (2015) and *Sicario: Day of the Soldado* (2018). Vela reveals how carefully Sheridan articulates the ethical codes at play in the "land of wolves," the intellectual and emotional space that Alejandro (Benicio del Toro) most especially occupies, and the physical space the border tolerates. Vela explores the ethical questions Sheridan sets in this space to show that his films tempt audiences to justify even the worst atrocities if the benefit appears to warrant it. Vela contrasts this message to the more restrained code of the *sicario* as it is realized in Latin traditions. The difference raises a number of issues that Vela navigates by giving special attention to Sheridan's depictions of border violence, his profiles of the cartels and the American government, and his attention to the young people implicated in the dramas these contests stage on both sides of the border. In the end, Vela creates space to challenge the ideologies supported by reductive views of those placed along geographic, political, and ethical borders.

The last two chapters of this anthology indirectly consider many of the issues discussed before them while turning their attention to issues of representation as they relate to history, both collective and more personal. Tina Olsin Lent investigates representations of the women in "Media Portrayals of the Woman Suffrage Movement." Lent contrasts four relatively recent filmic representations of this movement: Ruth Pollak's 1995 episode of PBS's *American Experience, One Woman, One Vote*; Ken Burns's 1999 documentary, *Not for Ourselves Alone: The Story of Elizabeth Cady Stanton and Susan B.*

Anthony; Katja von Garnier's 2004 HBO feature, *Iron Jawed Angels*; and Sarah Gavron's 2015 feature film, *Suffragette*. Lent relates the new pattern of films to a number of cultural shifts that arise by the mid-1990s. Women assume more prominent positions within the film industry. Stories centered on women begin to find their way into films circulated in wide release. Women also become more active in politics. And notable anniversaries of various woman suffrage movements around the world begin to occur. Lent pays particular attention to the ways in which the histories found in the above four films bend to fit the narrative and political priorities surrounding each production. Lent's final point is that, somewhat disappointingly, each of these projects seems more interested in entertaining a public than in inspiring political activism. The histories they represent are thereby left in the past.

Marc DiPaolo concludes this anthology with a consideration of the ways in which political moments influence how audiences adapt their views of filmmakers and genre film. Specifically, DiPaolo examines through the #MeToo movement of 2017 two films from two different directors, John Landis and his 2005 episode for the *Masters of Horror* anthology television show "Deer Woman," and Quentin Tarantino and his 2007 film *Death Proof*. DiPaolo's study casts both directors as monsters, at once attractive and repelling, especially so after supervising well-documented on-set tragedies. Landis supervised a helicopter stunt that killed Vic Morrow and two child actors. Tarantino oversaw a car accident that severely injured Uma Thurman while filming *Kill Bill*. DiPaolo wonders if Landis's "Deer Woman" and Tarantino's *Death Proof* do not serve as attempted confessions or even veiled apologies for these atrocities. If they do, he further wonders if filmic confessions and apologies, or any such instances of contrition, are worth the film they are set on. DiPaolo's tentative answer is that it depends on what the audience does with each confession. The cinematic adaptations of atrocities might matter only when the audience uses them as an opportunity to disavow themselves from deplorable behavior.

Taken together, the chapters in this anthology might very well reach a similar conclusion. An adaptation experienced as an adaptation foregrounds the kinds of space that exists between texts, between political commitments, between ethical obligations that every filmic text can open. The chapters esteem the expansive dialogue adaptations accelerate when they realize their capacity to bring together two or more texts, two or more peoples, two or more ideologies without allowing one expression to erase another. The most minute detail becomes significant the moment that detail captures someone's attention. The prevailing story becomes more inclusive the moment a new face fills the frame. The supposedly unique issues experienced in one place become global the moment more people identify with those issues. The projections mean to continue discussion rather than settle them. The chapters in this volume hope to do the same.

Works Cited

Bakhtin, Mikhail. *The Dialogic Imagination: Four Essays*, translated by Caryl Emerson and Michael Holquist, U of Texas P, 1981.

Bazin, André. "In Defense of Mixed Cinema." *What Is Cinema? Volume 1*, edited by Hugh Gray. 2nd ed. U of California P, 2004, pp. 53–75.

Bluestone, George. *Novels into Film: The Metamorphosis of Fiction into Cinema*. Johns Hopkins UP, 2003.

Brontë, Charlotte. *Jane Eyre*. Penguin, 1985.

Byatt, A. S. *Possession: A Romance*. Chatto & Windus, 1990.

Cartmell, Deborah. *Interpreting Shakespeare on Screen*. Palgrave Macmillan, 2000.

DeBona, Guerric. *Film Adaptation in the Hollywood Studio Era*. U of Illinois P, 2010.

Dovey, Lindiwe. "Towards an Art of Adaptation: Film and the New Criticism-as-Creation." *Iowa Journal of Cultural Studies*, no. 2, 2002, pp. 51–61.

Gilbert, Sandra M., and Gubar, Susan. *The Madwoman in the Attic: The Woman Writer and the Nineteenth-Century Literary Imagination*, 2nd ed., Yale U P, 2000.

Henry V. Directed by Kenneth Branagh, performances by Kenneth Branagh, Derek Jacobi, and Simon Shepherd. Renaissance Films, 1989.

High Fidelity. Directed by Stephen Frears, performances by John Cusak, Iben Hjejle, and Todd Louiso. Touchstone Pictures, 2000.

Hornby, Nick. *High Fidelity*. Victor Gollancz, 1995.

How Tasty Was My Little Frenchman [Como era gostoso o meu francês]. Directed by Nelson Pereira des Santos, performances by Arduíno Colassanti, Ana Maria Magalhães, and Eduardo Impasse Filho. Condor Films, 1971.

Hutcheon, Linda. *A Theory of Adaptation*, 2nd ed. Routledge, 2013.

Jeffers, Jennifer. *Britain Colonized: Hollywood's Appropriation of British Literature*. Palgrave Macmillan, 2006.

Leitch, Thomas. "Against Conclusions: Petit Theories and Adaptation Studies." *The Oxford Handbook of Adaptation Studies*. Oxford U P, 2017, pp. 698–710.

Leitch, Thomas. "Literature versus Literacy." *Film Adaptation & Its Discontents: From Gone with the Wind to The Passion of the Christ*. Johns Hopkins UP, 2006, pp. 1–21.

Naremore, James. "Introduction: Film and the Reign of Adaptation." *Film Adaptation*, edited by James Naremore, Rutgers UP, 2000, pp. 1–18.

Niklas, Pascal, and Oliver Lindner, editors. *Adaptation and Cultural Appropriation: Literature, Film, and the Arts*. DeGruyter, 2012.

Possession. Directed by Neil LaBute, performances by Gwyneth Paltrow, Aaron Eckhart, and Jeremy Northam. Focus Features, 2002.

Rhys, Jean. *Wide Sargasso Sea*. Penguin, 1987.

Ryan, Michael, and Douglas Kellner. *Camera Politica: The Politics and Ideology of Contemporary Hollywood Film*. Indiana UP, 1988.

Sadlier, Darlene J. "The Politics of Adaptation: *How Tasty Was My Little Frenchman.*" *Film Adaptation*, edited by James Naremore. Rutgers UP, 2000, pp. 190–205.

Sanders, Julie. *Adaptation and Appropriation*. Routledge, 2016.

Stam, Robert. "Introduction: The Theory and Practice of Adaptation." *Literature and Film: A Guide to the Theory and Practice of Film Adaptation*, edited by Robert Stam and Alessandra Raengo, Blackwell, 2005, pp. 1–52.

Star Wars: Episode IV—A New Hope. Directed by George Lucas, performances by Mark Hamill, Harrison Ford, and Carrie Fisher. Lucasfilm, 1977.

Van Weyenberg, Astrid. *The Politics of Adaptation: Contemporary African Drama and Greek Tragedy*. Rodopi, 2013.

NEXT GENERATION ADAPTATION

JIM JARMUSCH'S *PATERSON*

Poetry, Place, and Cinematic Form

JACK RYAN

A PASSION FOR POETRY TEXTURES NEARLY ALL JIM JARMUSCH FILMS. SOME CONNECTION TO poets and poems can be seen scattered across films even when deeper connections do not exist. For example, in *Down by Law* (1986), Roberto (Roberto Benigni) exuberantly expresses his passion for Walt Whitman and "Bob" Frost. The film concludes with a shot that visually echoes "The Road Not Taken," one of Frost's most renowned poems. In *Mystery Train* (1989), a pair of Japanese tourists walk down Chaucer Street in Memphis. Jarmusch creates a more intricate nod to poetry in *Dead Man* (1995). The film features a protagonist named William "Bill" Blake (Johnny Depp), and Jarmusch inserts language from the poet William Blake throughout the screenplay. He even allows Nobody (Gary Farmer), Bill Blake's aboriginal guide, to quote from Blake's "Proverbs from Hell." As Hugh Davis notes, these nods to Blake move beyond a mere adaptation of Blake's poetry: "The film represents a synthesis of the very different media of poetry and film into a form that transcends what either can do individually" (94).

A similar kind of synthesis of media exists in *Ghost Dog* (1999), as brief poetic passages from the *Hagakure*, a collection of meditations meant to instruct samurai warriors, are superimposed on the screen. *Broken Flowers* (2005) features a main character, Don Johnston (Bill Murray), who doubles as an aged Don Juan, in the Byronic sense, and who sets off on an American road trip to visit his former lovers. Adam (Tom Hiddleston) and Eve (Tilda Swinton), the eternal vampire protagonists of *Only Lovers Left Alive* (2013), immerse themselves in art and culture, and they remark on the renowned artists they have known, including Shelley and Byron.

One sees a more substantial connection to poetry in two earlier Jarmusch films. Jarmusch's first feature, *Permanent Vacation* (1980), offers a protagonist,

3

Aloysius Parker (Chris Parker), who reads Comte de Lautréamont, the French poet who influenced both the Surrealists and the Situationists. Parker is also clearly influenced by the Beat movement. He presents himself as a jazz hipster wandering New York City in search for something unnamable. *Stranger than Paradise* (1984), which launched Jarmusch's independent career, does not present an overt thematic or narrative connection to poetry, but his empty mise-en-scène does expose every grungy detail of the Lower East Side of 1970s New York with observational precision. His use of blackouts to separate narrative episodes produces the effect of stanza breaks that lends the film a poetic visual style. The film moves with a poetic sensibility.

With *Paterson* (2016), Jarmusch combines these narrative and stylistic sensibilities in such a way that he begins to answer the question so many of his films propose: "What makes poetry?" Jarmusch's protagonist, a public bus driver and unassuming poet named Paterson (Adam Driver), moves through the city of Paterson, New Jersey, listening carefully to his passengers' conversations and observing the city and its people with anonymous dedication. Jarmusch's bus-driver-poet does not seek self-conscious ideas and meaning from his urban environment. Rather, he discovers poetic inspiration from mundane things like a box of matches, a yellow raincoat, a shoebox, a beer glass. In this way Jarmusch's film concerns itself less with the political or ethical questions poetry might raise and more with the adaptive process of creating poetry, with the reason poetry exists. Jarmusch clarifies this interest by offering his audience a poet who does not share his poetry. Paterson's poems mean to enrich his life. They help him examine and engage the world around him. As such, *Paterson* allows poetry to exist outside the demands of any audience.

Jarmusch's inspiration for his *Paterson* occurred more than twenty-five years before the release of the film, while he was reading the beginning of William Carlos Williams's epic poem *Paterson*. Williams's opening words intrigued Jarmusch enough that he took a daytrip to Paterson, New Jersey. Motivated by the diversity of the city, its history, its poets, and especially the Great Falls of the Passaic River, Jarmusch began to make notes about "a guy named Paterson who lives in Paterson: a working-class guy but also a poet," and, as he told Geoff Andrew, the idea remained with him for a long time (20). Jarmusch began to work with some aspects of Williams's poem and against others as the years passed. The writer-director keeps Williams's idea that "a man in himself is a city" and that there are "no ideas but in things" (xiv, 6). Jarmusch uses some of Williams's images and metaphors to examine creativity. The director insists on the importance of personal relationships and the power of art. Still, his film is not so much a straight adaptation of

Williams's poem. Jarmusch admits to Amy Taubin that Williams's poem is "a bit too abstract, or maybe a bit too philosophical for [him] somehow" (3). Jarmusch wanted a film that celebrates imaginative possibility, a quixotic sensibility anchored to everyday experience. He wanted his protagonist to give shape and meaning to the beauties of the seemingly dreary world around him. To achieve these aims, Jarmusch needed to work against the modernist inclination in Williams's poem. He refuses to offer his protagonist a world that changes, or to let some hero's quest fulfill him. Any sense of fulfillment Jarmusch's Paterson finds is more private, extending from his poetry, and arises to the extent that he can add thoughtful and mindful substance to ordinary existence.

Jarmusch's *Paterson* ends where Williams's ambitious poem begins, before the Great Falls of the Passaic River in Paterson, New Jersey. Jarmusch sets within this scene a lyrical encounter between his protagonist and a Japanese poet (Masatoshi Nagase) visiting the site that inspired Williams. After sitting down next to Paterson on the only available park bench, the visitor opens a Japanese translation of Williams's *Paterson*, which includes an English translation on every other page. He sees Paterson glancing sideways at the book. The visitor asks, "Are you from here in Paterson, New Jersey?" Paterson replies, "Yes, I am. I was born here." The visitor asks if Paterson knows "the great poet William Carlos Williams here in Paterson, New Jersey." Paterson answers, "Well, I am aware of his poems." The visitor says, "May I ask if you too are a poet of Paterson, New Jersey?" Paterson does not accept that title, responding, "I am just a bus driver." But the audience knows differently. They have listened as this unassuming man composed poetry in his head, watched him carefully record his work in a notebook, and heard his calm recitations in voiceover. The Japanese visitor also seems to know different: "A bus driver in Paterson. Aha. This is very poetic. This could be poem by William Carlos Williams."

The conversation continues and Paterson and the visitor reveal a knowledge of poetry. Paterson mentions the subject of Frank O'Hara's poem "Naphtha," painter and sculptor Jean Dubuffet. The Japanese visitor knows O'Hara and this specific poem. He returns Paterson's mention of O'Hara with a comment about Allen Ginsberg, who was born in nearby Newark, New Jersey, and befriended Williams. Paterson admits knowing his poems as well as the New York School of Poets. The remark is interesting if only because these poets are known for utilizing everyday experiences in their work in just the way Jarmusch's Paterson develops such things. Even more, many of the New York School of Poets worked everyday jobs just as Paterson does, effectively concealing their poetic lives from the people with whom they interacted on a daily basis. Dubuffet, the founder of the Art Brut movement, championed so-called low art, which he believed to be more authentic and humanistic than traditional forms of image making. Paterson appreciates Dubuffet having worked as a meteorologist at the Eiffel Tower in 1922—a job seemingly unrelated to poetry. The Japanese man is convinced that Paterson is indeed a poet. He presents Paterson with an empty Japanese notebook, which replaces the one Paterson's dog, Marvin, destroyed the night before. The visitor leaves Paterson with the reminder that the blank page can inspire creativity. At this point Jarmusch's character, like Williams's own, awakens from a kind of slumber that had washed over him before the scene began. Jarmusch's poet begins to create poetry again as he walks the streets of Paterson, New Jersey.

To appreciate the care Jarmusch takes to portray the method of poetry to which his Paterson awakens, one does well to trace the connections Jarmusch's film makes to the priorities of the New York School of Poets, and, just as importantly, against the poet Williams creates, a man named Dr. Noah Faitoute Paterson, and the tradition in which he sets him. Jarmusch aspired to be a writer, first exploring journalism, then literature at Columbia University. He studied poetry with Kenneth Koch and David Shapiro, figureheads of the New York School. Other New York School Poets include Frank O'Hara, James Schuyler, and Ron Padgett, all of whom have a clear influence on Jarmusch's thinking. Padgett and Shapiro edited the *Anthology of New York Poets*, a collection, Jarmusch notes, that "became a bible for what is now the New York School" (Kelsey 3). Jarmusch admits his connection with these poets in an interview for *Tribeca Shortlist*: "When I'm gone, if people considered my films to be a sort of the cinematic extension of the New York School of Poets who try not to take anything too seriously and try to write to another person, I would be very honored if they thought of my films that way" (Dawson).

Many of the scenes in *Paterson* include small unremarkable moments, indicators of the approach the New York School of Poets brought to their observational work. Jarmusch recreates the aesthetic of the New York School in the slow pace of the film, its spare plot, wry humor, empty spaces, quiet moments, and the economy of language and gestures used by Paterson himself. Adam Driver's performance as Paterson typifies a Jarmusch protagonist, for he is not demonstrative and registers little emotion. In this way the performance recalls Buster Keaton, a Jarmusch favorite, who was "funny in an extremely human way" (Hertzberg 194). Such a character contemplates, observes, and listens with meditative focus; this is just what Jarmusch's Paterson does as well. Unobtrusive tracking shots of Paterson as he walks and drives through Paterson, New Jersey, an urban space that is (in the film) diverse and accepting, are understated, formally pure. Stationary cameras and slow tracking shots have been a stylistic hallmark of Jarmusch's films since the beginning of his career. He is particularly captivated by figures who walk, but his attention to Paterson takes a clearer purpose. His walks match Williams's Paterson, who also moves through the city on foot in *Book Two*. "Walking—" is repeated throughout the first section of that book, illustrating the way Williams positions his poet as a surveyor and interpreter of the landscape.

Jarmusch refuses to offer his poet the quest Williams gives his protagonist. One sees this difference in the scene that has Paterson compose "The Run," which verbally and visually captures driving his 23-bus route. After starting the poem inside his parked bus while waiting to begin his shift, Paterson returns to the work in voiceover after exiting the garage: "I go through / trillions of molecules / that move aside / to make way for me / while on both sides / trillions more / stay where they are." Jarmusch uses a series of long and close-up shots edited to the rhythm of the poem. He presents images from both inside and outside the bus itself, at times presenting the parts of the bus mentioned in the poem: "The windshield wiper blade / starts to squeak. / The rain has stopped. / I stop. / On the corner / a boy / in a yellow raincoat / holding his mother's hand." At the conclusion of the poem, Jarmusch utilizes a montage, blending Paterson, the 23-bus, and the city of Paterson, which underscores how significant the city is to Paterson and his creative process. Additionally, with the special clarity that only cinematic form can provide, Jarmusch's imagery captures the strange beauty of a neglected, ordinary city, which continually inspires his worker-poet.

Jarmusch consistently uses Paterson's daily routine to consider how to protect the creative consciousness from the crush of modernity. Paterson's imagination is ignited by the everyday: he displays a mindfulness that is unusual in the twenty-first century. As Paterson tells Doc (Barry Shabaka Henley) during one of his nightly stops at Shades Bar, he does not own any technology—no phone, no iPad, no computer. While Paterson's choices seem old-fashioned, not being technologically tethered frees him to contemplate life. Numerous scenes from the film depict Paterson either walking or sitting while he observes the world around him or internally composes poetry, both mindful actions that countervail the technologically obsessed twenty-first century. The resulting awareness of his environment allows Paterson to mark his poems with a sense of place that approximates Williams's sense. Adam R. McKee claims that Williams scaffolds every book of his epic with "a particular space as the central organizing feature, pulling together history, language, and geography to produce the seemingly chaotic form" (142).[1] Williams himself explains in a 1951 statement the significance of Paterson, New Jersey, in his poem:

Thus the city I wanted as my object had to be one that I knew in its
most intimate details. New York was too big, too much a congeries of
the entire world's facets. I wanted something nearer home, something
knowable. I deliberately selected Paterson as my reality. My own sub-
urb was not distinguished or varied enough for my purpose. There
were other possibilities, but Paterson topped them. Paterson has a def-
inite history associated with the beginnings of the United States. It has
besides a central feature, the Passaic Falls, which as I begin to think
about it became more and more the lucky burden of what I wanted to
say. I began to read all I could about the history of the Falls, the park
on the little hill beyond it and the early inhabitants. (Paterson xiii)

The remark echoes a similar comment Williams made in a letter to Horace
Gregory describing the sources of *In the American Grain,* his prose collection
of historical literary fiction. He explains how embracing the place one lives
allows a creative artist to imaginatively possess it:

Of mixed ancestry, I felt from the earliest childhood that America was
the only home I could possibly call my own. I felt that it was expressly
founded for me, personally, and that it must be my first business in life
to possess it; that only by making it my own from the beginning of
my own day, in detail, should I ever have a basis for knowing where I
stood. (*Selected Letters* 185)

Unlike many of his contemporaries, particularly T. S. Eliot and Ezra Pound,
who opted for older, seemingly richer cultures as imaginative wellsprings,
Williams chose to remain in America "in order to lift his own environment,
by use of the imagination and the vernacular language," and to "discover a
culture as locally related as a tree in the earth" (Conarroe 1–2). Upholding
the modernist tradition, Williams's Paterson strives to capture heroic values
by elevating his city's history, rather than fully accepting the urban space as
it was. His poet-hero is a romantic monologist confounded by modernity, a
figure common to the high-modernist tradition.

Book One of *Paterson* opens with Williams's poet rousing from sleep under
the Great Falls of the Passaic River. Upon waking, he assumes the persona
of the epic quester, "walking" the landscape in search of wonders, a figure
that craves the "miraculous" (10). Yet Williams's Paterson exists in an age
that seldom yields such wonders to the poet-hero. As Roger Salomon notes,
Williams creates a poet that is rebellious, youthful, hopeful, a symbol of re-
newal. His persona accepts an ironic dimension that suggests "diminishment,

attenuation, someone who perhaps essentially models himself on a memorialized ideal"—he is "foreign and anachronistic" to the environment in which he exists (146).[2] In the Preface to "Book 1," Paterson expresses awareness of his precarious situation:

> To make a start, / out of particulars / and to make them general, rolling / up the sum, by defective means— / Sniffing the trees, / just another dog / among a lot of dogs. What / else is there? And to do? / The rest have run out / after the rabbits/ Only the lame stands—on / three legs. Scratch front and back. / Deceive and eat. Dig / a musty bone / For the beginning is assuredly / the end—since we know nothing, pure/and simple, beyond / our own complexities. (4)

Williams's Paterson continually confronts impediments that diminish his romantic heroism; in fact, he accomplishes almost nothing in his epic quest, walking aimlessly, strolling toward a sterile void "foot pacing foot outward / into emptiness" (64). Williams's *Paterson* ultimately centers on a relentlessly pursued but futile romantic quest; its multibook structure impedes the search for essential meaning. Williams, of course, recognizes this conundrum, as his Paterson says at one point, "Blocked. / (Make a song out of that: concretely)," which he utters as a recognition of the challenge that exists to make sense of his physical world he chooses to avoid or ignore rather than observe and render meaningful (63).

Jarmusch's Paterson is the exact opposite manner of poet. He commits himself to an observational poetry that is deeply in tune with his environment. Jarmusch marks this shift, in part, by stripping his poet of the trappings of the high-modernist hero that mark Williams's Dr. Noah Faitoute Paterson. Jarmusch's poet is a bus driver, which immediately contradicts the popular perception of who or what a poet is. Poets are often depicted as highly educated artists who sequester themselves to write. Emily Dickinson might be the most well-known example of this common stereotype. Jarmusch's Paterson functions as a visual synecdoche for liberating the representative image of a poet. His bus driver quietly resonates a sentiment Jarmusch expressed to Jonathan Rosenbaum in a 1996 *Cineaste* interview, after Rosenbaum asked him about what critic Phillip Lopate called Jarmusch's cinematic lowlifes:

> Once I was in a working-class restaurant in Rome with Roberto Benigni at lunchtime. . . . We sat down with these people in their blue work overalls, they were working on the street outside, and Roberto's talking to them, and they are talking about Dante and Ariosto and

twentieth-century Italian poets. Now, you go out to Wyoming and go
in a bar and mention the word poetry, and you'll get a gun stuck up
your ass. That's the way America is. Whereas even guys who work in
the street collecting garbage in Paris love nineteenth-century painting. (Hertzberg 160)

Paterson is a typical American working-class figure. His dark-blue work
uniform, military-green Stanley lunchbox, and daily routine all show his
everyday status. However, like an Italian construction worker or a Parisian
garbage collector, he also keeps an interior creative life far more intellectual
than one might assume he possesses. Paterson consciously and deliberately
chooses to remain firmly in the space of his social experiences and interactions, and he chooses to create his poetry from within that space.

Jarmusch avoids some of the political or ethical observations poetry might
make by creating a protagonist who is so reserved and methodical that the
viewer's attention is often on the process of creating poems rather than the
poems themselves. The most important details tend to be the small objects
Paterson notices that might otherwise be overlooked. Paterson does not
make comments about the condition of his city or its inhabitants. However,
Jarmusch's protagonist is a progressive representation of a working-class
figure because he is someone society ignores or takes for granted—he is
a bus driver, nothing more. In this way, Jarmusch's Paterson is one of the
director's signature marginal, outsider figures. One sees the impact of this
societal position in the abovementioned scene with the Japanese visitor.
The visitor's presentation to Paterson of a new, empty notebook is a pivotal
moment in the film, because the act awakens in Paterson a willingness to
see himself as a poet, someone who can again engage Paterson, New Jersey,
as a significant place, one rife with artistic possibility. The gift-bearer repeats the words "Paterson, New Jersey," creating a poetic refrain in his brief
conversation with Paterson that provides a rhythm to the scene that makes
their entire dialogue a prose poem, and that reminds the viewers of the
potential significance of place. Referencing Bruce Kawin, Jennifer O'Meara
argues that Jarmusch's "use of repetition," common to many of his films, "is
generally in keeping with Kawin's description of 'repetition for poetic value'
as depending on 'artful variations'" (173). Visually, Paterson and the visitor
are connected by master shots, medium shots, and two-shots. These stylistic
choices form filmic stanzas that lead toward a spoken couplet in which each
poet repeats "Aha," a quiet appreciation for the act of creative observation
and artistic discovery.

This move is one Jarmusch performs in many of his films. The director often juxtaposes artist-seekers with the practical roles society offers them. *Dead Man* (1995), *Ghost Dog: The Way of the Samurai* (1999), and *The Limits of Control* (2009) all feature these metaphoric seekers. Each of these films uses violence to comment on social restrictions and, tellingly, how power, technology, capitalism, and conquest, among other things, work to diminish the creative imagination. As Julian Rice suggests, "Jarmusch's method of resisting ugly societal conditions that form the background of his films is spiritual rather than political" (13).[3] None of the protagonists in these films is presented as an artist, but they are avatars for creative thought. In this way, then, *Paterson* becomes an extension of these projects. The film is not as overtly political as these earlier works, but thematically the film suggests that artistic creation is not limited to trained artists; rather, art and creativity are open to anyone willing to observe and engage the world, even a worker-writer who dissolves the boundary between his work domain and his literary domain.

Routine, repetition, and workdays structure *Paterson* and anchor its titular character's week as a public bus driver. Paterson lives by mundane routine; ironically, though, Jarmusch means to suggest that this routine adds a fundamental level of creative freedom to his life, as the writer-director explains: "He likes routine, because routine allows him to drift. Because he doesn't have to think about what clothes he wears each day, what time does he go to work, what is the route of his bus. Even walking the dog, going to the bar is part of his routine. Everything is laid out for him, and that lets him be a poet" (Taubin 7). The meditative poetry Paterson creates requires this type of quiet, reflective sameness. Paterson is a dedicated poet, whose poetry is fed by his life and vice versa. The reciprocity provides the character a spiritual dimension. Indeed, Paterson practices an almost monastic call to create for himself alone because the act of artistic creation is enough. Visual and spoken references imply that Paterson's repetitive days are judiciously deliberate choices that harness his connection to his city as both a historic and contemporary crucible for creative thought. What is essential for him are his own thoughts, his poetic reflections.

Structurally, the film frames the artistic process as a seven-stanza poem, one stanza for each day of the week, and each day is presented with its own languid beauty. Jarmusch's images, for the most part, record what Paterson sees while composing his poetry. Sometimes the poems are complete. Sometimes they are in process. At still other times they undergo revision. Similarly, Jarmusch's images are sometimes master shots, sometimes portions of things, and sometimes repeated with slight variations. As Jarmusch told critic Amy Taubin, "as far as *Paterson*, somebody said it's like a poem in the form of cinema, but I think it's more like cinema in poetic form" (2).

Writing about Jonas Mekas's film criticism for the *New Yorker*, Richard Brody notes that for Mekas "poetic" cinema is the "most advanced form of cinematic art."[4] Mekas argues that movies, "with their emphasis not on images, drama, and representation, but on '*light, motion, celluloid, screen*' brought the movies to the place that had been reached by painting, sculpture, and the other visual arts." When Jarmusch visually illustrates Paterson's poems, the pure cinema Mekas describes fills the screen. For instance, when Paterson sits down on a park bench near the Great Falls to complete "Love Poem," Jarmusch overlays an image of the waterfall in present time with a close-up from earlier that morning of an Ohio Blue Tip matchbox; it is as if Paterson is seeing the matches in his mind as he writes the poem. Then Paterson's handwriting appears on the screen, and the frame completely blends the poetry being written with the present and the past moment of inspiration. By sampling Paterson's poems and depicting the process of making a poem as if he is inside Paterson's mind, Jarmusch places poetry and the creative process at the center of his cinematic narrative.

Jarmusch keeps this process at the center of *Paterson* through Paterson's encounters with other poets. Paterson has three such encounters in the film. The first encounter succinctly captures the strategy at work in these encounters. Paterson hears a spoken-word artist working out a rap inside a city laundromat. The man uses the sounds from a washing machine to set the rhythm for his rap; he melds the racial anguish of Paul Laurence Dunbar's "We Wear the Mask" with quotes from Williams's *Paterson*: "They call me Paul Laurence Dunbar / I wear the mask / No ideas but in things." The rap is rich with cultural references, including film, sports, music, and poetry; it is presented with pulsating vigor. The rapper eventually turns toward Marvin, Paterson's dog, who is standing in the doorway, calling him "Pugsley." When Paterson reveals himself, the rapper calls the man the dog's "human ball and chain." Paterson compliments the rapper on his work. Paterson glances around the interior of the ramshackle laundry and asks, "Laboratory?" The rapper responds, "Wherever it hits me is where it's going to be," suggesting that creative opportunities can emerge anywhere.

The scene makes it abundantly clear that poetry can be intimately tied to lived experience, especially for people in tune with place, history, and physical space. When it is, the art form possesses the power to cross cultural boundaries. It can bring people together people, in this case, poets who might otherwise be divided. As it relates to this scene, though, the fact that the rapper is Black and Paterson is white hardly comes into play. What is captured instead is a brief interaction between two poets. As bell hooks notes, Jarmusch has used brief interactions like this one in other films: "This filmic moment challenges our perception of blackness by engaging in the process of defamiliarization (the taking of a familiar image and depicting it in such a way that we look at it differently)" (99). This defamiliarization continues after Paterson compliments the poetic rapper and walks to Shades Bar, where he sits alone, listening to jazz, glancing into his beer glass, the only white man in the place. He watches two men play chess using a timer. He examines the pictures Doc has hung on the Paterson, New Jersey, "Wall of Fame." He simply observes and in so doing becomes a manifestation of hooks's defamiliarization.

Jarmusch uses defamiliarization as a literary technique throughout the film, presenting an American cityscape through the eyes of an amateur poet, someone in tune with the urban environment and open enough to be inspired by what he experiences. The city directly inspires two poems, "The Run" and "Another One." The point of these poems, though, when set against Jarmusch's mise-en-scène, would seem to be that his poet-protagonist is, in fact, the city. The idea extends from Williams's 1946 "Author's Note," wherein he asserts that *Paterson* "is a long poem in four parts—that a man in himself is a city, beginning, seeking, achieving and concluding his life in ways which the various aspects of a city may embody—if imaginatively conceived—any city, all the details of which may be made to voice his most intimate convictions" (xiv). Jarmusch's Paterson moves and writes as "a man in himself is a city." He takes inspiration from his urban environment, which stimulates his poetic creativity. His work life, domestic life, and social connections all inform his poetry. The cityscape that Paterson slowly moves through, whether on foot or driving his bus, is rich with the unexpected, the unfamiliar, the "things" Williams referenced that help produce poetry. In one of Paterson's first walks to the bus depot, for example, a point-of-view shot captures the beauty of the early-morning sun on an abandoned textile mill with Edward Hopper–like grace, and then Paterson begins to compose "Love Poem" in his head.

Cinematically, "Love Poem," the first poem made in the film, is used to introduce Paterson's artistic process and to connect to William Carlos Williams's notion of avoiding abstraction in order to elevate the ordinary and the tangible. The poem is an ideal example of Williams's most famous dictum: "—Say it, no ideas but in things—" (7). "Love Poem" begins as a simple observation. Paterson considers a single box of Ohio Blue Tip matches, turning it slowly in his left hand, while eating his breakfast of Cheerios from a glass, which he does every morning. The workingman's inspection of the matchbox, though, distinguishes the moment from an otherwise commonplace occurrence. As he walks toward the bus depot, Paterson begins to compose: "We have plenty of matches in our house / We keep them on hand always / Currently our favorite brand / Is Ohio Blue Tip." Paterson describes the letters on the matchbox: "In the shape of a megaphone / As if to say even louder to the world / Here is the most beautiful match in the world." The poet opts for the collective pronoun "we" to indicate that the match selection was a joint effort, and he connects his poetry with his domestic environment. Poetry serves as the connective tissue for almost anything in Jarmusch's narrative. The poem illustrates this as Paterson reflects on the utility of the match and its ability to light the "cigarette of the woman you love." Bestowing importance upon an otherwise insignificant object, a match, becomes the basis for an unexpectedly passion-filled conclusion to the poem: "I become the cigarette and you the match / Or I the match and you the cigarette / Blazing with kisses that smolder toward heaven." In life the narrator is insignificant, like the match, yet his passion (love) demonstrates his value and purpose, just as a simple matchstick has value and purpose.

After starting the poem, Paterson tells Laura (Golshifteh Farahani), his wife, his partner, his flower, and his friend, that he has been working on a poem for her. She takes joy in this fact and in the possibility of seeing his creation. Laura wants Paterson to preserve his work, to copy it, to share it. Paterson resists this impulse. He elects to keep his writing private. He prefers to keep his poems in what he calls his "secret notebook." Laura practices a more visible art. While Paterson drives his bus route, Laura remains inside their modest home painting the walls, the curtains, the cabinets, and the shower curtains with circular designs in black and white. She dresses in black and white and accents herself with black and white accessories. Her long-term plans involve starting a cupcake business and becoming a country music performer, even though she does not know how to play the guitar. She prepares dinner, experimenting with recipes of her own making, which Paterson chokes down with loving acceptance. Her exuberance and energy and the variety and change she brings into their lives complicate and stand in contrast to his simple, routine-driven existence. Yet Laura's whimsicality also seems to feed Paterson's creativity in a safe, supportive way. Their relationship is harmonious and sympathetic—she wants him to publish his work, she demonstrates for him the reward of taking chances with art, and she reminds him to make a record of his writing. Hers is a world of joyful disorder, and his is an attempt to add poetic order to the mundane reality both inside and outside their home.

The interchange between the world Laura occupies and the world Paterson inhabits comes into clear view during the onscreen recitation of "The Run." Jarmusch intercuts images of the bus, the city, and Paterson with images of Laura at home as she models dresses featuring her own black-and-white designs. Eventually, she appears with her harlequin guitar in a dress with a similar harlequin design. The images are significant in a variety of ways, particularly by recalling Juan Gris's painting *Harlequin with Guitar* (1918). Gris, who was William Carlos Williams's favorite cubist artist and the inspiration behind his poem "The Rose" (1923), frequently used the harlequin figure in his work. In this sequence, Jarmusch fuses his unique visual style with Paterson's poetry and creates an homage to Williams and modern art.

Other images also extend features of Williams's poetry in noteworthy ways. When each new day breaks, Jarmusch films Paterson and Laura from above their bed. He leaves for work, and she works at home creating elaborate designs inside the house, on her clothing, and on her cupcakes. The recurring image of Paterson awaking captures an essential Williams line: "A man like a city and a woman like a flower / —who are in love" (8). Jarmusch presents other features of Williams's poem as well by assigning minor characters lines that mark the significance of Paterson, New Jersey. A young boy on the 23-bus recalls the infamous story of Hurricane Carter, a Paterson boxer who, in 1966, was wrongfully arrested and convicted of a triple homicide in a Paterson bar. Another bus rider mentions the ninetieth-century Italian anarchist Gaetano Bresci, who ran a newspaper in Paterson before assassinating King Umberto I of Italy in 1900. Throughout the poem *Paterson*, Williams inserts passages detailing historical facts about the city and the United States. These details note the city's complex and unusual history and piqued Jarmusch's curiosity: "It was the first industrial utopian city envisioned by Alexander Hamilton, and indeed it became a utopian city in the 19th century, using the falls as a form of energy" (Andrew 20). By having his minor characters celebrate the city's significance, Jarmusch mimics a technique Williams used on a larger scale in his epic poem.

Jarmusch's imagery and script at times also echo the beginning of *Book One*: "To make a start, / out of particulars / and make them general, rolling / up the sum, by defective means—" (3). Movement from the particulars to the general is exemplified in Paterson's poem "Another One":

> When you're a child
> you learn
> there are three dimensions:

height, width, and depth.
Like a shoebox.
Then later you learn there's a fourth dimension:
time.
Hmm.
Then some say
there can be five, six, seven . . .
I knock off work,
have a beer
at the bar.
I look down at the glass
and feel glad.

Jarmusch visually captures this poem on screen by showing Paterson driving his bus through different portions of the city and then sitting at Shades gazing directly into a beer glass active with carbonation and capped with foam. Jarmusch does not display overt interest in the contemporary social or economic problems of Paterson; instead, he uses the city to illustrate Williams's notion of concrete things being more significant than abstractions.

Visually, Jarmusch's mise-en-scène also promotes details and concrete things, which help define Paterson himself. When at home on his day off, Paterson writes in a cramped basement space surrounded by household supplies, hardware, and books and images of his favorite writers and poets, including William Carlos Williams, Wallace Stevens, Kenneth Koch, Ron Padgett, Luc Sante, and David Foster Wallace. Paterson composes all of this poetry in isolation, either in a safe physical place or inside his head, which links him to Williams, O'Hara, and Wallace Stevens—all poets who maintained working lives that cloaked their artistic natures. However, unlike these poets, Paterson never shares his work. Jarmusch's character accepts the mystery of things and the power of poetry to give shape and substance to that mystery: the mere act of writing wakes one from a sleep one might not otherwise be aware of.

Jarmusch plays with this idea of waking and awareness by observing how his two lead characters begin each day. On Monday ("day one"), Paterson kisses Laura on her forehead, and she sleepily tells him that she had the most beautiful dream about their having twin children. Jarmusch's use of twins throughout the film establishes an internal visual rhyme that adds a dash of the enigmatic to the narrative.[5] Twins appear randomly throughout the film, and most of the twins, like the older twins Paterson sees while composing "Love Song," are seen from Paterson's point of view. Only the brothers Sam (Trev Parham) and Dave (Troy T. Parham), patrons of Shades Bar, named after the Stax Records soul singers, speak, and they are used both cultural touchstones and for subtle humor. The other twins materialize when Paterson is either walking or driving his bus. The poem Jarmusch wrote for *Paterson*, "Water Falls," appears when Paterson walks from the bus depot after completing his shift. He sees a girl about ten years old sitting near one of the industrial buildings he passes on his daily journey. Paterson is concerned that she is alone and asks her if he can sit down with her to wait until her mother arrives. She agrees, and as in the scene with the rapper and the Japanese visitor, they bond over poetry. Similar to Paterson, she writes poetry in a "secret notebook." She reads him her poem "Water Falls":

> *Water falls from bright air.*
> *It falls like hair, falling across a young girl's shoulders.*
> *Water falls making pools in the asphalt, dirty mirrors with clouds*
>   *and buildings inside.*
> *It falls on the roof of my house.*
> *It falls on my mother and on my hair.*
> *Most people call it rain.*

The split compound noun, two words that should go together like twins, evokes some of Williams's own poems, particular breaking "wheel barrow" into two words in his most famous poem, "The Red Wheelbarrow." Paterson compliments the girl on her work, particularly the "internal rhyme." When her mother and twin sister appear—she is another example of duplication seen throughout the film—she turns to Paterson and asks him if he likes Emily Dickinson. He says, "Yes, she's one of my favorite poets." She responds, "Awesome, a bus diver that likes Emily Dickinson."

These words echo the language the Japanese visitor voices at the end of the film, "A bus driver in Paterson. Aha. This is very poetic. This could be poem by William Carlos Williams." This *could be* a poem by William Carlos Williams, but it is a cinematic homage to poetry by Jim Jarmusch. His cinematic choices in the final encounter elevate the moment. While Paterson sits on his favorite bench staring at the Great Falls, the powerful crucible for Williams's epic poem, the Japanese visitor enters the frame from the right, atypical in American cinema, which visually upsets Paterson's contemplative state, yet upholds and illustrates the Japanese tradition of reading right-to-left.[6] With Ozu-like precision, Jarmusch moves his static camera behind the two men, to maintain the scene's continuity and to reinforce the connection being established between them and the Great Falls before them.

Visually and verbally, Jarmusch depicts Paterson's awakening, spurred on by the Japanese poet, while echoing the opening of Williams's *Paterson*. The visitor presents the bus driver with a Japanese notebook, and he says, "Sometimes the empty page presents more possibilities." The benefactor turns back to Paterson after having started to walk away to say once more, "Excuse me. Aha." Paterson whispers to himself, "Aha," and then slowly reaches for the pen in his jacket pocket. A possibility is born with every "Aha." Paterson returns to his craft, beginning a poem titled "The Line," which asks, "Would you rather be a fish?" The question is the kind of remark one might expect from a poet, even if the poet, in this case, is an unassuming bus driver. This bus driver happens to celebrate the beauty and mystery of everyday life. He is an amateur in the oldest sense, a true lover and student of life. He creates poetry by observing and connecting with his city, with himself. Jarmusch's film creates a similar connection, opening a cinematic window on the world of a poet given to his craft, given to observation, given to the discovery of the next "Aha." Poetry, place, and cinematic form as Jarmusch realizes each depends on all that this short utterance contains.

Works Cited

Andrew, Geoff. *Sight & Sound* 26, no. 12, (2016): 20–23.

Brody, Richard. "Jonas Mekas, Champion of the 'Poetic' Cinema." April 21, 2016. newyorker.com/culture/richard-brody/jonas-mekas-champion-of-the-poetic-cinema.

Conarroe, Joel. *William Carlos Williams' Paterson: Language and Landscape*. Philadelphia: University of Pennsylvania Press, 1970.

Davis, Hugh. "Some Are Born to Endless Night: The Blakean Vision of Jim Jarmusch's *Dead Man*." *Verse, Voice, and Vision: Poetry and Cinema*, edited by Marlisa Santos, 81–94. Toronto: Scarecrow Press, 2013.

Dawson, Courtney. "Interview: Jim Jarmusch on *Paterson* and Poetry." January 17, 2017. outtake.tribecashortlist.com/tagged/jim-jarmusch.

Hertzberg, Ludvig. *Jim Jarmusch: Interviews*. Jackson: University of Mississippi Press, 2001.

hooks, belle. *Reel to Real: Race, Sex, and Class in the Movies*. New York: Routledge, 1996.

Jarmusch, Jim. "Jim Jarmusch on The New York School Poets. Radio Open Source. September 11, 2017. radioopensource.org/john-ashbery-is-you/.

Kelsey, Colleen. *Interview Magazine*. "Jim Jarmusch's Poetic Verse." December 2016. interviewmagazine.com/film/jim-jarmusch-paterson#.

Lippy, Tod, ed. *Projections 11: New York Filmmakers on Filmmaking*. London: Faber and Faber, 2000.

McKee, Adam R. "Paterson: William Carlos Williams's Image of the City." *William Carlos Williams Review* 31 (2014): 141–58.

Northover, Benn. "Jim Jarmusch and Jonas Mekas on Film, Poetry and Trump." *AnOther*. March 2017. anothermag.com/design-living/9589/jim-jarmusch-and-jonas-mekas-on-film-poetry-and-trump.

O'Meara, Jennifer. "Poetic Dialogue: Lyrical Speech in the Work of Hal Hartley and Jim Jarmusch." *Verse, Voice, and Vision: Poetry and Cinema*, edited by Marlisa Santos, 165–178. Toronto: Scarecrow Press, 2013.

Paterson. Directed by Jim Jarmusch. Performances of Adam Driver, Golshifteh Farahani, Barry Shabaka Henley. K5 International. Amazon Studios, 2016.

Quart, Leonard. "Creating a Cinematic Prose Poem: An Interview with Jim Jarmusch." *Cineaste* 42, no. 2 (2017): 28–30.

Rice, Julian. *The Jarmusch Way: Spirituality and Imagination in Dead Man, Ghost Dog, and The Limits of Control*. Toronto: Scarecrow Press, 2012.

Rosenbaum, Jonathan. "Jim Jarmusch's Lost America: The Pleasures of *Paterson*." 15 June 2017 jonathanrosenbaum.net/2017/06/jarmsuchs-lost-america-the-pleasures-of-paterson/.

Salomon, Roger B. *Desperate Storytelling: Post-Romantic Elaborations of the Mock-Heroic Mode*. Athens: University of Georgia Press, 1987.

Taubin, Amy. "Jim Jarmusch on Paterson." *Film Comment* November/December 2016: filmcomment.com/article/jim-jarmusch-paterson-gimme-danger-interview/.

Williams, William Carlos. *The Autobiography of William Carlos Williams*. New York: New Directions, 1967.

Williams, William Carlos. *In the American Grain*. New York: New Directions, 1956.

Williams, William Carlos. *Paterson*. Revised edition prepared by Christopher MacGowan. New York: New Directions, 1992.

Williams, William Carlos. *The Selected Letters of William Carlos Williams*. New York: New Directions, 1985.

Notes

1. McKee's argument deals with the physical space of Paterson, New Jersey, and the implications of landmark theory, which is an original approach to understanding the four primary sections of Williams's *Paterson*. He acknowledges the contentious nature of gender roles within the poem, but he provides a number of scholarly sources to demonstrate various approaches for this interpretation. See McKee, page 157.

2. Roger Salomon's book traces the use of the mock-heroic mode by focusing on postromantic storytellers, including James Joyce, Wallace Stevens, and Vladimir Nabokov. Many of Jarmusch's characters are foreign or anachronistic and, indeed, *Ghost Dog* presents many mock-heroic traits. However, Jarmusch's characters lack the despair displayed by numerous high-modernist protagonists.

3. Julian Rice's book concentrates on only three of Jarmusch's films, but the sweeping analysis is robust. Rice identifies the celebration of art found in the films and establishes Jarmusch's underlying spirituality as an essential component of his film work.

4. In the March 1, 2017, issue of *AnOther*, an online fashion and culture publication, Jim Jarmusch and Jonas Mekas, interviewed by Benn Northover, covered a wide-ranging collection of topics. Mekas told Jarmusch: "When I first read *Paterson* I thought I should meet William Carlos Williams and maybe make a film of his poems. I knew LeRoi Jones, Amiri Baraka—so we went and visited Carlos. We discussed the project, he had no patients that day. We agreed I would make some notes and then he would make some notes, and then we would meet again. But I do not remember what happened next."

5. Jonathan Rosenbaum, the most perceptive Jarmusch interpreter, points out the film-maker's interest in pairing characters who may or may not be related. The twins that appear in *Paterson* extend Jarmusch's use of characters that look alike. In his original screenplay, Jarmusch did not include the twins. A couple of extras happened to be twins, so he put them in the film as part of the narrative.

6. In an interview with *Cineaste Magazine*, Jarmusch told Leonard Quart that he based this scene "on a little Zen parable where you encounter a stranger who puts you back on your path."

CARNIVALIZED ADAPTATIONS OF OSCAR WILDE'S *THE PICTURE OF DORIAN GRAY* ON SCREEN

EMINE AKKÜLAH DOĞAN

"No more let Life divide what Death can join together."

(SHELLEY "ADONAIS" 1075–83)

CRITICISM FOR THE SCREEN ADAPTATIONS OF WILDE'S ONLY NOVEL, *THE PICTURE OF DORIAN Gray*, has been limited in focus. Most critics follow the lead of mainstream commentary on the novel and focus on issues of perceived immorality. As Robert Mighall states, "questions of the role of art and its relation to morality, and to the author's life dominated debate about *The Picture of Dorian Gray* at the time of publication" (x). Mighall reminds readers that legal counsel even used the novel as evidence meant to "prove that [Wilde] was guilty of 'a certain tendency' believed to be represented in *Dorian Gray*," namely, homosexuality (ix). Karl Beckson shows that reviewers were quick to grasp the novel's "homosexual subtext" (407). Beckson repeats the *Daily Chronicle*'s description of the novel as "a tale spawned from the leprous literature of the French *Decadents*—a poisonous book [. . .] [of] effeminate frivolity [. . . and] unbridled indulgence in every form of secret and unspeakable vice" (qtd. in Beckson, 407). Such responses are not entirely shocking. Overt homosexuality would have captured the attention of readers in the late nineteenth century. What is more shocking is the way in which contemporary commentators and critics of recent cinematic adaptations of Wilde's novel also emphasize the homosexuality of their project's titular character. To put it simply, even present-day depictions of Dorian Gray on screen are presented as examples of Wilde's flamboyant and aesthetic personality as well as a reference to his homosexual identity.

This contemporary reaction to the screen adaptations of Wilde's novel are surprising if only because they ignore the privilege each filmmaker gives "the Picture" in the story.[1] In all three moving images this chapter considers—Albert Lewin's *The Picture of Dorian Gray* (1945), Oliver Parker's *Dorian Gray* (2009), and John Logan's *Penny Dreadful* (2014–16), the Picture enjoys a presence and power as a material thing that subjugates every other aspect of the story, including the main character. This rendering actually recovers an all-too-often overlooked aspect of Wilde's novel. Wilde explores the "immoral" tendencies of his protagonist, but he does so more as an attack on the supposed moral values of his society than as some kind of personal confession. Wilde's assault on the hypocrisy of that society is, in fact, placed in the Picture, wherein the decay and corruption that poisons humanity is revealed. Such a view fits Wilde's own admitted assessment of the immorality in his story: "Each man sees his own sin in Dorian Gray. What Dorian Gray's sins are no one knows. He who finds them has brought them" (*The Letters* 266). The three screen adaptations considered in this chapter also make the Picture a central part of their story, and they do so in such a way that they reinvigorate that element in Wilde's story in provocative ways.

Such a proposal fits Wilde's own assessment of the way an adaptation can revitalize a source text, which also fits the multidirectional influence Jørgen Bruhn describes. Bruhn explains, "Any rewriting or adaptation of a text is always influencing the original work and even the most 'loyal' or repetitive adaptation imaginable is bound to be unsuccessful in terms of copying the original" (70). As such, while an adaptation acquires differences from the source text, it also changes the source text if only because it changes a reader's reception of that text. In this multidirectional model, the adaptation is always equal ground with the source text. The adaptation assumes an agentic power that gives an alternative voice to the source. This chapter insists that the Picture in the filmic adaptations of *The Picture of Dorian Gray* works similarly.

This chapter uses Mikhail Bakhtin's idea of the carnivalesque as a way to recover this voice in the three screen adaptations being explored. This study takes particular interest in the cinematic techniques of Technicolor and the camera positioning on the Picture as a means to subvert the authority of the source text by carnivalizing the films both in terms of form and content.[2] These screen stories construct the Picture as something of a Gothic doubling that performs the type of "confluence" Akıllı and Öz ascribe to some gothic narratives (16). The resulting agency turns the Picture into a kind of adaptation of the character that allows the adaptations themselves to become self-reflexive comments on the ethical contributions art and adaptations make. These moves not only decenter the human character at the center of their story, but they also transform Wilde's novel into a more degenerated exploration of a range of sexual subtexts by focusing on the animalistic tendencies in their story. In other words, the producers of the above three adaptations create through the Picture a carnivalized world that breaks the boundaries around both "ideal" adaptations and the ethical responsibilities some critics expect such texts to honor. This chapter insists that the only commitment the adaptations of Wilde's *The Picture of Dorian Gray* keeps is a willingness to become more immoral, more degraded, subversive, and corrupted. The result is the exact type of elevated text Wilde himself describes when discussing or creating adaptive art.

Wilde scholars have begun to note the extent to which *The Picture of Dorian Gray* is already an adaptation before it is ever adapted. Richard Ellmann and Graham Hough deem the novel as a "fantastic variation," to quote Ellmann, of *À rebours* (1884) by Joris-Karl Huysmans (298). Richard Aldington lists three other novels that influence Wilde: Benjamin Disraeli's *Vivian Grey* (1826), Balzac's *La Peau de chagrin* (1831), and R. L. Stevenson's *The Strange Case of Dr Jekyll and Mr Hyde* (1886). Keeping with Aldington's assessment, part of what marks Wilde's style is a willingness to adjust other literary expressions to "his unique personality[,] transform[ing] them into something fresh and attractive" (30). In this way, Wilde's novel serves as a proof for an exploratory adaptation that imbues an existing text with a new way of thinking. Such a view fits Wilde's belief that art does not imitate life in the way a mirror captures some reality; rather, it serves as "a veil" that hides the ugliness of the real world ("Decay of Lying," 228). Wilde's claim is particularly important to this chapter since it argues that the Picture in Wilde's novel means to serve as the combination and materialization of Wilde's ideas on art and aesthetics. The Picture, in other words, can resemble the dialogic and dynamic relationship between the adaptation and the source text contemporary adaptation theory seeks. An analysis of the novel and screen adaptations shows that each text frustrates a clear line between source and adaptation. The Picture simulates the actions of the human character on canvas, but Dorian also "adapts" the actions and emotions of the Picture. The dynamics of their relationship do not work in a one-way direction.[3] One can find evidence of this mutual influence in the novel, but the filmic versions are able to show this interrelationship in especially clear terms. Dorian and the Picture enlighten each other in just the way Bakhtin's notion of the carnivalesque would allow them to inform each other.

Bakhtin's concept of the carnivalesque very nearly approximates Wilde's own understanding of the revelatory influence subversive art can assume in its society. For Bakhtin, the carnivalesque exists as an artistic performance or a role-playing that builds "a second world and a second life outside officialdom" (5–6). As such, the carnival serves as an alternative life, if not utopia, where people can be their true selves, where they can go back to their origins, and they can be freed from official responsibilities. Carnival time does not have a moral aspect; neither does it concern itself with social values. Instead, following Bakhtin, it is a place of imaginative freedom that exists "between art and life" (7). This freedom is realized through a willingness to adopt a sense of the grotesque that provides a positive function for those that perceive it in that it reveals "something universal, representing all the people" even if it is also a form of degradation (19). Following Bakhtin's own assessment, degradation has a more positive connotation than more popular uses of the term tend to suggest:

> To degrade also means to concern oneself with the lower stratum of the body, the life of the belly and the reproductive organs; it therefore relates to acts of defecation and copulation, conception, pregnancy, and birth. Degradation digs a bodily grave for a new birth; it has not only a destructive, negative aspect, but also a regenerating one (21).

The carnival becomes, then, to imbue Bakhtin's words with Wilde's sensibilities, an unreal, dreamy space that subverts reality in just the way art subverts reality. The carnival reveals the true faces of humanity by exposing the animality inside every human. An encounter with the grotesque thereby initiates a process that never runs its course. It always regenerates itself. Like the earth, the grotesque body reforms itself after each corruption and putrefaction. These acts are but the first step of revitalization. Each revitalization likely ends at some different point. The resulting steps, then, are not unlike the different paths various adaptations of the same source text might take. Every adaptation realizes a different vision even if they utilize the same elements.

Together, *The Picture of Dorian Gray*, *Dorian Gray*, and *Penny Dreadful* illustrate the various paths competing adaptations of the same text can pursue. This idea is at the center of Linda Costanzo Cahir's identification of three types of adaptations:

1. literal translation: which reproduces the plot and all its attending details as closely as possible to the letter of the book;
2. traditional translation: which maintains the overall traits of the book (its plot, settings, and stylistic conventions) but revamps particular details in ways that the filmmakers see as necessary and fitting;
3. radical translation: which reshapes the book in extreme and revolutionary ways, both as a means of interpreting the literature and of making the film a more fully independent work. (200)

Tanja Meissinger uses these classifications to distinguish the various screen adaptations of Wilde's novel from each other. Meissinger deems Lewin's *The Picture of Dorian Gray* as a literal translation, and Parker's *Dorian Gray* as a traditional adaptation (43, 80). In keeping with this approach, one could deem Logan's *Penny Dreadful* a radical adaptation. Such an account would fit the eclectic manner of Logan's series. The show departs from Wilde's novel to become a collage of fictional characters from the Victorian period. Dorian Gray is an important protagonist, but he is not the only lead character. The show is equally interested in Dr. Frankenstein, Dracula, and Mina Murray. The cast of characters leads Benjamin Poore to conclude that the "series is neither an adaptation of *The Picture of Dorian Gray*, nor of *Dracula*, nor of *Frankenstein*" (70). Logan's show is something more.

The truth is that all three adaptations can be analyzed as something more than Cahir's or Meissinger's assessment allows. A discussion of each adaptation in turn will illustrate. Lewin's 1945 adaptation marks a transition from black-and-white movies to movies with color, since Lewin employs some scenes in Technicolor. As it relates to the film itself, rather than its place in film history, Lewin's use of Technicolor intends to mark the Picture as something different from the other elements in the film. The Picture is dressed in color while the other elements remain in black-and-white. Judith Mayne suggests Lewin's use of Technicolor "introduces a striking opposition between black-and-white and color, for the display of the portrait at three crucial moments [. . .] the use of color gives the painting(s) a certain autonomy" (122). The use of Technicolor does more than surprise the viewer; it also shifts the focus of the film to the Picture, which begins to overwhelm Dorian (Hurd Hatfield) and the audience alike.

Lewin indicates the particular focus he brings to the Picture each time it is placed on screen. Dorian sees the Picture while still young and beautiful. The use of color on the Picture in this scene allows the Picture to compete with Dorian's presence. The Picture appears again when Dorian tests Sibyl's (Angela Lansbury) virtue by asking her to spend the night in his house as Lord Henry had suggested. When Sibyl accepts his offer, Dorian loses his interest in her and asks her not to see him again. At this moment the narrator notes that the Picture suddenly gains "a touch of cruelty in the mouth" (39:19). Lewin withholds the Picture from the surface of his film for some time after this moment. The director does not reintroduce it again until it has been totally transformed into the grotesque image. Mayne defines the transformation in the Picture as follows: "The style of the painting has also changed. It is now in an expressionist mode, with excessive strokes, bold colors, and a myriad of indistinguishable objects within the frame" (125). Different from the change after Sibyl's death, only a "cruel look about the mouth," after Dorian murders Basil (Lowell Gilmore), the hands of the Picture get bloody, and the color red is added to reflect the blood on the actual murderer's hands.

The Picture in Technicolor shows the audience that black and white are not the only colors. However, it also implies that experiencing these colors may come with a price. These colors provide a different and exquisite pleasure, but they also cause degeneration, degradation, and rottenness. Lewin admits to wanting the color in his film to function this way:

> I got involved with making the picture exquisite. I really went to town on every set-up. When you have two thousand set-ups in a picture, it can take rather long. I was even careful about the table linen and the cutlery and whatever was on the wall. All the upholstery was built for me. I decided that everything was going to be black and white because of the good and evil symbolism (qtd. in Felleman 72).

Lewin's words propose that the director meant the use of Technicolor on the Picture to do more than just help it stand out. The color comments on the significance of the Picture, which cannot be either totally black, symbolizing "evil," or totally white, indicating "good"; rather, the Picture is a negotiation between good and evil. It is the embodiment of "cultivation and corruption" (Mighall xiii). Lewin's aim echoes, in this context, Lord Henry's words: "Sin is the only real colour-element left in modern life" (*PDG* 53). In this way, one can see how Wilde and Lewin each evaluate sin as the true color of life. However, Lewin takes Wilde's statement a step further by colorizing the life of Dorian Gray, which is to say to represent the corruption in a visible way. Ostensibly, the canvas is transformed into a grotesque image subverting the authority, purity, youth, and beauty of the human Dorian. Thus, the Picture begins to realize a kind of carnivalization that subverts Wilde's novel in regard to its form and content, and does so through the use of Technicolor.

Parker offers a similar comment in his screen adaptation, *Dorian Gray*, albeit through the stylistic technique of silence. Unlike Lewin, Parker rejects an audible narrator. The only narrator in the film is the Picture. Following Kristen Marie Fish, Parker makes the Picture *the* narrative voice in the film: "the portrait is the omniscient narrator who watches, judges, and executes consequences upon the main structural dynamic between the eternally youthful Dorian Gray, the artist Basil Hallward, and the ever-cynical Lord Henry Wotton" (5). Fish further points to Parker's use of the camera as a way to attribute agency to the Picture. By allowing the camera to frame the Picture's point of view, Parker allows the audience to see key scenes from, if not through, the canvas. The scenes with the Picture suggest that the art is an agent that literally affects the characters. The destruction and the grotesque imagery on the canvas show more than a human narrator could. These details also begin to mimic the main character. The grotesque Dorian on the canvas grows dreadful and exposes the moral lack in the human character. One can trace this lack in the Picture and the human through Parker's inclusion of a new Dorian Gray birthed the moment the human Dorian (Ben Barnes) makes his wish to be young and beautiful forever. At that moment Parker brings forward a new Dorian Gray, one who is different from both the former human and the Picture. Later in the film, this new Dorian realizes that his exquisite experiences are observed and imitated by the Picture. Even though the Picture is physically absent in most of the scenes, the corporeal entity of the thing and the human, in other words, their physical, as well as spiritual, connection, reveals that the Picture is always with and within every human pleasure and sin he experiences. Rather than restrain the human Dorian, this knowledge frees the character to pursue his animalized being with even more abandon. The Picture gives Dorian a power that transforms him into an animalized being that only seeks pleasure.

One could contend that Parker diminishes the visibility of the Picture with the inclusion of this third Dorian, but the presence of this character actually increases the importance of the Picture, as Meissinger explains:

> While the Dorians in previous adaptations often did not even dare to look at their 'mirror' and 'other self', Oliver Parker's Dorian seems to be drawn towards it. With pleasure he is seen sitting in front of his picture taking drugs, as if he tried to observe the immediate changes in his portrait. Besides, he is haunted by the fear that someone might find out about the picture and destroy it. However, despite Dorian realizing the horrible truth of his rotten soul towards the end of the film, he cannot let go of his painting (84).

Meissinger's interpretation highlights the inseparable nature of the human and his Picture. Even when Dorian is away for a long time, traveling around the world to taste new experiences, he is always with the Picture that is watching him and mirroring that same action. Dorian returns to the Picture as soon as he ends his travels to observe the changes the trip has had on the canvas. The positioning of the camera in these scenes is of particular importance, as it often suggests that the Picture is alive and is watching the events around it. Parker's use of camera lens puts the audience in the place of the main character, Dorian, which leads the audience to experience and observe the action through the canvas. This audience experiences and observes the inner desires of the character together with his thoughts and deeds. It also attributes a power and ability to the camera for traveling to the heart and the mind of the character in order to "weave the narrative" (Fish 7). Parker combines the placement of his camera with the position of the Picture in the scene to suggest that the Picture is a "seemingly omniscient, morally aware narrator" (Fish 12). It is important to note that while Parker's Picture is morally aware, it also withholds any moral judgement. Parker's picture even seems to delight in the desires it ultimately embodies. The Picture becomes a representation of the degradation the character enters.

Differing from the novel and also from Lewin's version, Parker lets the characters display the Picture publicly. It is hung on a wall at the center of Dorian's living room, a place where it could observe the environment clearly. While Buckton reads this display as a "sexual openness" (354) on the side of male characters of the film, this placement and public display of the Picture more fittingly gives the canvas the ability to watch its human partner and also the whole society coming to see it. As the characters comment on how lively and original the Picture is, one has the sense that the Picture is also commenting on its observers. The Picture watches society as it is being watched. The public display also ensures that audiences see the Picture as a character in the scene. Parker marks this idea in a particular way by ending the scene with a posed picture of Dorian, Lord Henry (Colin Firth), and Basil (Ben Chaplin) that places the Picture in the resulting image. The Picture becomes a visual echo of the man situated on the same vertical line in perspective (*DG* 20:19). This moment at least begins to suggest that the human and the Picture experience an inseparable relationship. This relationship, however, is different from the one between a human and his object. The human and the Picture reciprocally affect and are affected by the presence of each other. There is no hierarchy in their relationship; instead, the one simply narrates the other.

For Parker's strategy to work, the Picture must appear lifelike, and one can see Parker ascribing this quality to the Picture in several key scenes. The first example of Parker's attempt to create a lively Picture occurs when Dorian realizes for the first time that he is under the focus of the Picture's evil eyes. After the death of Sibyl (Rachel Hurd-Wood), and while the human Dorian is under the influence of Lord Henry's degenerate ideas, the camera swiftly assumes the point of view of the Picture. The lens of the camera blurs, and a sound of horror registers on the soundtrack (*DG* 43:28). The Picture appears tense, and the characters react to this feeling by immediately turning to see where the Picture stands. Dorian observes the cruel change in the face and also the scar on the hands of the Picture. The scar on the human Dorian is simulated by the Picture, while the hand of the human is healed. Dorian realizes his connection with the Picture, which causes him to move the canvas to the old schoolroom in the attic. This displacement does not reduce the power and agency of the Picture as the narrator of the film if only because it continues to register every sin. The audience still knows that the canvas is corrupted by the human Dorian. In this way Parker aligns the portrait with the grotesque while also subverting any image of beauty the human may possess. The true face of the man is always present on the canvas.

When the Picture returns, Parker again positions his camera so that the audience sees the action from the Picture's point of view. The Picture and the human together look at Basil standing against the creator of their connection with a surprised look on his face. The Picture narrates the past corruption of the character. The human even asks the question "Don't you recognize me?" (57:38). Later the human stands next to the painter to examine the Picture. He asserts that "together we created something beautiful" (57:53). It is not clear, here, whether Dorian refers to Basil or the Picture. It can be suggested that the human Dorian refers to his connection with the Picture. The Picture and the man exist as cocreators of this original work. Although Basil is the one who paints the young and beautiful Picture in the beginning, the combination of "cultivated corruption" at the end of the film is the production of a dialogic relationship between the human and the thing, or at least between the adaptation and the source (Mighall xiii). At the same time, Parker continues to have the audience see from the Picture's perspective. In keeping with the novel, the Picture even proposes that Dorian kill Basil, which Dorian does: "Dorian Gray glanced at the picture, and suddenly an uncontrollable feeling of hatred for Basil Hallward came over him, as though it had been suggested to him by the image on the canvas, whispered into his ear by those grinning lips" (*PDG* 191–92). While standing as a witness to the murder, the Picture possesses "a cruelty in the mouth." This cruelty is put into action later when Dorian and the Picture kill each other and bring their dialogic relationship to an end. As earlier, the camera assumes a position in this scene that invests the Picture with some sense of narrative agency. The film may begin from Dorian's point of view, but the human surrenders his sense as narrator to the Picture by the end.

One sees a different use of the Picture in Logan's *Penny Dreadful*. Hardly anyone would regard Logan's series as a "loyal" adaptation of the novel. The series exists as a pastiche of Dorian Gray, Dr. Frankenstein, Dracula, and Mina Murray. The show is explicitly nourished with the elements of Gothic

horror stories and other "penny dreadfuls." Still, Logan makes similar use of
the Picture, which, in the midst of so many departures, actually heightens
the carnivalized and grotesque aspects of the series. Logan even admits a
desire to emphasize these aspects of his story when he says his show means
to reveal "the monsters in all of us [. . .] the thing we must embrace, the
thing that frightens us, the thing that makes finally who we are" (*Penny
Dreadful Comic-Con*). An analysis of Logan's series reveals the director realizes his aim. One might even describe the series as an exposé on humans as
"human-animals" that unsuccessfully try to fight the animalistic aspect of
their being. While they may escape their own self-awareness, in the end, the
Picture reveals them.

This exposé is particularly clear as it relates to Dorian (Reeve Carney) and
the Picture. Logan creates with Dorian Gray and the Picture a clear Gothic
doubling. Sinan Akıllı and Seda Öz account for this doubling in three ways:

> True to the Gothic's "essentially betwixt-and-between nature," *Penny
> Dreadful* creates what we would like to call a 'confluent' and urban
> diegetic world which is characterized by the merging of dualities. In
> the most general sense, it is possible to observe three layers or or-
> ders of confluence in *Penny Dreadful*: first, the confluence of London/
> Demimonde; second, the confluence of the double (and sometimes
> multiple) selves of the characters; and third, the confluence of
> Romantic poetry and nineteenth-century Gothic fiction (16).

Akıllı and Öz use the term "confluence" to refer to the dynamic relationship
between two entities that are not totally separate but are also not exactly
the same. In other words, the relationship is akin to the contemporary understanding of the interconnected relationship between an adaptation and
a source text. The two entities experience a kind of "confluence" akin to the
moment when "two streams of water [. . . flow . . .] as a single but hetero-
geneous body" (25). The stream metaphor means to highlight the merging
nature of the characters with some other sense of self. The intent is not to
draw boundaries between the character and the other self, or even to split
them into halves; instead, it is to see the "'complex fragmentation of the
subject' in the context of late-Victorian Gothic writing" (20). Akıllı and Öz
suggest that "in *Penny Dreadful*, John Logan creates a 'confluent' and urban
diegetic world which is characterized by the merging of dualities" (16). The
characters exist in a kind of liminal space that sees their identities split into
two different, but not entirely separate, entities.

This perspective matches the perspective Wilde and his adaptors take on the human Dorian and the Picture. The audience knows what Dorian knows, that there exists no line between him and the Picture. He is aware that he becomes the Picture. He is also aware that the Picture offers a representation of his sins, desires, and pleasures. Dorian explicitly reveals this understanding to the audience in his speech to Lily (Billie Piper) that explains his wicked secret of immortality. He claims that one day she will lose her passion and becomes like those paintings in Dorian's home: "Beautiful and dead. [. . .] You will become a perfect, unchanging portrait of yourself" ("Perpetual Night"). Even though Lily does not know what Dorian means, the audience who already knows his relationship with the Picture understands Dorian's reference. He admits his connection with the Picture. The series, then, becomes something of a reflection on the "confluence" of the human Dorian and the Picture.

By focusing on Akıllı and Öz's idea of "confluence" and the dual nature of characters, one can see in Logan's series that Dorian is different from the other characters in the show. Dorian tolerates a confluence with his other self that they do not. This difference can be understood on two levels. Firstly, unlike the others, Dorian and the Picture do not share the same body; secondly, Dorian is happy about his evil side so long as it provides him with new experiences. On the first level, Dorian is like other characters in the show, Vanessa (Eva Green) or Ethan (Josh Hartnett): he is a combination of good and evil. The difference is that unlike Vanessa and Ethan, Dorian's other self is located in a separate body or matter. The shared condition of Dorian and the Picture does not imply that they are separate entities but proves their connectedness into a single self that manifests beauty on the human and sins on the canvas. One sees this unique instance of "confluence" most clearly through a reference to a special kind of orchid called Rothschild's Sleeper ("Demimonde"). The orchid and the wasp fashion a rhizomatic relationship as such things are described by Gilles Deleuze and Félix Guattari (10). The orchid metaphor refers to the human and his portrait and their unique embodiment. Similar to the wasp and the orchid in Deleuze and Guattari's example, the human and the Picture come together to "form a rhizome" (10). Therefore, to read this relationship with Deleuze and Guattari's words, Dorian and the Picture "imitate" each other by "reproducing" what they see while looking at each other's faces. This duplicity is what makes the orchid beautiful and aesthetically similar to the Picture when Dorian is young and beautiful. According to Dorian, the orchid, which is also young and beautiful is "poisonous like all beautiful things" ("Demimonde"). One might say Dorian is aware of this truth of sorts because of his relationship with the Picture. Their connection is poisonous even as it is beautiful. Dorian's poisonous and evil provides the Picture with a certain beauty. It also provides him the courage to experience one exquisite thing every day. The borders between good and evil are no clearer in Dorian Gray than they are in the Picture. In both cases the body that holds these beings refuses to insist on a clear division between good and evil. Both entities are a combination of these two conditions.

Logan's Dorian seems to understand this reality. Unlike Vanessa and Ethan, he makes no attempt to save himself. He embraces what has been gifted him. Any regret he might feel is overcome by the moment he experiences some new occurrence. Throughout the three seasons of Logan's show, Dorian tries exquisite pleasures. He has sexual intercourse with multiple characters: Brona Croft (Billie Piper), a whore suffering from consumption; Ethan, a werewolf; Vanessa, who is possessed by Evil; Angelique (Jonny Beauchamp), who is a transwoman; and, eventually, Lily, who is, in fact, Brona after she has been brought back to life by Frankenstein (Harry Treadaway) and Justine (Jessica Barden). Logan's Dorian continues to delight in these acts even after they occur by returning to the Picture to see the affect he has created on canvas. He delights in the degradation he sees. Even more, unlike the versions that come before his story, Logan never has Dorian try to rid himself of the Picture. This choice honors Dorian's pleas with the other characters to just embrace the evil inside them. One sees such a moment in the botanical garden scene, when Dorian tells Vanessa that what he finds "so fascinating about flowers is their duplicity. [...] Their hidden depths, at any rate" ("Demimonde"). Dorian verbalizes his fascination through a question about the soft smell of the lethal nightshade:

> VANESSA: It is the adder beneath the rose, isn't it?
> DORIAN: All of this. They can seem so enticing and luxurious, yet within, there's a dark thing waiting.
> VANESSA: Things are so rarely what they seem.
> DORIAN: Which of us does not have our secrets, Miss Ives? ("Demimonde")

In this exchange, Dorian asks Vanessa to consider how exquisite and unique the dark side can be if one knows how to use it effectively. Sensing the dark nature of Vanessa, Dorian would like the character to save herself by embracing her evil nature. Dorian makes a similar request to Lily:

Do you not yet comprehend the wicked secret of the immortal? All age and die, save you. All rot and fall to dust, save you. Any child you bear becomes a crone and perishes before your eyes. Any lover withers and shrinks into incontinence and bent, toothless senility. While you, only you, never age, never tire, never fade, alone. But after a time, you'll lose the desire for passion entirely for connection with anyone. Like a muscle that atrophies from lack of use. And one day, you'll realize you've become like them. Beautiful and dead. You have become a perfect, unchanging portrait of yourself ("Perpetual Night").

Even though he seems sorry, it is clear that Dorian knows how to live with his evil side, in part, because it has been visualized for him in the Picture. He learns how to use the ephemeral things for his own good and how to take pleasure from them. The realization follows Akıllı and Öz's concept of "confluence" in that it allows two realities to coexist. In this case Dorian and his embodiment with the Picture form a "unified whole even though they are seemingly different entities" (Akıllı and Öz 25). Dorian believes that his beauty is the result of his devilish pact with the Picture. His evil makes him beautiful and young forever. From the perspective Logan assigns Dorian, all dualities must be embraced to be human. This attitude differs from the insight Lewin and Parker give Dorian. The shift allows Logan to keep the human and the Picture on equal footing, which is to say to exist as an example of confluence because of the duality they create together. This confluence is most especially realized when the two entities exist together in the mind of the audience. Their placement on the screen can never achieve the same seamless connection they realize in the audience's imagination.

The most sophisticated understandings of adaptation reach a similar conclusion. The ultimate placement of a character between a "source text" and an "adaptation" occurs in the mind of the audience. Even the most faithful adaptation of a character will remain isolated from the character as it is realized in the source text. By tracing the development of the relationship between Dorian and the Picture across a series of expressions of Wilde's *The Picture of Dorian Gray*, one begins to see a new way of reading Wilde's adaptations. The inferiority of any one version only marks the beauty of another. In this way any departure from Wilde's text actually aligns the performance of that text to his ideas on art and aesthetics in a more carnivalized way. By departing from the source text, the adaptations considered in this chapter actually free each version to participate in the carnivalesque, which raises art to the place Wilde wanted it to exist. The literary expression begins to operate with a sense of confluence that rejects talk of two distinct realities. There is only the mutual existence of converging streams. Such is the insight of Wilde and his adaptors.

Works Cited

Akıllı, Sinan, and Seda Öz. "'No More Let Life Divide . . .': Victorian Metropolitan Confluence in *Penny Dreadful.*" *Critical Survey and Berghahn Books* 28.2 (2016): 15–29. *Research Gate.* Accessed 20 Mar. 2018.

Aldington, Richard. Introduction. *The Portable Oscar Wilde.* Ed. Aldington. New York: Viking P, 1946.

Bakhtin, Mikhail. *Rabelais and His World.* Trans. Helene Iswolsky. Cambridge: MIT P, 1968.

Beckson, Karl, Ed. "Oscar Wilde: Overview." *Gay & Lesbian Literature* 1 (1994). *Literature Resource Center.* Accessed 30 Nov. 2017.

Bruhn, Jørgen. "Dialogizing Adaptation Studies: From One-Way Transport to a Dialogic Two-Way Process." *Adaptation Studies: New Challenges, New Directions.* Ed. Jørgen Bruhn, Anne Gjelsvik, and Eirik Frisvold Hanssen. 69–88. London and New York: Bloomsbury, 2013.

Buckton, Oliver S. "Wilde Life: Oscar on Film." *Oscar Wilde in Context.* Ed. Kerry Powell and Peter Raby. 347–355. Cambridge: Cambridge UP, 2013.

Cahir, Linda Costanzo. "The Nature of Film Translation: Literal, Traditional, and Radical." *In/Fidelity: Essays on Film Adaptation.* Ed. David L. Kranz and Nancy C. Mellerski. Newcastle: Cambridge Scholars P, 2008. 198–201.

Deleuze, Gilles, and Félix Guattari. Introduction. Rhizome. *A Thousand Plateaus: Capitalism and Schizophrenia.* 1987. Trans. Brian Massumi. Minneapolis: U of Minnesota P, 2005. 3–25.

"Demimonde." *Penny Dreadful.* Prod. John Logan. Dir. Dearbhla Walsh. Desert Wolf and Neal Street Productions. 1 Jun. 2014. *The Complete First Season.* DVD.

Dorian Gray. Dir. Oliver Parker. Perf. Ben Barnes, Colin Firth, and Rebecca Hall. Ealing Studios, 2009. *Amazon.* Accessed 20 Mar. 2017.

Ellmann, Richard. *Oscar Wilde.* London: Hamilton, 1987.

Felleman, Susan. "On the Boundaries of the Hollywood Cinema: Art and the Films of Albert Lewin." Diss. City U of New York, 1993. *ProQuest.* Accessed 24 Mar. 2018.

Fish, Kristen Marie. "The Fullness of Literary Film Adaptation: A Study of the Artistic Experiences within Oliver Parker's *Dorian Gray* and Alan Crosland's *The Jazz Singer.*" MA thesis. State U of New York, 2013. *ProQuest.* Accessed 24 Mar. 2018.

Hart-Davis, Rupert, Ed. *The Letters of Oscar Wilde.* New York: Harcourt, Brace & World, 1962.

Hough, Graham. *The Last Romantics.* London: Methuen, 1947.

Hutcheon, Linda. *A Theory of Adaptation.* 2nd ed. London: Routledge, 2013.

Mayne, Judith. *Cinema and Spectatorship.* London: Routledge, 1993.

Meissinger, Tanja. "Film Adaptations of Oscar Wilde's *The Picture of Dorian Gray.*" MA thesis. Universitat Wien, 2013. *Universitats Bibliothek.* Accessed 12 Apr. 2018.

Mighall, Robert. Introduction. *The Picture of Dorian Gray.* London: Penguin, 2000. ix–xxix.

"*Penny Dreadful* Panel at San Diego Comic-Con 2014 SDCC." Inside the Magic. 25 July 2014. *Youtube.* Accessed 10 Oct 2017.

"Perpetual Night." *Penny Dreadful*. Prod. John Logan. Dir. Damon Thomas. Desert Wolf and
    Neal Street Productions. 19 Jun. 2016. *Amazon*. Accessed 20 Mar. 2018.
The Picture of Dorian Gray. Dir. Albert Lewin. Perf. George Sanders, Hurd Hatfield, and
    Donna Reed. Metro-Goldwyn-Mayer, 1945. *Amazon*. Accessed 21 Mar. 2017.
Poore, Benjamin. "The Transformed Beast: *Penny Dreadful*, Adaptation, and the Gothic."
    Victoriographies 6.1 (2016): 62–81. *Edinburgh University Press*. Accessed 12 Feb. 2018.
Shelley, Percy Bysshe. "Adonais." *English Romantic Poetry and Prose*. Ed. Russell Noyes. New
    York: Oxford UP, 1956. 1075–1083.
Stam, Robert. "Introduction: The Theory and Practice of Adaptation." *Literature and Film:
    A Guide to the Theory and Practice of Film Adaptation*. Ed. Robert Stam and Alessandra
    Raengo. Malden: Blackwell, 2005. 1–52.
Wilde, Oscar. "The Decay of Lying." *Oscar Wilde: The Major Works*. Oxford: Oxford UP,
    2000. 215–40.
Wilde, Oscar. *The Picture of Dorian Gray*. London: Penguin, 1949.

Notes

1. Throughout the chapter, I capitalize "Picture" to emphasize the argument that this object possesses an agentic nature over the human character.

2. This statement has in mind Çağrı Koparal's argument in "Robbing the Source Text of His Authority: The Robin Hood Story as Dialogic Intertext." MA thesis, Hacettepe University, 2015.

3. This statement accepts Linda Hutcheon's idea that adaptations are to be evaluated in terms of both the changes an adaptation makes and that adaptation's resistance to change, rather than simply one or the other (xxvi).

INTO THE FUTURE FROM *OUT OF THE PAST*

Double Binds, Double Crosses, and Ethical Choice

LARRY T. SHILLOCK

As for *Out of the Past*, the book and film are entirely different.
The film is a lot better, a lot less confused.

DANIEL MAINWARING

Don't you see you've only me to make deals with now?

KATHIE MOFFAT

TO READ CRITICISM OF *OUT OF THE PAST* (1947), JACQUES TOURNEUR'S CANONICAL FILM NOIR, is to enter a domain that privileges detectives and gangsters over women characters. A 1947 review in *Variety* sets this tone for Tourneur's film by emphasizing that the "plot depicts Robert Mitchum as a former private detective who tries to lead a quiet, small-town life" ("*Out of the Past*" 447). Bosley Crowther, writing shortly after the film's premiere, admits to understanding only its first half; still, "this story of an ex-private detective who is shanghaied from a quiet, prosaic life to get involved with his old criminal associates is intensely fascinating for a time" (18). In an online reconsideration, Roger Ebert (2004) refers to its "noir hero" and uses six masculine pronouns in three sentences before summarizing the film as "the story of a man who tries to break with his past and his weakness and start over again in a town, with a new job and a new girl." Scholars have been no less taken by detectives and the gritty streets they walk, albeit with more attention to the women in the story. In an influential attempt at a pure model of the detective film cycle, for instance, James Damico states that such a man's work can be inseparable from a femme fatale's attractions (103). Blake Lucas concurs, naming *Out of the Past* as "one of two films that best evoke a subject central to the genre: the destruction of a basically good man by a corrupt woman he loves" (218–19).

36

Introducing *Women in Film Noir*, E. Ann Kaplan, too, foregrounds the erotic dynamic of hardboiled film narratives, noting that "the femme fatale was often evil and deliberately used her sexuality to draw the hero into the enemy's hands" (10). Even a recent survey of film-noir scholarship falls victim to the idea, to borrow Elizabeth Cowie's astute observation, "of see[ing] women characters as occupying a subordinate position" (135)—as if, that is to say, it were axiomatic that the pursuit of a femme fatale or the investigation of her crimes is more about the pursuer-investigator than the person who sets the plot in motion, defends her story against those who would retell it, and evinces as much intelligence as the beauty or pathology with which she is so often credited.[1]

The present chapter challenges this long-held commonplace. Focusing on *Out of the Past*, which Robert Ottoson names as "quite simply the *ne plus ultra* of forties *film noir*" (132), it explores the ethical issues that get obscured when viewers exaggerate the centrality of Jeff Bailey (Robert Mitchum) to the film. It treats Kathie Moffat (Jane Greer) more equitably, not as a girl or love object or baby-faced killer whose function is to be an obstacle to a man's heroic quest, but as an agent of the plot, someone defined no less by the double binds she first negotiates than by the double crosses she later designs.[2] The chapter begins with a discussion of the film's source text and screenplay before tracing the adaptational choices that raise a gangster's dame to narrative prominence. What her character achieves will, more than once, be taken from her, producing a sense of loss and fear of violence that compel her self-allegiance. While Moffat's ultimate fate is deserved, the revenge plot that she supplants speaks to the limits of mobility that postwar film would impose upon one of its most defiant characters.

In 1946 Daniel Mainwaring published *Build My Gallows High*, a pulp novel, under the pen name of Geoffrey Homes; produced by RKO, *Out of the Past* premiered one year later. The rapidity with which the novel became an A-list film would suggest that the process was an efficient one, but that was not quite the case. As Jeff Schwager has shown, producer Warren Duff and Tourneur rejected an early screenplay by Homes-Mainwaring and were correct to do so. James M. Cain followed by penning two versions with not much more success. It would fall to Frank Fenton, a reliable scenarist who was little known outside of the studios that employed him, to add "the bulk of the film's best dialogue," "many of the film's key plot elements," and a rounded believability to the leading characters (16).

Build My Gallows High begins at the point when so many narratives so often end: with two lovers discussing marriage. Jeff "Red" Bailey, 42, is fishing for trout on a creek rising from the eastern Sierra Nevadas. Ann Miller,

20, joins him, fishing rod in hand. A veteran of the war, he was a detective in New York and California before buying a gas station in Bridgeport. As his love interest, Miller is slight, freckled, and boyish. From the first, she proves outspoken in her desire, going so far as to propose that he propose to her. Bailey notes that her youth and his living under an assumed name are impediments. "Nothing matters, but us, does it?" (3), she responds. A statement as well as a question, her utterance is unambivalent; her ethical standpoint, resolute. Bailey, by contrast, knows that the bonds of allegiance extend beyond love and, once contested, can threaten it. His troubled past, including a stint at war, and her parents' opposition pose obstacles to marriage. Surprisingly, he relents, thinking, in the novel's omniscient narration, "The past was dead. Ten years dead, and buried deep" (4).

The lovers cannot marry because they have not overcome a series of obstacles, as romance genres require, and because the past often imposes itself in pulp novels (and film noir), making choice a trial of cognition and ethical character. Accordingly, and within the span of one sentence and two hours, his identity is compromised, their stasis disrupted, when Joe Stefanos—"the little Greek" (5)—arrives from out of that dead past and insists he meet with Parker, a corrupt former police chief from Los Angeles who "runs a gambling joint in Reno" (51). Parker knows Bailey—the name our detective prefers and that I use throughout—as Red Markham of Peter Markham and Jack Fisher, Private Investigators, and wants to hire him. Exposed, Bailey faces the first of the dilemmas that punctuate the action and test characters' allegiances. Here, he must decide whether to accept a highly paid job that will involve breaking the law. Should he refuse, he risks retribution from a corrupt ex-cop. His plight recalls that of other figures from classical Hollywood cinema (e.g., the retired sheriff recalled to defend a town one last time in a western, the criminal mastermind blackmailed into a final job in a heist film). Bailey too cannot stay retired, since his debts take precedence over his ethical bonds to Miller. Thus, the novel's present focus must, like its genre allusions, expand to encompass the past.[3] Bailey agrees to take down New York attorney Lloyd Eels, who, Parker says, has "been sniping at a friend of mine" (12–13). In short order, he also meets "the dame" (13), Mumsie McGonigle, a former lover, and becomes enmeshed in an elaborate revenge plot.

McGonigle is at once well- and ill-appointed. Like Miller, her instructive contrast, she is slim but possesses "long lashes," "pale hair," and a "full breasted body sheathed in satin and lace" (109). Shown in her negligee, she recalls a 1940s pinup, the very image of feminine excess and masculine fantasy. A lover named her Mumsie, thereby asserting his patriarchal rights over her. His new name elides her old identity and serves as an index of character that men miss. Specifically, Mumsie can be "mum"—self-possessed, tactical—even while speaking. During the scene with Bailey, her first three statements are brief, unconvincing lies. Disadvantaged by being a woman in a man's milieu and a possession, since Parker bought her from a fellow gambler, she knows that women like her navigate the terrain of gambling dens by being desirable. Men who revel in a dame's surfaces and words—ignoring her motivational depths and silences—thus imperil themselves. The novel poses similar obstacles for its readers by treating McGonigle largely as a two-dimensional, offstage presence, obscuring how much she has learned from hardboiled experience that is both ethical detriment and prologue to violence.

Novels do not find their way to the screen unchanged, and the multiply authored screenplay incorporated cuts that Schwager does not consider. In keeping with studio protocol, for instance, it deleted characters assertively. Minor figures, and the pulp atmosphere they contributed, were among the first to go. Doormen, secretaries, elevator operators, passersby on the streets, cops, kids, cab drivers—those persons who provide a novel's connective tissue—all were out. Less predictably, the screenwriters excised the plot's dominant antagonist, Guy Parker, as well as his hired killer, "Slats" Ryan, and reduced the role of a second gangster's henchman. The writers addressed less tangible matters as well, including the ethical constraints imposed by the Production Code. At issue was its decree that no villain could go unpunished for crime.[4]

Out of the Past opens briskly as Stefanos (Paul Valentine) drives into Bridgeport during the credit sequence and interrogates The Kid (Dickie Moore) working for Bailey. Shortly thereafter, the film cuts to Bailey and Miller's fishing excursion and no less efficiently outlines their relationship. But the screenplay inverts aspects of the novel's first scene, replacing a fly rod with a spinning reel, a stream with a tarn, and Miller's request for marriage with a thoughtful proposal from Bailey that goes unanswered. As played by Virginia Huston, Miller is older, less boyish and athletic, still dependent on her parents' approval. Tellingly, she consents to being kissed, rather than kissing Bailey herself. Often backlit—even when outdoors—she is tied to domesticity and so feminine she could be in the wrong film cycle. In a second casting change, Stefanos is not little or Greek. He is tall, droll—a killer working for an employer, Whit Sterling (Kirk Douglas), with a long and ruminative memory. Tightly composed by Nicholas Musuraca, the deep-focus two-shots of Stefanos and Bailey amid the garage's machinery foreshadow little room for maneuvering and signal that gas stations are "a fixed locality servicing the mobility of others" (Turim 178). Wearing a black coat, Stefanos circles, rejecting an offer of dinner and a quick parting. "I'm still working for that guy, Jeff," he says, smiling. "He'd like to see you." Even viewers unfamiliar with the novel see that Stefanos, by imposing on Bailey's workspace, has an agenda. Bailey, his eyelids suspicious, relents.

Unlike its source, where Stefanos drives Bailey to Reno where he will accept the Eels job and go to New York, the film cuts to Miller's parents' house. In a scene shot day-for-night, Bailey asks her to go to Tahoe. The filmscape darkens when, in an extended voice-over, he takes us back three years (not ten) to the prediegetic sources of the film (and not the novel). The temporal shift is a cornerstone of film noir, a sign of its "singular concern with or awareness of the nature of narration" (Telotte 12). The drive provides details crucial to the exposition as it asserts the story's actual beginnings. *Out of the Past*, it follows, does not begin in Bridgeport with Bailey, as reviewers and scholars reflexively insist, but with Moffat and Sterling, whom we have not met, and their less-than-sterling relationship. Framed by the driver's-side window, Bailey uses the cover of night to tell Miller about his past. "Some of it is going to hurt you," he says. His experience and her role as audience matter more than affect. Characteristically, she defers to him as he speaks of his past as if it had been lived by someone else.

The flashback begins with Bailey and Fisher at the apartment of a powerful New York racketeer. Readers expecting "that guy" to be Guy Parker have been misled by these references, since the screenwriters deleted him. The Sterling house call occurs "because some dame had taken four shots at him with his own .38," Bailey explains. "Made one of them good." Lou Baylord (John Kellogg), a henchman, has been cut from the scene too, and so his lines explaining the job go to Sterling and Stefanos. "She ran out on me," Sterling says; "with 40,000 bucks," Stefanos introjects. "I want her back," the crime boss adds, commanding the scene until the unnamed woman's return comes up. "What happens to her?" Bailey asks, an ethical concern upon which his acceptance of the deal turns in the novel. "I won't touch her," Sterling replies. Made in level tones, his promise implies that he has touched her harshly before.

Removing Parker and Ryan, a gambler and hit man, recharacterizes the novel's leading characters. Without its dominant villain, the story can bring Sterling out of his gambling dens and into the action. Excising Ryan cuts the number of hit men, enabling Stefanos to span the plot from its exposition to just shy of its reversal-climax. Two men now work in concert, not four. Most importantly, the changes create a gender-inverted opportunity for McGonigle's complex successor to be other than a dependent dame. Since Parker and McGonigle were a criminal team as well as lovers, the plotting they did in the novel, dominated by Parker, will fall to Moffat alone—and to whichever man she allies with.[5] If we accept Sterling's account, and there is little reason not to, the double crime of attempted murder and burglary signals that she will impose her will on others. Disabled, the racketeer cannot pursue her and so must pay a detective to do it for him. Extending the affront, she stole his gun and cash, without which there is little midcentury gambling business. Now that Parker, the corrupt representative of the law, cannot be in the dame's mind, and Sterling is injured in heart and pocketbook, the central female character is free of domestic control and enjoys a mobility unavailable to a gambler's moll. Her departure changes the story by changing how women are represented and, in Moffat's case, will represent themselves.

By accepting the job, Bailey sides with a known thug, a choice unbefitting a hero.[6] He sets out to find and interview Moffat's personal maid, Eunice Lennon (Theresa Harris). Their meeting in a segregated nightclub is not in the novel and would not have been cheap to film. To borrow from important work on critical inference (Bordwell 2–3), we might say that the scene exists to distinguish Moffat from McGonigle, to suggest why she fled, and to show the detective at work. As the novel intimates, McGonigle is an older man's younger woman whose primary skill is eliciting desire by lounging about; she *could* be bought and possessed. Moffat's outlines, by contrast, are indistinct and framed by two racketeers. Her character comes into more focus by virtue of what Lennon does. Despite disliking Sterling, her employer, she nursed Moffat through a bad reaction to being vaccinated and safeguards their relationship by lying to a white man about where she went. The point is not only that the maid protects her mistress but, in black and white, that Moffat inspires affection and loyalty.[7] The vaccination datum and gun combine to show that she planned to shoot Sterling; hers was thus not an act of compulsive desire alone.

The meeting with Lennon points Bailey south and west to Acapulco, seeking a woman he knows only by photograph and, inexplicably, expects to find by waiting in a café, La Mar Azul (The Blue Sea). His waiting succeeds: "And then I saw her, coming out of the sun," he states in voice-over to Miller, "and I knew why Whit didn't care about that forty grand." Wearing white, Moffat enters in an off-centered, frame-within-a-frame long shot that balances her beauty and self-possession. His reaction shots register surprise, concern, interest, and uncertainty. While viewers see from his point of view, she is not a victim of the political economy of the gaze, even though, in Laura Mulvey's terms, she is spectacular (19). Any such illusion ends as Moffat commands the negative space before her. Her first sentence, "I don't want a guide," is paired with a critical glance at Bailey for calling her a "very difficult girl." Posing as a lonely tourist earns him little information, and, as he talks, sizing her up, she sits composedly. Who she is and what she wants go unsaid until she implies that he try Pablo's, a bar she sometimes visits.

That a detective should approach such a woman warily is a given. Moffat may be a poor shot, but she is, nonetheless, a would-be killer, thief, and flight risk. Still, larger forces affect the will and ethical choice; and being right and doing right conflict for Bailey two nights later at Pablo's. Newly attentive to him, she listens and laughs easily, his equal in their banter. When she calls him curious for not being curious about her background, he asks questions and appreciates her answers. Here, despite Moffat's accomplished femininity and Bailey's rough-hewn appeal, despite the film's sudden lyricism, it would be a mistake to think he is taken in by her (or she by him). Even after they trade kisses passionately on the beach, he maintains his reserve. Abruptly, she looks down and asks, "When are you taking me back?" Moffat has made him as Sterling's henchman come to end her freedom. Cornered, her next statements are deeply felt and true: she hates the gambler and wishes him dead; she could have already fled. When Bailey responds coolly, she changes tactics. A tremulous note intrudes, and she shifts from what she has done to how he feels, intimating romance. He avoids her searching gaze until the $40,000 comes up, and she denies having stolen it. The girlish tourist who failed, earlier, to know how to gamble so as to "lose more slowly," is gone. In her place is a person who reads others intelligently, answers questions almost before their last words take form, tells truths and lies without signaling which is which, all while speaking complete sentences. In practice, her utterances and emotions converge, and her gestures and facial expressions reinforce what she would have him believe. To make recourse to beauty privilege or gender performance is inadequate here, since how Moffat acts and, crucially, reacts stems from a powerful understanding of others' interests and bonds of obligation.

Rather than indict either character for manipulation, we should recall the crucial detail that Moffat fled because "she got pushed around." The directness with which a Black maid tells an unknown white man about a noted gambler's violence is telling; and given Moffat's hatred of him, we can infer that the abuse occurred more than once. The omnipresence of Stefanos, a killer on payroll, itself presses that conclusion. To Moffat, then, Sterling would possess and display her; she would possess her self for herself. Which to choose? Viewers should not side with a gangster over an abused, unemployed, unmarried woman. Indeed, Moffat was right to fear for her safety, right to defy a powerful racketeer, right to establish a life alone. As the detective's intrusion signals, her dilemmas endure. She may therefore make a claim on audiences' sympathies, one that critics, influenced by her actions in the second half of the film, deny quickly.

Bailey insists that he too is unsympathetic; but when their encounter ends, she leaves the beach alone. The two see each other nightly and soon fall in love. The Acapulco set-piece, as a whole, enchants. If *Casablanca* (1942) gets enduring credit for its Paris flashback, *Out of the Past* deserves no less for its romantic equivalent. No longer feeling cornered, Moffat becomes open and playful. Bailey responds with a wry warmth. As James Harvey observes, "they seem to do a lot of laughing together, and to be genuinely having fun—more like a couple out of the great romantic comedies of the thirties than the doomed noir lovers that we know they are" (16). But we do not *know* they are doomed, only what we have seen and heard. Patently, the characters have chosen each other. Therein lies the plot's complication and attendant dilemmas, since Bailey is working for, and has been paid by, Sterling. He is thus ethically and contractually bound to him. He is as well a lover to a remarkable beloved, and therefore must choose between irreconcilable allegiances. What surprises us is not so much the joy they feel together but that our on-the-run pair is able to love at all, since she loves him despite having been hurt by his employer, and he loves her knowing that she tried to kill a man and could do so again. While neither lover is heroic, their love is almost certainly so, since both risk self and freedom for its fulfillment. In their most intimate moments, the lovers transcend circumstance together.

Their best such moment occurs when she invites him home. There, to the sound of rain, he asks her to go away with him. "Why," she asks, hesitantly. "To make a life for ourselves; to get away from Whit," he says, adding, "He knows I'm here." Struck into silence, Moffat crosses the room, her pained face matched to the low-key lighting. His features—like his understanding—are obscured by darkness. Laughter thus gives way to her need to determine if he acts as detective or lover. Remarkably, Moffat foreswears the approach she used on the beach. "Can we get away with it?" she asks, sounding little like a dame. Bailey is confident that Sterling will forget them. She is not. "Are you afraid?" she asks, her eyes on him. "I'm only afraid you might not go," he replies. "Don't be," she says. He thus sheds his reserve, and she affirms their love. But Bailey should fear the obsessive gangster, since the lovers face an unknown future, and ethical allegiances, as such, change.

Despite what we have seen, Bailey remembers the time with Moffat less idyllically. As he tells Miller in voice-over: "I knew where I was and what I was doing, and what a sucker I was." When a character comments upon the past, the adaptational issue is less fidelity to the source text (the novel has no comparable scene) than congruence of representation and memory. Bailey's unconvincing account of his time with Moffat is mediated by later developments, and it is influenced further by his audience. Miller would not know a gambler's girlfriend if she met one, but her response to his love for another woman matters. On one point he is correct: an accounting is due, since among the debts that remain to be paid is the double-crossing of his gangster-employer.

The first such accounting occurs after Moffat and Bailey return to California. Fisher, hired by Sterling, tracks them to a remote cabin. In the novel, a fight ensues, he goes for his gun and, overcome by Bailey, shoots himself. The film's version is expansive, a change enabled by cuts to the script.[8] Now the writers send Fisher too out of the dark past to arrive at a poor time, since the lovers are elated at being reunited. In no hurry to discuss terms, he insults Moffat and scorns Bailey for being involved with her. As the scene darkens, she watches the men press for verbal advantage. "Jeff," she says, shifting her purse, "he isn't going to tell Whit anything." Sterling could handle being shot, losing money, and even Bailey "falling down on the job," Fisher says, but "you ganging up together? He might not like that." The pitch is simple: he wants the entire forty grand. Bailey responds with a punch. Once the fight begins, high-contrast lighting dominates, an index of the stark dilemmas Moffat and Bailey face, separately and together. Musuraca cross-cuts from the men to no-reaction reaction shots of her. Shown without fill lights to soften her appearance, she stands grimly against the wall. Fisher, grinning, hits Bailey repeatedly. Without averting her gaze, she reaches into the purse for Sterling's gun. Just as Bailey gains the advantage, she fires a bullet past his side and into a falling Fisher. Bailey freezes in reaction. "You didn't have to kill him," he exclaims. "Yes, I did," Moffat replies, jumping on his line. Musuraca dramatizes their differences by deepening the lighting contrast and matting the upper part of the image. The resulting black frame isolates her in an over-the-shoulder shot whose dimensions match the one that first showed her walking through the archway at La Mar Azul.

Bailey is right to say that an unconscious Fisher posed no immediate threat. Moffat is no less right to say that his partner, if alive, could have continued to blackmail them. Should Sterling have learned of the double cross, it follows, he would have sought revenge. Indeed, he dismissed Bailey's offer to return what he had been paid and end their deal by saying, "I fire people, but nobody quits me." This offer was less ethical than it seems, because it was made even as the lovers planned to board a steamer and go into hiding. As such, to say that each lover is "right" is not to say that either is ethical. It is instead to draw attention to their irreconcilable views and to recall Hegel's tragedy of two rights, especially its crucial point that characters in conflict can be incapable of taking in, and ethically accounting for, another's closely held position (see, e.g., Bradley 72; Taylor 175; Butler 31).[9] How the lovers assess the ending of the brawl turns on their respective identities. He is a detective; his professional code allows for retributive violence but rarely murder. She is a woman who wishes never to be victimized again. The most telling thought—almost an epiphany-image—flickers unspoken across her features and must be inferred by us: "I remain vulnerable, and you are not capable of protecting me."[10]

Moffat's assertion that you either kill a blackmailer or let him live to hurt you in multiple ways may be a false dichotomy. (It does not appear in the novel.) Once the question of killing becomes a crucial plot point, further dilemmas form. The lovers fail these tests of character when, as Bailey examines Fisher's body, Moffat flees, leaving him to cover up, not report, the murder. As she drives off, signaling a newly opportunistic mobility, he finds a $40,000 deposit in her bank book, the money she denied having stolen. He is abandoned; their allegiance is thus broken. Whatever hope of ethical progress we may have held out for Moffat, once she was free of the racketeer, dissipates, since, for an abused woman to lie for self-protection can be ethically justified; to kill someone deliberately cannot be. A third option was available to the lovers all along: her suffering, their shared flight, paid for by Sterling's money. Fisher's death gave them an opportunity to set aside their competing positions and resolve, dialectically, to move ahead and far away, despite the crimes and lies that estrange them here. Moffat's bond was once with Bailey, but by rejecting the obligations of love for a deadly self-preservation, it is now apparently to herself alone.

Moffat is no dame, moll, or beloved. By hoarding truth and loving and killing strategically, she becomes a femme fatale. Unwilling to play a bit part in someone else's narrative, femmes fatales seek to achieve outsized ambitions through action (Place 56–57). Despite being conventionally, if not also excessively, feminine, they borrow from the domain of masculine behavior to advance their interests. Mobility, be it social or sexual, is crucial to them. Miss Wonderly/Miss Leblanc/Brigid O'Shaughnessy (Mary Astor) is one such precursor to Moffat. She steals the talismanic Maltese falcon, arranges for it to be shipped to San Francisco, hires detectives, kills Miles Archer (Jerome Cowan), sets her fellow thieves against each other, and romances Sam Spade (Humphrey Bogart). Despite being tied to the domestic sphere, Phyllis Dietrichson (Barbara Stanwyck)—for another—seduces Walter Neff (Fred MacMurray), convinces him to kill her husband, helps to dispose of the body, shoots her lover-partner, and remains free until the penultimate scene of *Double Indemnity* (1944). And Helen Grayle (Claire Trevor)—as still another—compels Moose Malloy (Mike Mazurki) to take the fall for a crime she committed, creates a new identity, marries a much older man, betrays him sexually with women and men, invents a crime, kills one man and bludgeons another with a sap, pockets the payoff, double-crosses blackmailers, and keeps a detective at bay until the climax of *Murder, My Sweet* (1944). The 1940s femme fatale both conceives of and drives the plot, leaving investigators and villains alike to react after the fact and to her crimes. Her agency and mobility, often played down by reviewers and scholars who would play up a hero's investigation, underscore hardboiled dramas in ways that should astonish.

Out of the Past flash-forwards to the present as Bailey and Miller approach Sterling's estate, where, astonishingly, Moffat now resides. It is not clear why, with riches and a fast car in a vast land, she has resubordinated herself. For his part, Bailey is tired of running, and despite his surprise at the setup wants to know what Sterling has on them. During a breakfast that opens with a claustrophobic three-shot, the gambler ribs Moffat and Bailey aggressively, his eyes measuring each utterance's impact. "Kathie's back in the fold," he gloats. "You're back in the fold too now, Jeff." Observing her dependent femininity and his averted gaze, he presses the point: "See, Jeff, you owe me something. You'll never be happy till you square yourself." Having staged Bailey's alienation, the screenwriters create a means for his reintegration by imposing new dilemmas. At issue is not if he will work for the racketeer so much as how he will do the job on offer. Sketching its outlines, Sterling assigns Bailey to Meta Carson (Rhonda Fleming) in San Francisco. She will give him access to tax records that Leonard Eels (Ken Miles) is using to extort $200,000—a remarkable sum—from Sterling. Once the records are in the right wrong hands, Bailey's debt will be paid.

Two reversals vie for viewers' attention: Moffat's return and Bailey's reemployment. Reversals are motivated, not random, and knowledge should follow from a narrative's new direction (Aristotle 14).[11] The opposite happens as Moffat goes to Bailey. As she implores him to see that she was without options, audiences may as well be on the beach in Acapulco. "I had to come back," she claims. "What else could I do?" The hardboiled insults that Fisher did so well now come from him. Scornfully, he says, "You're like a leaf that a wind blows from one gutter to another." Her eyes widen, and she begs for him to trust her, but he wants to learn if Sterling knows of Fisher's death. She wouldn't tell anyone; "I swear it, Jeff. Believe me." Close-ups underscore her speech, and the theme song, "The First Time I Saw You," swells, reinforcing her romantic promise. Yes, he has been taken in by this calibrated performance before, but its appeal may not be the telling point. Even if Bailey were able to distinguish her truths from lies, his quandary remains: he will be working with criminals who have framed his future, and so he can know for certain only that Sterling's crew plots well ahead of him. The film, as if in recognition, slows momentarily to give us time to think over Moffat's performance and recalibrate her allegiances going forward.

Despite these epistemological limitations, Bailey evaluates his circumstances in his role as detective. Once in San Francisco, he suggests to Eels that he is in danger and watches as Carson departs the building where they work, folder in hand. Bailey knows too little, his intervention too late, to save Eels; and Stefanos sees to the murder. As film noir decrees, the detective cannot set law right, now that it is so corrupt, but he can be responsible to his identity and the community by creating obstacles to the racketeers' plans. In effect, he must shift the locus from his reactions to plot complications to theirs. Bailey changes the narrative's direction by moving Eels's body from the crime scene before breaking into Carson's apartment, intent on finding the tax records. There, he watches as Moffat calls the landlord so that the body can be found and the police called in.

Fearing that he is in a frame, Bailey investigates so that he might fill in what he calls its "picture." It is precisely now, in his contributions to the scenes in Eels's and Carson's residences, that reviewers and scholars are justified in foregrounding the detective. But the film is more complex than their explanations and his awareness allow. Indeed, as its narrative shifts from Sterling, Stefanos, Moffat, and Carson to Bailey and back again, the plot becomes a descending spiral more than a picture or a line whose direction has reversed. Moffat now twice impersonates Carson and, distraught to learn that there is no body, phones Stefanos, her brow furrowed in thought. When Bailey steps forward as the foil, she offers a feeble lie: the murder was not meant to implicate him. Manhandling her, he says that Eels has fled. She gathers her w(h)its: "I don't want to die," she cries, suggesting that her participation was extorted from her by Sterling. "I don't want to die either, baby," Bailey replies, "but if I have to, I want to die last."

He has the best hardboiled patter, but she has the better moves. Holding Bailey's gaze for fourteen seconds without blinking, a sign of remarkable self-control, Moffat says she is glad that Eels is alive because the plan was to blame his death on Bailey. "You're wonderful, Kathie," he says, hurt. "You're magnificent. You can change sides so smooth." He could as well add adroit, creative, and quick to the list of her cognitive virtues. "I'm almost getting it," he adds. "Very pretty." Framed by a window, Bailey names the steps of the plot aloud, as if he were confronting a villain in a mystery's penultimate scene. Viewers relish his grasp of the crime and concur that there has to be a motive implicating him, not Sterling, for the death of Eels. "There's only one thing missing: the plant," he says. Moffat confesses that, helpless and alone, she signed an affidavit naming him as Fisher's killer. With his strength and her weakness on display, viewers can miss the character insight that Musuraca signals by cutting to a low-angle, medium shot of his monologue. The long take with an embedded pan is from her point of view. The moving camera signals movement in the plot, from his thoughts to hers. Thus, while he talks, she measures how much he knows and plans a response. He *does* get it, and the feminine plot *is* pretty. A smarter man would have kept his knowledge of the plotting from such an adversary.

As Bailey walks out of the frame, the shot stays on her as she concludes that a new tack is needed. The lovers' failed allegiance has led to being controlled in the same way by the same man, and to escape blackmail, they need to cross him together.[12] Moffat's opening comes when Bailey, still off-camera, admits to coming around to her assessment of Sterling's taste for violence, saying, "That Whit can really hate. You said it once, he can really remember." The lovers parted ways precisely because of two disagreements—over Sterling's capacity for revenge and the necessity of Fisher's murder. Quickly, she takes Bailey in her arms, a fitting erotic inversion, and hits the right subjects and emotional notes in her speech: helplessness, shared hatred, entrapment, mutual self-interest, freedom. "We don't have to be against each other now," she says. "We can break out of it. All we need is the briefcase." She thus proposes that they double-cross a double-crosser, blackmail a blackmailer, resolve an irreconcilable disagreement, and return to the very obligations of love that she once spurned. Greer can play a girl who gambles and a woman who loves in an exotic locale, but to concentrate on her allure in the scene atop Telegraph Hill is almost unworthy of comment. What comes through as powerfully is Moffat's improvisational intelligence. As Peter Brooks has shown, plot is "the organizing dynamic of a specific mode of human understanding" (7). I read his sense of "understanding" as the master faculty of modernity. Extending his insight to characters, we might say that to plot a crime well is to think through the shifting iterations of time, circumstance, and motivation.[13]

Willing to bargain as part of plotting their future, Moffat agrees the affidavit must be stolen, since, once they have the tax file, "we've got them, Jeff. We can get anything we want from them." Expressed in five indexical pronouns, her goal is unambiguous. Viewers cannot know if the robbery offer is in earnest, but, as the theme song spirals in, it is conceivable that retribution and romance can coexist. Given their desperate straits, then, the two may be making the right wrong moves in solidarity and by way of a new revenge plot. Who initiates the parting kiss is unclear, but at least Bailey is smart enough to act the part of the lover and keep silent.

The romantic ideas that compromised his judgment are no more. In their stead is an emerging sense that what Moffat says is less situational than multiply temporal. Film-noir victim-villains like her differentially assess the past, plan, seek revenge, and position themselves at the point at which others' narratives converge. What Moffat does in her speech acts—confess, appeal, vow, propose—may or may not carry over to her actions, a fact that threatens a detective's agency. Henceforth, Bailey will need to think more like her if he is to predict what she will do. He is scarcely alone, since, as films noirs grow complicated and near their respective climaxes, detectives often realize that they need to learn from the femme fatale as part of becoming what they assumed themselves to already be: accomplished investigators.[14] Conversely, Moffat has learned from gangsters and from the abject position she occupied in their milieu. Construed in this context, Sterling schools her by his example—and by means of threats and violence. Overconfident, he is thus vulnerable to the very plot reversals he has helped to compel.

In maneuvers almost worthy of the critical idolatry that private detectives often receive, Bailey double-crosses the racketeer, beats Baylord unconscious, and steals the tax files. Moffat's off-screen actions may be equally accomplished, as she allies with Stefanos and sends him to kill Bailey, a change from novel to film. When the story's most dangerous man is ripped from a ledge and into the East Walker River, Bailey has an opening in which to double-double-cross her as well. He returns to Tahoe to negotiate an end to the job. There, even Moffat cannot finesse the fact that a dead detective would have left the tax records he possesses in limbo. Sterling's response to the twinned reversals indicates that a deal can be done: Stefanos can be blamed for Eels's death, Moffat will go down for Fisher's, and Sterling will pay $50,000 for the files. In this scenario, the killers go to jail, justly, and Bailey to Mexico, able to live unhampered. Less an ethical hero than an astute blackmailer, the detective thus sells twice-stolen tax records so he can assume his rightful command of the plot, compelling its denouement.

Apparently, the screenwriters have created a penultimate scene in which the femme fatale's powers of acting and reacting, planning and plotting, fail. Center stage now belongs to Sterling, the abuser, wounded lover, and killer. His slapping Moffat upon learning of Stefanos's death needs no amplification. Pressing forward, noting her characteristic duplicity, he says, "I took you back when you came whimpering and crawling. I should have kicked your teeth in." The threats that ensue are the most violent directed at a woman in film noir, too vile to quote. Suffice it to say she will confess and go to jail. Any sign of disobedience will lead to torture. Sterling thus acquiesces to blackmail, folding his cards to cut his losses, as an accomplished gambler intent on winning must.

The negotiations done, Bailey returns to Miller, where he declares his fealty. "You know," he says, "maybe I was wrong, and luck is like love: you have to go all the way to find it." "You do to keep it," she responds. The two, talking at cross-purposes, get the formula wrong. What he needs to stand for ethically is not luck or blackmailing criminals but devotion writ large. The screenwriters again complicate the action by imposing multiple dilemmas—obedience or slow death, bad or good women, going "all the way" or nowhere, good or bad fortune—and would have each be restricted to two choices. But Moffat, ever thoughtful, writes her own stories and resolves her own dilemmas, and now that Sterling has no bodyguard, she shoots him in the back. Verbally abused, beaten, threatened, and blackmailed, she nonetheless imposes her will on circumstance and frees herself. Fisher, Eels, Stefanos, and Sterling are dead. Each man, secure in his privilege, underestimates a woman. Being involved with her is deadly because she is less a fixture in a man's domestic life than a determined agent in her own.

Our protagonist-villain's breadth of character is evident when Bailey sees Sterling's body on the floor, and she says, "You can't negotiate with a dead man, Jeff." Moffat is thus ungeneric, at minimum resistant to gamblers', detectives', reviewers', and scholars' attempts to represent her in their terms. She left Bailey because he imagined rather than understood her. Moreover, she did not return, helpless, to Tahoe to be resubordinated but to groom partners who would enable her to end Sterling's life. A killer, she is also a lover, a point made by her insistence that Bailey return with her to Acapulco and renew their romance. Thus, love is not doomed but, out from under the threat of relentless racketeers, freed. "And I have nothing to say about it?" Bailey asks.

From the first, Bailey's mistake was to assume that his choice—ethical or otherwise—was paramount. Sterling's parallel mistake was to think his was the only revenge plot or, later, that Moffat, beaten, would stay bowed to him. The femme fatale, once brutalized, steps free of patriarchal ethics to do as she must, succeeding in her counterplots because she has learned to see from others' standpoints. The reading of necessity she keeps secret is that others too easily hold one point of view or commit to a single obligation and thus, as Hegel's focus on the ethics of tragedy show, are held in place or die. Like the two-dimensional McGonigle in the film's source-text, she shifts her allegiances as conditions change, conditions that would compel a gangster's moll, a girlfriend, a wife to defer to a criminal, a boyfriend, a husband. Moffat, a decidedly three-dimensional character as well as a next-generation adaptation, enjoys a man's society but looks to the future, knowing that the social is an abiding constraint to women. Almost the last man standing, Bailey must choose a side in an irremediable conflict. He can reject her and be blackmailed for four deaths or, by acquiescing to her double-cross, be controlled. He might also take Stefanos's gun from his trench coat and, abjuring his code, kill her. Whichever choice he makes—prison, subordination, murder—promises its own violation. Left alone with his thoughts, he chooses a fourth tack and calls the police. Thus, he renounces his shared past with Moffat, especially their idyll in Mexico. His ethically correct choice—his deliberate setting aside of the self-division she would impose—has wrong results: the loss of Miller with the loss of his life.

The femme fatale commands her actions so that she might command the story. Born in trauma and held in secret, her understanding turns on an assessment of intricated circumstances. The power that McGonigle and Moffat exert thus resides in the disparity between what they keep secret (mum), while plotting, and what a lover misconstrues while in thrall to their intelligent beauty. A femme fatale's strength (and attendant weakness) derive from other sources as well: a tough-minded defiance, a steadfast refusal to be responsible to any law not of her own making. By siding with the self over and against someone else she takes pains to know, she secures an extraordinary mobility—erotic and decisional—but at best a brief transcendence. What she gains through revenge plots she must ultimately lose, as the Production Code decrees. Allegiance in film noir tends to be temporary and interested; allegiances in tragedy, once tested, endure in death and memory. Slavoj Žižek would have us believe that the femme fatale is "not only a tragic figure but, more radically, an *ethical* figure" by virtue of "an unreserved acceptance of the death drive" (63). He may, from the perspective of another postwar Hollywood film, be right; but here the femme fatale, fooled by a detective's last-minute plot reversal—itself made possible by what he has learned from her example—kills in anger, not acceptance. A small tragedy but a large and essential film noir, *Out of the Past* ends as it must by making the costs of an unethical, and constitutionally vulnerable, self-allegiance visible in death.

Works Cited

Aristotle. *The Poetics of Aristotle*. Translated by Preston H. Epps. U of North Carolina P, 1970.

Best, Stephen, and Sharon Marcus. "Surface Reading: An Introduction." *Representations*, vol. 108, 2009, pp. 1–21.

Body Heat. Directed by Lawrence Kasdan, screenplay by Kasdan, director of photography Richard H. Kline. Warner Brothers, 1981.

Bordwell, David. *Making Meaning: Inference and Rhetoric in the Interpretation of Cinema*. Harvard UP, 1989.

Bradley, A. C. *Oxford Lectures on Poetry*. Macmillan, 1950.

Brookes, Ian. *Film Noir: A Critical Introduction*. Bloomsbury, 2017.

Brooks, Peter. *Reading for the Plot: Design and Intention in Narrative*. Vintage, 1985.

Butler, Judith. *Antigone's Claim: Kinship between Life and Death*. Columbia UP, 2000.

Chandler, Raymond. "The Simple Art of Murder." *Raymond Chandler: Later Novels and Other Writings*. Library of America, 1995, pp. 977–92.

Cowie, Elizabeth. "*Film Noir* and Women." *Shades of Noir: A Reader*, edited by Joan Copjec, Verso, 1993, pp. 121–65.

Crowther, Bosley. "'Out of the Past,' RKO Mystery Starring Robert Mitchum, New Feature at Palace." *New York Times*, 26 Nov. 1947, p. 18.

Damico, James. "*Film Noir*: A Modest Proposal." *Film Reader*, 1978, pp. 94–105.

Doane, Mary Ann. *Femmes Fatales: Feminism, Film Theory, Psychoanalysis*. Routledge, 1991.

Ebert, Roger. "*Out of the Past*." 18 July 2004. *RogerEbert.com*.

Felski, Rita. "Latour and Literary Studies." *PMLA*, vol. 130, no. 3, 2015, pp. 737–42.

Goldhill, Simon. "The Ends of Tragedy: Schelling, Hegel, and Oedipus." *PMLA*, vol. 129, no. 4, 2014, pp. 634–48.

Grossman, Julie. "'Well, Aren't We Ambitious,' or 'You've Made Up Your Mind I'm Guilty': Reading Women as Wicked in American *Film Noir*." *The Femme Fatale: Images, Histories, Contexts*, edited by Helen Hanson and Catherine O'Rawe, Palgrave, 2010, 199–213.

Harvey, James. *Movie Love in the Fifties*. Knopf, 2001.

Homes, Geoffrey. *Build My Gallows High*. 1946. Prion, 2001.

Hutcheon, Linda, with Siobhan O'Flynn. *A Theory of Adaptation*. Routledge, 2013.

Kaplan, E. Ann. "Introduction to the New Edition." *Women in Film Noir*, edited by Kaplan, BFI, 1998, pp. 1–14.

Lucas, Blake. "*Out of the Past* (1947)." *Film Noir: An Encyclopedic Reference to the American Style*, edited by Alain Silver and Elizabeth Ward, 3rd ed., 1992, pp. 217–19.

Maxfield, James F. *The Fatal Woman: Sources of Male Anxiety in American Film Noir, 1941–1991*. Fairleigh Dickinson UP, 1996.

Miller, A. V. *Hegel's Phenomenology of the Spirit*, translated by Miller, Oxford UP, 1977.

Mulvey, Laura. "Visual Pleasure and Narrative Cinema." *Visual and Other Pleasures*. Indiana UP, 1989, pp. 14–26.

Ottoson, Robert. *The Reference Guide to the American Film Noir, 1940–1958*. Scarecrow, 1981.

Out of the Past. Directed by Jacques Tourneur, screenplay by Geoffrey Homes, director of photography Nicholas Musuraca. RKO, 1947.

"*Out of the Past*." *Variety Movie Guide*. Variety staff writers. Prentice Hall, 1992.

Place, Janey. "Women in Film Noir." *Women in Film Noir*, edited by E. Ann Kaplan, BFI, 1978, pp. 47–68.

Porfiro, Robert. "Daniel Mainwaring (1902–1977)." *Film Noir Reader 3*, edited by Robert Porfiro et al., Limelight, 2002, pp. 149–61.

Schwager, Jeff. "The Past Rewritten." *Film Comment*, vol. 27, no. 1, 1991, pp. 12–17.

Seligman, Martin E. P., et al. "Navigating into the Future or Driven by the Past." *Perspectives on Psychological Science*, vol. 8, no. 2, 2013, pp. 119–41.

Shillock, Larry T. "The Global and the Local Femme Fatale in *The Maltese Falcon*: A Reappraisal. *Philological Papers*, vol. 55/56, 2012, pp. 135–52.

Taylor, Charles. *Hegel.* Cambridge UP, 1975.

Telotte, J. P. *Voices in the Dark: The Narrative Patterns of Film Noir.* U of Chicago P, 1989.

Turim, Maureen. *Flashbacks in Film: Memory and History.* Routledge, 1989.

Wagner, Jans B. *Dames in the Driver's Seat: Rereading Film Noir.* U of Texas P, 2005.

Žižek, Slavoj. *Looking Awry: An Introduction to Jacques Lacan through Popular Culture.* MIT P, 1991.

Notes

1. A curious subgenre, the film noir plot summary routinely asserts that a film noir is a detective's story, as if the division of labor in narrative were uncontested. For such an example, see Brookes 58. My distinction throughout is between a generic stereotype or male fantasy figure and a woman whose actions and cognitions are of intrinsic interest in themselves. My points of departure include Maxfield's claim that Tourneur's film is intended "to evoke simple responses from [its] audiences." He adds, no less incorrectly, that films noirs across fifty years are linked by "the threat which a woman (or love object) poses to the life, welfare, or psychological well-being of a male protagonist" (Introduction n.p.). Similarly, despite having observed that the femme fatale "is fully compatible with the epistemological drive of narrative" (1), Doane asserts that her "power is of a peculiar sort insofar as it is usually not subject to her conscious will, hence appearing to blur the opposition between passivity and activity" (2). My position is that the femme fatale's conscious awareness is exemplary. For early criticisms of the roles scholars ascribe to film-noir women, see Place 47 and 55–57. For a recent critique, see Grossman 204.

2. In screenplays, characters are defined more by what they do than what they say. Expanding upon this truism, I borrow strategies from surface reading, an empirical approach to "what is evident, perceptible, apprehensible in texts" (Best and Marcus 9). My goal is to make evident the thinking underlying the central characters' plotting as well as the ways Musuraca represents it. Additionally, I hold that the film, as the narrative unspools, is an ethical object in itself.

3. On this point see also Hutcheon's remark that "adapted texts" go on to "haunt" subsequent adaptations (6).

4. Given its dark subjects and mise-en-scène, films noirs comply with and contest the norms of classical Hollywood cinema, and so what we might see as compliance—such as fewer on-screen deaths and adultery treated indirectly—might be better read as parts of an adaptational strategy that presses against the limits of acceptable content.

5. Responding to Bruno Latour's actor-network theory, Rita Felski reframes agency, arguing, "Actors exist not in themselves but only through their networks of association" (738). In other words, what persons do is enabled by their relations to others. The formulation might be made more accurate by seeing persons, actors, and characters—as in the case of Moffat—as existing "in themselves" *as well as* "through their networks of association."

6. "He is the hero, he is everything" (991–92), writes Chandler of the detective-protagonist. His influential remarks here are part of a remarkable and overwrought conclusion to "The Simple Art of Murder."

7. For a political reading of this scene and brief support for the femme fatale's narrative role, see Wagner 2, 4.

8. The adaptational point is that condensing a source text can allow for other scenes in a film to take on greater importance and, especially, intensity.

9. In his *Aesthetics* and *The Phenomenology of Spirit*, Hegel extends what he learns from Sophocles and treats tragedy less as a dramatic genre than as part of a larger inquiry into ethics, in the process affirming that "human self-consciousness [is] divided against itself, and yet in progress through this division and its transcendence" (Goldhill 635).

10. It is difficult to film someone's silent thoughts, and it is evidence of the film's excellence that cinematographer Musuraca and Greer, working together, do so convincingly.

11. In *Poetics*, Aristotle asserts that tragic figures "must be certain kinds of persons in character and in thinking—the two criteria by which we determine the quality of an action; for character and one's thinking are two natural causes of action, and it is because of these that all men fail or succeed" (12–13). A rich body of scholarship exists on the role of character in tragedy but not on the impact of thinking on plot.

12. For two persons to double-cross a third requires that four conditions be met. The first is a false solidarity. Should Moffat waver, Sterling can use the affidavit to implicate her in the murder. The gangster must therefore believe she is resolute even as she works with a new partner. Simultaneously, Bailey must give Sterling the impression he is following orders. The second condition is a variation on the first: a new allegiance. For Bailey to ally himself with Moffat, he must accept that she is bound to Sterling. He can then consider his self-interest and re-ally or not. Concurrently, she must believe that he trusts her enough to risk a partnership. Conditions three and four involve planning and implementation, stages which a femme fatale and a detective could be expected to excel at.

13. As the arsonist Teddy Lewis (Mickey Rourke) observes in *Body Heat* (1981): "Any time you try a decent crime you got fifty ways to fuck up. And if you think of twenty-five of them, then you're a genius." A less profane take on the primacy of what cognitive psychologists call prospective thinking can be found in the powerful work on "the mental simulation of future possibilities" in Seligman et al. "A good prospector," its authors assert, "must know more than the physical landscape—what is to be found where, with what probability—but also at what cost in effort and risk and with what possible gain. The prospecting organism must construct an *evaluative landscape* of possible acts and outcomes" (120). Measured in the terms above, Moffat is at the very least masterful.

14. On this point, see Shillock.

"ACTING VICTORIAN"

Marketing Stars and Reimagining the Victorian in Classical Hollywood

NOELLE HEDGCOCK

AMONG THE GLITZ AND GLAMOUR OF CLASSICAL HOLLYWOOD MODERNITY, A DISCERNIBLE attachment to the past manifested itself in the form of "prestige pictures," one of the most popular production trends in 1930s Hollywood. In *Film Adaptation in the Hollywood Studio Era*, Guerric DeBona describes "prestige pictures" as a set of production practices that centered on big-budget, extravagant, but "authentic" re-creations of some form of "pre-sold property" or "classic" story (43). These productions tended to be marketed in such a way that privileged fidelity to a literary source. Chris Cagle's "Two Modes of Prestige Film" discusses the way the industry used prestige pictures and adaptations of literature as attempts to elevate the status of film in the twentieth century. The essay describes one "industrial" mode of prestige films defined by the film industry and a second "social" mode defined by consumers. According to Cagle, "the industrial mode looked outward, conspicuously, towards higher cultural forms to lend Hollywood narratives the aura of respectability. The socially-defined mode looked inward, internalizing an aesthetic and form of perception that itself was meant to be culturally more elevated." Both modes depend on how the aura of canonical value could legitimize twentieth-century cinema.

DeBona's appraisal explains how prestige pictures were especially important to David O. Selznick, one of the major figures credited with developing ways to effectively sell prestige pictures during the Classical Hollywood era. Selznick's success, according to DeBona, depends, in part, on the fact that the producer was able to "reap the financial and aesthetic dividends from overtly literary capital," meaning that part of the appeal of these films was their literary counterparts (43). For Selznick, successful prestige pictures (and their marketing) relied on not only a reproduction of the story and structure of a novel "but also the minor details [at the level of plot and mise-en-scène] that elicit the strong sense of identification forged with its readership" (Edwards 34–35). In short, Selznick recognized the potential lucrativeness of an already-existing audience. He tried to capitalize on the already-formed audience without alienating audiences who were unfamiliar with a text while still attracted to a title's "literariness." In *Victorian Vogue*, Dianne F. Sadoff reaches a similar conclusion regarding Selznick's "marketing genius," asserting that his tactics of marketing adaptations allowed him to "reach the wide audience that would guarantee box-office success, critical acclaim, and industry awards" (79).

In addition to a faithfulness to the source text, implicit in many prestige pictures was an authentic re-creation of a historical moment. In "Narrative Authority and Social Narrativity: The Cinematic Reconstruction of Brontë's *Jane Eyre*," Jeffrey Sconce discusses the effort that went into contextualizing Selznick's *Jane Eyre* (1944). Sconce writes that while attempting to re-create the setting of Charlotte Brontë's 1847 novel, Selznick's team researched "everything from what foodstuffs might be found on a country dinner table to fashions in facial hair from the period" (51). Sconce concludes this historical research intended to "'authenticate' the film as an accurate version of Brontë's work" (51) and, consequently, Victorian England. This meticulous historical representation and contextualization references a larger claim that Sconce makes about adaptation in Classical Hollywood, that literary adaptation required "the economic capital of the studio to convert the cultural capital of the novel back into the economic capital of a successful motion picture" (47). Sconce asserts that this conversion involved "a complex reconciliation of the interrelated demands between fidelity to the material, practices of the medium and expectations of the audience" (47). As *Jane Eyre* demonstrates, a core component of prestige picture marketing relied on an adaptation's ability to claim fidelity to a source text while simultaneously appearing as an authentic recreation of a specific historical moment.

Though prestige pictures were appreciated by some, studios inevitably encountered multiple issues when trying to effectively market the past to a wide range of audiences in the mid-twentieth century. Some of these difficulties were linked directly to film production. Growing censorship in Hollywood was one of these major issues, as the Motion Picture Production Code, or "Hays Code," started to strictly define what was acceptable on screen between the 1930s and 1960s. Concurrently, Hollywood experienced large structural changes to the business side of the studio system. Significant cultural changes complicated these challenges as studios faced serious resistance from the moviegoing public to advance old-fashioned ideals and conservative ideology. Studios producing prestige pictures had to navigate this resistance to a "conservative" past while also capitalizing on some desire for nostalgia and the "aura of respectability" attached to classic literature and historical prestige. However, a simultaneous resistance also existed, one that refused to relinquish entirely the "traditional" past and its conservative ideology, which complicated marketing and persona construction surrounding Hollywood's modern stars. These complications were particularly apparent for female stars. Cultural shifts in gender ideologies especially complicated the process of marketing actresses who starred in filmic adaptations of Victorian literature during the Classical Hollywood era. Publicity campaigns around such films needed to market actresses as inherently "Victorian"—to adhere to the tactic of selling "authenticity"—while also promoting its female stars as glamorous, independent modern women.

This need to capitalize on some nostalgia for the past and its canonical literature while simultaneously maintaining images of modern stars in Classical Hollywood marketing tactics exemplifies what Raymond Williams has defined as "dominant, residual, and emergent" cultural formations. Dominant cultural formations represent the social norms and expectations of a given period, but residual (historical) and emergent (in opposition to historical ideology) cultural formations can be present as well. Residual and emergent cultural formations are significant because they often work to reveal the characteristics of dominant ideology. According to Williams, though residual cultural formations have been formed in the past, they remain active "not only and often not at all as an element of the past but as an effective element of the present. . . . It is in the incorporation of the actively residual—by reinterpretation, dilution, projection, discriminating inclusion and exclusion—that the work of the selective tradition is especially evident" (122–23). In short, the residual formations a period "selects" for continued interpretation, recognition, or dialogue can reveal how that period chooses to remember its past. This process of "selective tradition" is especially evident in Classical Hollywood's marketing of prestige pictures, which routinely highlighted certain elements of historical canonicity while just as routinely minimizing or removing others. By "selecting" which "traditional" elements to include, Classical Hollywood found ways to present adaptations of historical periods and texts as authentic replications of the past that could still appeal to modern tastes and sensibilities.

Consequently, prestige pictures that relied on the adaptation of prominent literary classics and intricate re-creations of moments in history also occasionally contradicted notions of "fidelity" and "authenticity." After all, antiquated aspects of the source text still needed to appeal to a wider mid-twentieth-century audience as well. In essence, a mid-twentieth-century interest in Victorianism necessitated a mid-twentieth-century reimagining of what *was* Victorian. Guy Barefoot explains a similar tendency in his essay "*East Lynne* to *Gas Light*," where he discusses the "persistence, transformation, rejection, revival and creation of 'Victorian' melodrama in the 20th century" (94). *East Lynne* functions for Barefoot as an example of a popular Victorian novel that was constantly adapted in an attempt to capitalize on "a fragrant memory of the dear old past" (97). Despite multiple efforts to transform *East Lynne* in setting and tone, Barefoot notes, "the prestige of the name had apparently become a liability, and the contrast between Victorian literature and modern film production was accompanied by the perception of *East Lynne* as a deeply conservative work upholding the Victorian, patriarchal values of female forbearance and the sanctity of marriage" (98). In contrast to *East Lynne*'s inability to escape negative associations of Victorianism, the 1938 play-turned-film *Gaslight* (1944), which admittedly seeks to adapt the Victorian era rather than a Victorian text, reveals a "more general revival of interest in Victorian art and artefacts, and how the revival involved the deliberate construction of a notion of the past rather than simply the persistence of Victorian influences" (99). This claim is crucial to an understanding of how Victorian-themed prestige pictures are marketed, because it suggests that Classical Hollywood films were interested in a "twentieth-century construction of a notion of Victorianism rather than the continuation of a direct line of descent" (102). Studios could re-create a brand of Victoriana for a twentieth-century audience with different, more modern tastes.

The fact that nineteenth-century elements required some alteration in representation to ensure the films appealed to a more "modern" viewer gives insight into how re-creations of Victorian ideas, themes, and aesthetics were influenced by the Classical Hollywood discourses constructing them. The deliberate decision to reimagine rather than revitalize the Victorian era naturally influenced marketing tactics and promotional materials. One area in which this impact is notable is the publicity surrounding female stars and the larger practice of film studios attempting to brand stars and construct star personae in order to make them more marketable in relation to certain films and genres. In the specific case of female celebrities, discrepancies in how certain actresses' star images were constructed based on different moments in their careers reveal the intricate process of creating a star's persona. These discrepancies also expose differences in how social expectations of gender applied to an average American woman versus a female celebrity. While many scholars have focused on analyzing how female characters in a film conform to or resist certain gender roles and expectations operative at the moment the film was produced,[1] looking at the lives of female stars and the marketing that surrounded them offers new insights into how historical women navigated, and were expected to navigate, gender constructs in the US during the mid-twentieth century.

Film actresses were part of a star system that focused on building personae and branding female film stars in very specific ways. These women occupied a unique space in society in that they were expected to perform certain, sometimes transgressive, behaviors on screen, while still assuming average American gender expectations off screen. Karen Hollinger highlights a variation of this duality in star image in her book, *The Actress: Hollywood Acting and the Female Star*. Hollinger discusses how film stardom involves a "mixture of fiction and reality" because there is always the "on-screen performance" and the "private self of the off-screen image" (29). Hollinger, quoting Richard Dyer, presents the star image as a "structured polysemy [. . . an . . .] infinite multiplicity of [possible] meanings and affects [. . . that create . . .] an uneasy tension [of] discordant elements, temporarily foregrounding some, while masking and displacing others through an ongoing process of negotiation, reconciliation, condensation, oscillation, and fragmentation" (30). From this perspective, a female star was never only herself; she was an amalgamation of the images of the characters she played and the marketing that surrounded her work and personal life.

One iteration of stardom that makes the division between female character, female star, and average female especially clear is actresses who were part of Classical Hollywood prestige pictures. Because these films necessarily are about the relationship of the present to another cultural moment, they had to balance dualities analogous to the dichotomies female stars had to balance. Prestige pictures and the publicity surrounding them have the power to reveal these tensions specifically because they are part of the changing discourse surrounding gender constructs and ideals of femininity around the turn of the century. Given the proximity of the Victorian era to the mid-twentieth century and yet the desire of many to insist on the Victorian era's pastness, these tensions were especially pronounced in the case of prestige pictures based on Victorian literature, particularly when the female star was also "acting Victorian." The most interesting moment to consider occurs around mid-twentieth-century America's dual use of the term "Victorian," which meant to reference female actresses portraying Victorian characters on screen and also to criticize female stars for being "cold" or "conservative" off screen. This discourse captures one of the ways that shifting gender ideologies and mid-twentieth-century perceptions of Victorianism complicate the studios' attempts to craft a useful persona for their female stars.

While it is true that Classical Hollywood marketing sought to create the "picture perfect" female star, the idea of self-fashioning existed long before the mid-twentieth century, perhaps most explicitly in the form of women's conduct literature. Barbara Welter's influential article "The Cult of True Womanhood: 1820–1860" includes a comprehensive survey of nineteenth-century conduct literature, which aimed to relay to women the ideals and expectations of femininity and how to adhere to them. Authors of Victorian conduct literature often used the phrase "True Womanhood" to describe the essential attributes of being a woman. Through her research, Welter defines "four cardinal virtues" of femininity present in popular mid-nineteenth-century conduct literature, which include "piety, purity, submissiveness, and domesticity [. . .] put them all together and they spelled mother, daughter, sister, wife—woman. Without them, no matter whether there was fame achievement or wealth, all was ashes. With them [a woman] was promised happiness and power" (152).

Though most of Welter's article focuses on describing the virtues of womanhood, she ends with a discussion of the late-Victorian transition into "New Womanhood." This transformation, Welter asserts, was "as startling in its own way as the abolition of slavery or the coming of the machine age" (174). Citing various social, political, and industrial movements, Welter describes how the role of women was destined to change in the US as the nineteenth century unfolded. These changes naturally caused tension with regard to gender relations and how women viewed their own ability to live up to the expectations of "True Womanhood." Welter writes, "Real women often felt they did not live up to the ideal of True Womanhood: some of them blamed themselves, some challenged the standard, some tried to keep the virtues and enlarge the scope of womanhood" (174). Despite increasing skepticism, Welter continues, expectations of what women were "supposed" to be continued to persist even as the very "dislocation of values and blurring of roles" that conduct literature feared began to occur (174). In short, the turn of the century witnessed significant changes in ideals of femininity, cumulating in a shift from a social vision of idyllic True Womanhood to the bold New Woman figure that reverberated well into the twentieth century.

The shift from True to New Womanhood manifested itself in a variety of cultural settings. Most practically, it resulted in a rise in educated, working women influenced by an emergent feminist ideology. The progressive position of women in the public sphere appeared as an ideological and philosophical response to shifting gender relations in the face of modernity,[2] and was strongly reinforced by the role women played domestically and in the military during WWI.[3] Film historian Miriam Hansen has studied this shift, characterizing the changes in gender relations and their representation in Hollywood:

> Partly in response to the upheaval of gender relations during the war, such as the massive integration of women into the work force and their emergence as a primary target in the shift to consumer economy; the partial breakdown of gender-specific divisions of labor and a blurring of traditional delimitation of public and private; the need to redefine notions of femininity in terms other than domesticity and motherhood; the image of the New Woman promoted along with demonstrative liberalization of sexual behavior and lifestyles; the emergence of the companionate marriage (7).

As a response to the emergence of this new, modern brand of femininity, Hollywood became fascinated with the vision of the New Woman during the Classical Hollywood era. Studios began to produce films with strong, sexy, bold heroines. Mary P. Ryan's "The Projection of a New Womanhood: The Movie Moderns in the 1920's" underscores just how much the silver screen's brand of heroine changes after WWI: "By the mid-twenties the sweet heroines of the Victorian age had been totally banished from the screen by these new women" (501).

In *Classic Hollywood: Lifestyles and Film Styles of American Cinema, 1930–1960,* Veronica Pravadelli underscores the appeal and autonomy of the New Woman during the Classical Hollywood era, referencing films like *Glorifying the American Girl* (1929) and *What Price Hollywood?* (1932). Pravadelli identifies a greater interest in the figure of the New Woman in the US after WWI:

> Feminist historians have shown that modernity changed women's lives much more than men's [lives]. This scenario also explains Hollywood's craze for stories of female emancipation and images of the New Woman. In fact, between the end of the 1920s and the early 1930s, American cinema continued to focus on the image of the young, self-assertive, and sexy woman, thus perpetuating the cult of New Womanhood that emerged in the early years of the century (21–22).

According to Pravadelli, the film industry's interest in the figure of the New Woman came from a desire to depict "the female subject" as she experienced "an epochal transition from a Victorian conception of the relation between the sexes to a modern vision that implicated her departure from the domestic sphere and entrance into the public" (22). Significantly, New Woman characters were intended to attract both men and women to theaters. Often, men found the heroines' sensuality seductive, while women saw them as a type of woman they could aspire to be, direct and independent, and all the more attractive for it. By watching these types of women on screen, audiences began to enjoy the idea of the uninhibited New Woman, at least when these traits were partially or entirely contained on screen or within the apparatus of the Hollywood star system.

Even as Hollywood began to focus on producing films starring the New Woman figure, and audiences appeared to enjoy watching these strong, sexy, independent female characters, social perceptions of what a "true" woman should be continued to contradict this image of female autonomy. The New Woman could exist only in very specific spaces in Classical Hollywood cinema. Pravadelli outlines these parameters, suggesting that: 1) the New Woman's lifestyle "seemed possible only in a limited window of time, between early adulthood outside the parental home and marriage," 2) "Hollywood cinema granted sexual freedom and independence only to upper-class women," and 3) "The New Woman's trajectory could occur only in the urban milieu of modernity, far from the physically and morally constrictive spaces of the family and the small town" (24). By containing the New Woman's freedom and adventures in the years of early adulthood and "outside the parental home and marriage," films that included this type of heroine could refrain from actively challenging American values of domesticity and gender constructs that assumed a woman's duties were first and foremost tied to her husband and the home. Furthermore, by limiting sexual freedom and agency to upper-class women, Hollywood could avoid criticism that suggested certain films were negatively influencing the American middle-class family. Finally, by allowing the New Woman figure to thrive only in the "urban milieu of modernity," Hollywood could feature and still disavow and displace characters that might have appeared to threaten American life in small-town, middle-class, conservative America. A majority of the time, then, the New Woman figure was acceptable only if she appeared as a young adult free of domestic responsibilities, contained in a distinctly modern urban—and, moreover, onscreen—setting.

This construction and containment of the New Woman aligns with what Ryan describes as a "popular film formula" that is "constructed around the aspirations and anxieties of the contemporary audience" (508). Certainly, the figure of the New Woman embodies this paradigm because film audiences reveled in the spectacle of the New Woman film afforded, but they continued to circulate concerns about the effects the New Women might have on American society. Thus, while social perceptions of gender constructs seemed resistant to the figure of the New Woman inhabiting a space in the real world, fan magazines and promotional materials actively tried to sell certain actresses as New Women. These publications became a site for a progressive ideology about femininity to manifest in mid-twentieth-century American society as studio publicity positioned female stars as embodiments of the New Woman off screen. These tactics underscore the mediated nature of the image of the "New Woman" in Hollywood and ultimately illuminate the constructedness of star personae—a condition that affected many star personalities in Classical Hollywood.[4]

Interpretations of Victorianism often coincided with conservative ideals that some mid-twentieth-century moviegoers and reviewers wanted to condemn. For example, a 1937 *Modern Screen* article titled "Bette Davis' True Life Story: A Girl's Rise to Stardom through Sheer Determination" includes a short parable about how one of Davis's first major romances fell apart because she was an actress. Supposedly, Davis fell in love in Rochester, New York, while she was acting with George Cukor's stock company theater in a show called *Broadway*. The article calls the romance an "old, old fictional angle of the young business man of a good family falling in love with the actress. The old story of parental opposition and cross purposes and broken young hearts and tears" (Hall 56). After falling in love, Davis and the young man decided to get married. However, her fiancé's family did not support the match. The article states that the family "admired her, admitted her charm, her gentle birth but deplored and rejected her profession. Especially the father, who held the mid-Victorian axiom that, married to an actress, his son were better dead. It was as bad as that, and in the twentieth century" (Hall 56). The couple did not get married. The young man wrote Davis a letter saying "it was over," and she never heard from him again. The article laments that Davis was effectively exiled from a family because she was an actress, blaming an "old Victorian axiom" for the modern star's plight.

While some contemporary sentiments sought to shame constrictive Victorian tradition, these objections did not always set modern actresses against Victorian ideologies. For example, a review of Joan Crawford's performance in MGM's *Our Modern Maidens* (1929) demonstrates the complex problem of women "acting Victorian" during the mid-twentieth century. In *Our Modern Maidens*, Joan Crawford plays Billie Brown, a modern "flapper" who attempts to use her charms to seduce an influential businessman named Glenn Abbot (Rod La Rocque) with hopes of securing a promotion for her fiancé, Gil Jordan (Douglas Fairbanks Jr.). In response to the film, one male reviewer writes, "In cajoling *Glenn*, she [Billie] receives a kiss which brings to the surface a great show of Victorian prudery and strengthens my distaste for this sort of picture, because the 'Modern Maidens' aren't good sports. They flaunt their independence, but when a man takes advantage of it, they bridle and shudder like old maid schoolmarms" (Lusk 96). This review alludes to the complex problem of women "acting Victorian" during the mid-twentieth century. Just as the reviewer critiques Billie as a woman who "flaunts her independence" but "shudders like an old schoolmarm" when a man tries to "take advantage" of her independence, critiques of certain female stars also implicitly and explicitly accused women of being "bad sports" on account of their "Victorian prudery."

A 1935 *Picture Play Magazine* feature on actress Evelyn Venable reveals that female characters were not the only women chastised for "acting Victorian" in Classical Hollywood. On the contrary, the *Picture Play* article exposes the need for Hollywood to counter claims that suggested Venable possessed Victorian tendencies, going so far as to title the article "Not Annoyingly Noble" to prove how un-Victorian the star was. The article begins by describing Evelyn Venable as "Victorian with a vengeance," and "maligned by publicity which made her something of a prig and very much a highbrow. She couldn't be kissed in pictures and she carried a gun for protection against bold males. Now she speaks for herself and introduces a very different sort of girl" (Maddox 27). Similar to the critique of Billie in *Our Modern Maidens*, there is an explicit critique of Venable's personality being "Victorian" in that it needs to be expelled through a reintroduction. Such a claim reveals how the idea of "acting Victorian" was stigmatized, specifically because the term implied a prude or cold woman.

Simultaneously, the *Picture Play* article creates a space for Venable to introduce herself as a "New Woman" figure in Hollywood, calling her "a very different sort of girl [. . .] infinitely more interesting than we have been led to believe" (Maddox 27). The article reveals her New Womanhood by discussing how much she loves wearing "modern" clothes and acting on the screen (she started her career as a Shakespearean stage actress). These inclusions are an attempt to capitalize on the image of the New Woman—an archetype centered around the growth of female agency, heightened visibility in the workplace and the public sphere, and more open displays of sexuality. Ultimately, then, this article shows an attempt to change Venable's reputation from a woman with Victorian values to a modern, desirable woman and actress.

However, while the *Picture Play* article does seem to be invested in constructing Venable as a New Woman by emphasizing how un-Victorian she is, it also attempts to characterize Venable's life as an "average woman" through a description that seemingly undermines her "new" agency. After the article briefly mentions her marriage, Venable is quoted as saying, "I want a happy married life. That's been my main ambition and I'll never let a career interfere. Secondarily, I want to be a good actress on screen and on stage. I'm glad my husband is sympathetic with this wish" (Maddox 56). Although the article— again, like the *Our Modern Maidens* critique—wants to portray Venable as a modern New Woman instead of a woman with Victorian values, it still negotiates a delicate balance between the modern, glamorous movie star and the still-perceived problem of female independence and autonomy. The above passage works to reinforce an ideology that dictates that a woman's duty first and foremost centers on her husband and their domestic life. This is evident in the way Venable's quote positions a "happy marriage" as her "main ambition" with which she will "never let a career interfere." Further- more, while it is important that Venable puts domestic life before a career, her statement about her husband being "sympathetic" with her desire to be an actress is also meaningful because it positions her husband as the dominant one in the relationship. That is, even though Venable is a working woman with a happy marriage, there is some suggestion that this is only because her husband supports her decision to work. Again, this condition of patriarchal approval creates a situation where a female star has to walk a fine line between conservative ideals and modern independence.

Additionally, while Venable's statement is important because it demon- strates her husband's power over her independence, it is also significant that Venable is working as an *actress*. Unlike the *Modern Screen* article, which seemed sympathetic to Davis's profession, the feature on Venable reveals a contemporaneous mid-twentieth-century discourse that opposed women acting professionally, further revealing the complex gender constructs and expectations female stars had to navigate. A 1935 *Picture Play* article titled "Spot Your Hero" focuses on six of "the most successful leading men" in Hol- lywood in the 1930s. When asked about his personal love life, actor David Manners, "the new order of hero" in Hollywood, is quoted as saying: "I've been in love with several beauties out here, but not too seriously. I must have a Victorian complex, for I don't think I'd want my wife to be an actress" (Maddox). This response was supported by two other actors interviewed for the article, meaning three of the six actors shared the "Victorian" sentiment of being wary of acting as a female profession. Among other things, the senti- ment refreshes the complex problem of Hollywood actresses being judged against certain persistent Victorian gender expectations.

These examples ultimately reveal how mid-twentieth-century Hollywood's New Woman actresses encountered residual gender constructs rooted in conservative, True Woman ideologies associated with Victorian principles. These ideas created a clear divide for women between "acting" and being properly "Victorian," ultimately positioning the two as incompatible. In turn, this divide would have posed obvious problems at those times Hollywood had to attempt to market a female actress in a Victorian drama. How could Hollywood balance creating and marketing a glamourous star in an authentic Victorian adaptation when the two seemed to be so paradoxical? How could studios market a star as the perfect Victorian actress when Hollywood was allegedly the place where glamorous New Women thrived? One way to begin to answer these questions is to focus on how actresses in Classical Hollywood adaptations of Victorian literature were marketed. These marketing materials reveal the complications and constraints of promoting twentieth-century female stars as women who were "born to be"—or play—Victorians. One prominent example of a star in this situation is Joan Fontaine, an actress who received acclaim for her performance in the Victorian-inspired *Rebecca* (1940), and whose star persona would help authenticate her performance as Jane in *Jane Eyre* a few years later. This fashioning of Fontaine as the perfect actress to play Victorian women is just one example of a common process of star persona construction in Classical Hollywood wherein studios attempted to manipulate a star's image in everything from overt advertisements to seemingly "nonfictional" features in fan magazines.

The various materials that marketed Joan Fontaine as the leading lady in the Classical Hollywood adaptation of Charlotte Brontë's 1847 novel, *Jane Eyre*, clearly demonstrate how the dualities in the term "Victorian" could co-alesce, however uneasily. The novel's Jane is often read as an unconventional Victorian woman due to (among other things) her long, recurring speeches about equality and the encumbrances of domesticity. However, in order to sell the film as a prestige picture, Classical Hollywood promoted a very different view of Jane, relying on a specific conception of a more conventional Victorianism when trying to reimagine and sell the text and era.[5] Classical Hollywood's reimagining of the character of Jane as a conventional Victorian woman, and the subsequent fashioning of Joan Fontaine as the perfect actress to portray specific historical ideals of femininity, reveal how shifting gender ideologies and mid-twentieth-century perceptions of Victorian gender complicated the process of adapting nineteenth-century literature.

Advertisements surrounding the release of the film emphasize how its two stars (Orson Welles and Joan Fontaine) were "born to play" the leading roles of Edward Rochester and Jane Eyre. An ad that ran in multiple fan magazines, including *Variety* and *Motion Picture Herald*, underscored this claim, announcing: "The greatest love story of all time! The picture property of the year! Made for every heart that ever found romance! With two stars who were born to play it." While the ad stresses how both actors are "born to play" the leading roles, publicity surrounding Joan Fontaine as Jane reveals the problematic nature of marketing an actress as Victorian in twentieth-century Hollywood.

A spread in a 1943 edition of *Screenland* exclaims, "Miss Fontaine is the ideal selection for gentle, tormented Jane" ("Jane Eyre Comes Back!" 46). Indeed, much of the publicity surrounding Fontaine appears to focus on proving that she is the perfect actress to play this character. For example, an article in a July 1941 issue of *Hollywood* positions Fontaine as a potential Academy Award winner for the role, stating, "The versatile actress seems destined for the outstanding role of the year—*Jane Eyre*, a part as ready-made for her talents as *Rebecca*" (Wilkinson). In addition to suggesting Fontaine's skills as an actress are perfect for the role of Jane, the *Hollywood* article attempts to draw similarities between Fontaine and the Classical Hollywood interpretation of Jane. The article gives Fontaine's childhood a "tragic" backstory in an attempt to show how the actress is able to sympathize with Jane's character. The article also positions Fontaine as a "bookish child" and a "dreamer" with an overactive imagination. Both traits are regularly taken as essential elements to Jane's character in Brontë's novel. Likewise, the article claims that "Joan's imagination and intensity are both assets and liabilities. She feels everything too much and, being one of the shyest people in Hollywood, often ties herself in knots of nervous excitement, suspense or over-eagerness." This description again draws an implicit connection between Fontaine's personality and Jane's character (as Jane is often overexcited by Gothic fantasies or moments of suspense), as if to suggest that Fontaine will barely need to act to play this Victorian character.

In addition to comparing Fontaine's life and personal characteristics explicitly to the Victorian woman she plays in *Jane Eyre*, other articles reveal the ways in which publicity tactics attempted to assign "Victorian" traits to Fontaine's personality more generally (while still managing to make these Victorian traits endearing). A feature story in a 1942 issue of *Screenland* titled "Be True to Yourself (As I Am)" captures a brief retelling (presumably from Fontaine herself) of her self-creation throughout her career as an actress and woman in Hollywood. Early in the feature, Fontaine reveals some of the ways she attempted to push back against publicists who wanted to create an identity linked to performances with her sister, Olivia de Havilland. She says, "If I could not get there on my own, in my own way, I preferred not to get there at all" (Service 21). Problematically, the image Fontaine was interested in building for herself was not one of a glamorous, overtly New Woman figure in Hollywood. Fontaine recalls her resistance to pressure to take on that kind of persona when working on *Damsel in Distress* (1937) with Fred Astaire. Fontaine states:

> People expected, they said reproachfully, to see some other type of girl on the screen, more of a musical comedy type. I need not have been so—so blinking *ladylike*, need I? Yes, I did "need." I could not have played an English lady any way but *as* an English lady. I could not have had her come trucking down the bannisters. It would have made me all cross and snarly inside. I will NOT make myself unhappy. I will NOT sell my integrity for a mess of phony pottage (Service 21).

These remarks reveal that Fontaine appears willing to resist Hollywood's attempts to craft a specifically modern persona for her characters on and off screen. They also highlight the actress's desire to play roles that are "right" for her, which neatly aligns with the major theme of the *Screenland* feature. Fontaine appears more than willing to admit a telling tension between who she wants to be, the roles she plays, and the ways those roles are marketed.[6]

These tensions would appear to lessen in Fontaine's discussion of *Rebecca*, an adaptation of Daphne du Maurier's well-known novel. After saying that actresses "must" take on roles that are right for them, Fontaine asserts, "'Rebecca' was right for me. I *knew* it. . . . There were none of the queasy qualms and uneasy questioning" (Service 58). In many ways, Fontaine's role in *Rebecca* is similar to her role in *Jane Eyre*, which is only fitting given that du Maurier often acknowledged her novel's debt to the Brontës. In both Fontaine plays a somewhat naive young girl who falls in love with a brooding and slightly abrasive older man who is still "haunted" and antagonized by a first wife. Though the *Screenland* feature does not focus on *Jane Eyre*, when briefly recapping Fontaine's successes, it explicitly mentions that *Jane Eyre* was "directly ahead of her," or soon to be released, at the time of the interview. The feature article thus implicitly positions Fontaine as the perfect actress to play characters in British literature adaptations related to the Victorian era.

It cannot be denied that the *Screenland* feature seems to reveal the ways Fontaine often embodied more conservative traits and tendencies, which aligned more closely with ideologies surrounding Victorian True Womanhood. However, Fontaine's assertion that all of her career choices were made because she wanted to do things "her way" allows her to maintain the authentic innocence attached to the idea of True Womanhood while simultaneously asserting her own opinion of her identity in an independent, New Woman fashion. Fontaine claims, "If, in the early days of my career, I had listened to what they said; if I had gone to Hollywood parties, worn extreme clothes, tried to be something I am not, I might have had quicker and easier success but it would have been, I know, easy come and easy go. . . . If I had not been true to myself, *I would never have got anywhere*" (Service 59). Here, Fontaine separates herself from the type of behavior typically associated with glamorous, modern female stars, such as going to high-profile parties or wearing extravagant clothes. She says she achieved her success by staying true to herself, even though her personality appeared to align more closely with conservative ideologies. While this type of persona might have conflicted with general perceptions and expectations of mid-twentieth-century Hollywood stars, it was a perfect characterization for an actress who had gained acclaim for her more conservative roles, as in *Rebecca*, and who was soon to be received as a star for her ability to act perfectly Victorian in an adaptation of a nineteenth-century novel.

Interestingly, while studio publicity attempted to construct for Fontaine a desirable "Victorian" persona, the studio was simultaneously attempting to represent *Jane Eyre* as a proto-modern "Victorian classic" in order to appeal to more modern sensibilities. For example, one advertisement developed for the movie was printed in black-and-white, with an accent of red appearing only on Fontaine's lips and to highlight the title. In the picture Welles is looking intently at an apparently weak Fontaine who has collapsed in his arms. Printed above the couple are the words: "I'm sure most people would have thought him an ugly man . . . but when his lips caressed my hair . . . his fingers touched my throat . . . I knew he was the most thrilling man a woman ever loved" ("Jane Eyre by Charlotte Bronte" 18). The quotation marks positioned around the phrase seem to indicate that it is a line taken from the film, though it is not. Consequently, because the film was being marketed as an authentic reproduction of a Victorian classic, one might also assume this line comes from the novel, which, again, it does not, at least not as it is presented. The only words from the marketing material in the novel are "I [am] sure most people would have thought him an ugly man," which appear in chapter 14 of Bronte's version. No other references to sensuality or sexuality appear, at least not as overtly as the marketing material would make it. In combining a phrase from the source text with verbiage designed to be more titillating to a modern audience, the advertisement underscores how prestige picture marketing could capitalize on a text's literariness while simultaneously working to reimagine it in a way that would appeal to modern tastes and perceptions. Though Bronte's themes would have seemed radical or scandalous to a mid-nineteenth-century readership, Hollywood needed to update these themes to affect a modern audience in a similar way, hence the addition of lips caressing hair and fingers on throats to describe a thrilling, dark love story. The full quote codes *Jane Eyre* as a dark, intense, sensual romantic drama that somehow is also an accurate representation of the Victorian story.

This paradox of needing to promote an authentically Victorian experience while still appealing to modern sensibilities can also be seen in advertisements that ran in publications where *Jane Eyre* was promoted. For example, in an advertisement for Woodbury Color-Controlled Powder, a portrait of Fontaine is illustrated in vibrant color above the phrase "How YOU can have her American Beauty Skin-Tone" ("Woodbury Color-Controlled Powder" 86). A small box on the right side of the advertisement groups Fontaine with other prominent actresses of the period (such as Hedy Lamarr and Lana Turner) and lists each star's specific shade of powder and what desirable skin tone each powder creates. Fontaine's shade, "*Windsor Rose*, gives an American Beauty skintone." While "Windsor Rose" seems to reference her British heritage, this ad specifically positions Fontaine as a contemporary "American beauty," a modern star rather than a Victorian actress. However, a small line of text above the advertisement reads: "Joan Fontaine, under contract to David O. Selznick, soon to appear in Twentieth Century Fox production, 'Jane Eyre.'" The discordance between the reference to Fontaine as the conservative star of a Victorian drama and the portrayal of her as a glamorous American actress literally depicts the problem of female film stars "acting Victorian." Even though features like the aforementioned *Screenland* article explore the ways Fontaine was unlike many of her modern counterparts, this ad tries to display her as a vibrant, glamorous young star. Similarly, the only way to mediate the problem of needing to market Fontaine as "authentically Victorian" in publicity designed for, or to run alongside advertisements for, *Jane Eyre* was to make the reference to *Jane Eyre* so minuscule in the actual advertisement that it could very easily be entirely missed. The choice to highlight one side of a star's persona while in effect minimizing or subsuming the other reveals how stars' personae were as much a product of Hollywood studios as the films they appeared in.

Hollywood tried to market Fontaine as "perfectly Victorian" and therefore the best choice to play the leading role in *Jane Eyre*. Interestingly, Fontaine apparently relinquishes this persona after the film's release and exhibition, which further reveals the intricate nature of persona construction and the star system in Classical Hollywood. A 1945 gossip article in *Screenland* illustrates:

At long last, Joan Fontaine is a free soul. She just received her final divorce decree from Brian Aherne. The expiration of her contract with David Selznick is near. She's riding the crest of the wave but if we know our Joanie, she won't be signing any one of the many studio offers that would curb her freedom. What a far cry from the strange, anti-social Fontaine who originally starred in those first bad "B" pictures! Everything she once envied sister Olivia for is now her own. She claims she is heart-whole and contract free. And that's the way she wants things to remain. (East 57)

While this article does reference Fontaine being able to be a star "her own way," it seems that her representation as a "free soul" also relies on her relinquishing many of the traits that initially made her the perfect actress to play the character of Jane. First, the article celebrates Fontaine's divorce, which contradicts True Woman ideology that would mourn the loss of a husband and, potentially, traditional domesticity. Notable, however, is the strikingly similar way the article handles the impending end of her studio contract. The article asserts that once her contract with Selznick expires, "she won't be signing any one of the many studio offers that would curb her freedom." In this way, her contract to Selznick mirrors the oppressive masculine force she is allegedly escaping with her divorce from Aherne. Both American domestic life and the Hollywood star system become structures that inhibit independent women, such that the only way women, like Fontaine, who are implicated in one or both of these systems can be entirely "free" is to be rid of them completely.

The *Screenland* gossip article also says that Fontaine's transition from a timid star to an independent woman is "a far cry from the strange, anti-social Fontaine" who appeared in Hollywood when she was married and under contract. Such a statement continues to deconstruct the parts of the persona that were previously built for Fontaine in the line "Everything she once envied sister Olivia for is now her own." To return to the aforementioned article, "Be True to Yourself (As I Am)," Fontaine explicitly states that she did not want to be likened to her sister, neither did she attempt to fit the mold of a typical Hollywood star. Here, however, the article exalts Fontaine because she can be just like her sister. While it is unclear which article reveals the truth—whether Fontaine wanted to be like her sister or wanted to be an entirely different kind of star—this discrepancy reveals the intricate nature of celebrity persona construction in Classical Hollywood.

Ultimately, this case of analyzing how Hollywood attempted to market Joan Fontaine as the perfect actress to play a Victorian character reveals the ways film studios struggled to produce a discourse that branded her as one thing. They assign Fontaine authentically Victorian qualities in one moment and market her as a glamorous female star and modern woman in the next. This "contradiction" points to the larger issue of celebrity persona construction and how the process was complicated by the contest between genre expectations and shifting gender ideologies. In addition to needing to be a Victorian True Woman character and modern New Woman celebrity all in one, Fontaine and the actresses like her were still subjected to certain nineteenth-century sentiments that sought to contain the New Woman on screen or within the star system. The marketing materials around these female stars reveal that studios very intentionally opted to focus on, dispel, or reimagine the mythos of Victorianism as it suited them. The process reveals just how intricate the construction of star personae needed to be in the midst of shifting gender ideologies and, more specifically, mid-twentieth-century perceptions of Victorianism.

Works Cited

Barefoot, Guy. "*East Lynne* to *Gas Light*." *Melodrama: Stage, Picture, Screen*. Jacky Bratton, Jim Cook, and Christine Gledhill, editors. British Film Institute, 1994. pp. 94–105.

Brosh, Liora. *Screening Novel Women: From British Domestic Fiction to Film*. Palgrave Macmillan, 2008.

Cagle, Chris. "Two Modes of Prestige Film." *Screen*, vol. 48, no. 3, 2007. doi-org.libezproxy2 .syr.edu/10.1093/screen/hjm031.

DeBona, Guerric. *Film Adaptation in the Hollywood Studio Era*. Chicago: U of Illinois P, 2010.

Des Jardins, Julie. *Women and the Historical Enterprise in America: Gender, Race, and the Politics of Memory, 1880–1945*. U of North Carolina P, 2003.

Dyer, Richard. *Stars*. British Film Institute, 1979.

East, Weston. "Here's Hollywood: Gossip by Weston East." *Screenland Magazine*, vol. 49, 1944–1945, pp. 54–57, archive.org/stream/screenland49unse#page/n1023/mode/2up.

Edwards, Kyle Dawson. "Brand-Name Literature: Film Adaptation and Selznick International Pictures' 'Rebecca' (1940)." *Cinema Journal*, vol. 45, no. 3, 2006, pp. 32–58. *JSTOR*, www .jstor.org/stable/3877748.

Ellis, Kate, and E. Ann Kaplan. "Feminism in Brontë's Novel and Its Film Versions." *The English Novel and the Movies*. Ungar, 1981, pp. 83–94.

Hall, Gladys. "Bette Davis' True Life Story: A Girl's Rise to Stardom through Sheer Determination." *Modern Screen*, vol. 16–17, 1937–1938, pp. 45–60. archive.org/stream/modern screen1617unse#page/n63/mode/2up.

Hansen, Miriam. "Pleasure, Ambivalence, Identification: Valentino and Female Spectatorship." *Cinema Journal*, vol. 25, no. 4, 1986, p. 6.

Hanson, Helen. *Hollywood Heroines: Women in Film Noir and the Female Gothic Film*. I. B. Tauris, 2007.

Hollinger, Karen. *The Actress: Hollywood Acting and the Female Star*. Routledge, 2006.

"Jane Eyre." *Motion Picture Herald*, vol. 153, 1943, archive.org/stream/motionpictureher153unse #page/n41/mode/2up.

"Jane Eyre." *Variety*, vol. 152, 1943, p. 16, archive.org/stream/variety152-1943-11#page/n63/mode/2up.

"Jane Eyre by Charlotte Brontë." *Screenland Magazine*, vol. 47–48, 1943–1944, p. 18, archive.org/stream/screenland4748unse#page/n905/mode/2up.

"Jane Eyre Comes Back!" *Screenland Magazine*, vol. 47–48, 1943–1944, pp. 46–47, archive.org/stream/screenland4748unse#page/n231/mode/2up.

Jensen, Kimberly. "Volunteers, Auxiliaries, and Women's Mobilization: The First World War and Beyond (1914–1939)." *A Companion to Women's Military History*. Brill, 2012. pp. 189–231.

Lusk, Norbert. "The Screen in Review." *Picture Play Magazine*, 1929, vol. 30–31, pp. 64–67, 96, 98, archive.org/stream/picturep31stre - page/n69/mode/2up.

Maddox, Ben. "Not Annoyingly Noble." *Picture Play Magazine*, vol. 41–43, 1935. pp. 27, 56 57. archive.org/stream/pictureplay4143stre#page/n603/mode/2up.

Maddox, Ben. "Spot Your Hero." *Picture Play Magazine*, vol. 35, 1932, pp. 22–23, 69–69. archive.org/stream/picturep37stre#page/n27/mode/2up.

Pravadelli, Veronica. "Classical Hollywood and Modernity: Gender, Style, Aesthetics." *Routledge Companion to Cinema and Gender*. Ed. Kristin Lené Hole et. al. Routledge, 2017.

Pravadelli, Veronica, and Michael Theodore Meadows. *Classic Hollywood: Lifestyles and Film Styles of American Cinema, 1930–1960*. U of Illinois P, 2014.

Ryan, Mary P. "The Projection of a New Womanhood: The Movie Moderns in the 1920's." *Our American Sisters*, edited by Jean E. Friedman and William G. Shade, D. C. Heath, 1982, pp. 500–518.

Sadoff, Dianne F. *Victorian Vogue: British Novels on Screen*. U of Minnesota P, 2010.

Sconce, Jeffrey. "Narrative Authority and Social Narrativity: The Cinematic Reconstruction of Bronte's Jane Eyre." *Wide Angle*, vol. 10, no. 1, 1988, pp. 46–61.

Service, Faith. "Be True to Yourself (As I Am)." *Screenland Magazine*, vol. 45, 1942, pp. 20, 58–59, archive.org/stream/screenland45unse#page/n279/mode/2up.

Welter, Barbara. "The Cult of True Womanhood: 1820–1860." *American Quarterly*, vol. 18, no. 2, 1966, pp. 151–74, jstor.org/stable/2711179.

Wilkinson, Lupton. "Next Year's Academy Award Winner." *Hollywood*, vol. 30. Jan.–Dec. 1941, pp. 19, 37, archive.org/stream/hollywood30fawc#page/n459/mode/2up.

Williams, Raymond. *Marxism and Literature*. Oxford UP, 1977.

"Woodbury Color-Controlled Powder." *Photoplay Magazine*, vol. 23, 1943, p. 86. archive.org/stream/photopla123phot#page/n559/mode/2up.

Notes

1. In reference to *Jane Eyre* specifically, Kate Ellis and E. Ann Kaplan's "Feminism in Brontë's Novel and Its Film Versions" discusses the ways in which the film strips Jane of the agency she is afforded in the novel, turning her instead into a passive heroine subjected to patriarchal structures and the male gaze. More broadly, Liora Brosh offers a variety of readings of multiple British domestic fiction film adaptations in the 1930s and 1940s in *Screening Domestic Fiction: From British Domestic Fiction to Film*. Similarly, in "Classical Hollywood and Modernity: Gender, Style, Aesthetics," Veronica Pravadelli focuses on various formal and plot elements to develop readings of multiple film heroines' social narratives. Finally, in *Hollywood Heroines*, Helen Hanson offers a variety of readings of Gothic heroines and

femme fatale figures in multiple Classical Hollywood gothic and noir films. Notably, Hanson spends time "reading" these characters within the text themselves but also focuses on how their interpretation is complicated by various changes within the film industry as well as societal changes during the mid-twentieth century.

2. Julie Des Jardins discusses this in *Women and the Historical Enterprise in America*. Though it is focused on female historians and their endeavors to reclaim and retell male-dominated histories and the process of historicizing, Jardins's book offers insight into how women were allowed to and dissuaded from engaging in public work and civic discourse between 1880 and 1945. Notably, Jardins's work locates the figure of the "New Woman" as a site of tension as well, stating that even women taking on more progressive roles seemed to have been "torn between the values of older and modern times" (19).

3. Kimberly Jensen's "Volunteers, Auxiliaries, and Women's Mobilization: The First World War and Beyond (1914–1939)" discusses the roles women played within or closely related to the military in the US and other countries involved in WWI.

4. Richard Dyer details the star system and the construction of star personae in his canonical monograph *Stars*.

5. Classical Hollywood and contemporary audiences' interest in *Jane Eyre* can also be linked to a resurgence of interest in Gothic romance in mainstream media, evidenced by texts such as du Maurier's *Rebecca* and its popular film adaptation.

6. This is evidenced by the *Damsel in Distress* example and another instance in which Fontaine reveals she rejected a role in *Gone with the Wind* because she could not "sympathize" with the character (Service).

RUTHLESS RAM AND SEXUAL SITA

Alternate Readings of the *Ramayana*

RASHMILA MAITI

INDIA HAS A RICH HISTORY OF ORAL FOLKTALES AND EPICS. TWO EPICS, THE *RAMAYANA* AND the *Mahabharata*, sit at the center of this tradition. Several factors contribute to the significance of these two texts. The long history of each provides one point of importance. The *Ramayana* dates to the third or second century BCE; the *Mahabharata* dates somewhere between 400 and 200 BCE. The sheer volume of these two epic texts also ensures their ongoing significance. The *Ramayana* contains nearly 24,000 verses. The *Mahabharata* comprises over 100,000 verses. Perhaps most importantly, the epics establish codes and guidelines widely accepted as the basis for leading a moral life. These moral contributions inform religious and social codes alike, presenting ideas on the balance of good and evil in the universe, and the ideal conduct of individuals in their local communities. For example, these epics address how to lead a morally upright life, how to contribute to the larger extended family, and how to be a part of the society. These aspects become especially apparent when these two texts are brought to the screen. This chapter explores one such aspect, namely, the ways in which cinematic adaptations convey lessons about the expectations and duties of women. While India, in particular, wrestles with how to bring this history to the screen, most depictions tend to provide surprisingly consistent messages about the social role of women, at least until recently.

Because of the length, the numerous characters, and the countless important events that serve as moralistic stories, *Ramayana* has been abridged and adapted into various forms. Film adaptors have chosen to focus on the themes from the epic that can be read in a variety of ways. Garrett Kam observes in *Ramayana in the Arts of Asia* that the *Ramayana* has been recreated in different regions and languages in India, apart from the original Sanskrit version. It has also traveled to different countries, including Pakistan, Sri Lanka, Nepal, Iran, Thailand, Myanmar, Malaysia, Philippines, China, Japan, and Mongolia. Not unsurprisingly, Kam notes that in each case the adaptors modify the text to suit the culture and society of each country (Kam 5–9). The epic has been transformed into different genres, such as ceremonial dramas, puppet shows, shadow puppetry, plays, narrative songs, and dances; it has also been converted to cultural artifacts such as festivals, toys, temple sculpture, and paintings (Kam 10). On the other hand, there have also been rewritings of the epic so that it can be told from new perspectives, as in when the epic is expressed from Sita's perspective. Nabaneeta Dev Sen's analysis of contemporary rural women's *Ramayana* songs in Bengali, Marathi, Maithili, and Telgu provides one such example. These rural songs are outside the canon of patriarchal mainstream society where Sita is the idealized woman and Ram can do no harm.[1] As such, the songs tend to depict Ram as a villain who "comes through as a harsh, uncaring and weak-willed husband, a far cry from the ideal man"; for her part, Sen continues, "Sita is no rebel; she is still the yielding, suffering wife, but she speaks of her sufferings, of injustice, of loneliness and sorrow" (19). These songs, which allow Sita's story to be sung, tend to achieve more viability as they are not considered threatening to mainstream society. Neither do they marginalize, domesticate, or subordinate women's actions to the male power structures regularly recognized in the epic as it is understood in its more traditional context. As the songs are in regional languages and restricted to localities, they rarely reach the mainstream society, and, therefore, they are left to find new perspectives.

The three adaptations of *Ramayana* that this chapter considers—*Raavan* (2010), *Main Hoon Na* (2004), and *Sita Sings the Blues* (2008), are never permitted the outsider status, which the regional songs enjoy. Their popularity and praise ensure they find their way into mainstream ethical and political concerns. *Raavan* was critically acclaimed in India, even if it was not financially successful. *Main Hoon Na* was a commercial box-office success. *Sita Sings the Blues* was not released in India, initially, but it has gained considerable exposure on the internet, which brought it to the attention of groups it might otherwise miss. For example, *Sita* has faced serious backlash from various Hindu groups, including over the San Jose Museum of Art's screening in 2011, for the film's portrayal of Ram. The protestors feel that *Sita Sings the Blues* stages a negative representation of Hinduism that will only promote religious intolerance (Sohrabji).

What is most interesting about these three films is the ways they violate their source texts to appease the audience or, in the case of *Sita Sings the Blues*, to provoke the audience. In this way, the three films perform the kinds of violation Deborah Cartmell and Imelda Whelehan (2010) suggest are required if an adaptation is to gain increased visibility as an adaptation. Cartmell and Whelehan argue that sometimes in the "fidelity" debate, it is better for the adaptation not to be too faithful to the source text, as that can result in a failure (83). They support their argument with an example from the Harry Potter films. The earliest films were not as widely successful as later films, Cartmell and Whelehan reason, because they were too faithful. Not until they found ways to break from their source text did they begin to accumulate attention in their own right. Cartmell and Whelehan claim that the departures begin to perform something akin to Kristeva's intertextuality and Mikhail Bakhtin's dialogism (74). Intertextuality and Bakhtin's dialogism emphasize, alike, that a text is often created by the other texts. Not all of those texts must be literary. Social forces can be just as influential. This is just what appears to occur in each of the three films this chapter considers.

The responses given to *Sita Sings the Blues, Main Hoon Na,* and even *Raavan* validate Cartmell and Whelehan's argument, albeit for different reasons. The first two films were successful because they did not strictly follow their source text. *Raavan* did not achieve popular success, but it did realize critical success. One could argue that the divided response to *Raavan* extends from the adjustments those associated with the film made to the source text. Critics deem *Raavan* a success because it transposes the main ideas of the ancient epic to contemporary contexts. In this way, one could treat *Raavan,* and even *Sita Sings the Blues,* as what Thomas Leitch (2009) designates as updates, texts that "transpose the setting of a canonical classic to the present in order to show its universality while guaranteeing its relevance to the more immediate concerns of the target audience" (100). As updates they avoid being the curatorial adaptations, to borrow again from Leitch, that would strictly honor long periods of reception. These three recent adaptations push for new expressions of traditional characters.

Three features seem especially important to anyone wanting to see these films as updates. All three main protagonists of the *Ramayana*—the hero, Ram; his wife, Sita; and the main villain, Raavan—have each undergone a radical metamorphosis in these three Hindi/English film adaptations. Together, the three films tend to accept three shared traits. The contemporary films regularly refuse to present Raavan as evil as he is portrayed to be in the epic. Ram is just as regularly something less than an ideal husband. And contemporary adaptors consistently sexualize Sita while also granting her a voice. One can reason that all three changes reflect contemporary shifts in the roles of men and women in India. More than that, though, they exhibit a more nuanced understanding of good and evil. Modern India, like the rest of the world, notes how difficult it is to be entirely virtuous or vile. Most characters, even ones grounded in ancient epics, become a mix of virtue and vice when brought into contemporary light.

Before understanding the updates, it is important to understand the standard story of Ram and Sita as they are often received. The *Ramayana* narrates the story of the protagonist, Ram, and his wife, Sita. Ram, who is the crown prince of Ayodhya and the son of Dasaratha, wins Sita's hand in marriage. Through the plotting of Kaikeyi, Ram's stepmother, Ram is banished to the forest for fourteen years. Although the banishment is not extended to Ram's brother Laxman or to his wife, Sita, they also accompany Ram out of love and duty for Ram. The rest of the epic focuses on their adventures in the forest, including how Sita is kidnapped by Raavan, the evil king of Lanka, and how Ram, with the help of a monkey army, led by Hanuman, rescues Sita, destroys Lanka, and kills Raavan, only to return to Ayodhya. Upon their return, Ram orders Sita to prove her chastity by an ordeal by fire. Sita passes the test and is united with Ram. Later in Ayodhya, Ram's subjects raise doubts about the paternity of Sita's pregnancy, which causes Ram to banish Sita to the forest again. Ram orders Laxman to abandon Sita in the forest. Instead, Sita is sheltered by Valmiki, the poet of the epic, and gives birth to twin boys who are later united with Ram. However, when Ram asks for Sita to go through the fire once again, she agrees even as she states that if she is pure, she shall be swallowed by the earth, which is exactly what happens. This final event ensures that Sita is cast as the epitome of morality and an exemplar that is to be emulated. Conversely, Ram is celebrated as an ideal ruler, even if he is also seen as a horrible husband.

Not surprisingly, these stories have been used for political purposes. Sheldon Pollock traces in "Ramayana and Political Imagination in India" the long history and relationship between the epic and the usage of Indian political symbols. Pollock shows that the text offers two linked "imaginative instruments—whereby, on the one hand, a divine political order can be conceptualized, narrated, and historically grounded, and, on the other, a fully demonized Other can be categorized, counterposed, and condemned" (264). The strict demarcation between right and wrong is a consequence of a clear example of othering, whereby everything that is bad, evil, and horrifying is projected onto the other. In the epic this is what happens to Raavan, Beera in the film version of *Raavan*. Pollock's othering is also seen in *Main Hoon Na*'s Major Raghavan, who sees Pakistan as evil.

The abovementioned film adaptations refuse to draw characters that are either purely virtuous or evil. All three negotiate these categories as they exist in a world that has lost confidence in absolute values of good and evil, and, by extension, how women are to act or be treated in a patriarchal society. Meghnad Desai observes that by the time the *Ramayana* was written

> patriarchy had registered its authority over women's bodies and over their reproductive rights. Rama considers Sita his property until he loses her to Raavana. Despite Sita's purity, Rama rejects her twice, doubting her fidelity, twice. . . . Yet Sita is a silent heroine as she refuses to bear Rama any child until he secures his throne. She brings up her sons on her own as a single abandoned mother and finally returns to her mother's womb [the earth], thus establishing the autonomy of the female (9).

Unlike the original, *Main Hoon Na* and *Sita Sings the Blues* foreground the changes in Sita and her narrative. The source text has been freely adapted, and the plots do not hide this act. Their rendition fit Robert Stam's ideas that adaptations, "inevitably translate the competing languages and discourses typical of the past of the source text into the competing languages and discourses typical of the present of the adaptation" (247). The source text participates in an ancient time; the three adaptations renegotiate that world in order to come to terms with a more complicated present. In this way, the adaptations can be viewed as a means to keep the traditional epics relevant in today's world even if their relevancy depends on some significant reforms.

One can account for some of these reforms through the categories of adaptations recognized by contemporary adaptation theorists. The films subscribe to Leitch's ideas of adjustment, liberation, and colonization. Both *Main Hoon Na* and *Sita Sings the Blues* are examples of adjustment, "whereby a promising earlier text [*Ramayana*] is rendered more suitable for filming by one or more of a wide variety of strategies [allusions to earlier texts and films, and animation]" (98). *Raavan* shows how the concept of the hero and the villain has changed from the original *Ramayana*, blurring the lines between good and evil. This shift sheds new light on the politics of gender in the two films, which reflects a change in the attitude of the audience to be more accepting of Sita, who is an ideal character and also a victim of the patriarchy.

The three films can also participate in what Leitch terms liberation, namely, a suppression or repression of "the original text" (98). Despite the gravity of the epic, both *Main Hoon Na* and *Raavan* are a part of the Hindi film industry, and as such they do have some common tropes. Both films have song-and-dance sequences. Both rely on high-paid, well-known actors in the lead roles. The two films also follow some generic conventions even though they are not traditionally billed as musicals or melodramas.[2] One might even say that the three adaptations satisfy the conditions of Leitch's description for colonization adaptations where, "colonizing adaptations, like ventriloquists, see progenitor texts as vessels to be filled with new meanings. Any new content is fair game, whether it develops meanings implicit in the earlier text, amounts to an ideological critique of that text, or goes off in another direction entirely" (109). *Main Hoon Na* goes off in the direction of a musical fun-filled family entertainment with typical Bollywood tropes, *Sita Sings the Blues* provides an ideological critique of the epic, and *Raavan* also critiques even as it develops meanings implicit in the epic. The three films, then, perform a series of adaptative moves that can push the audience to reconsider ancient interpretations while also entering contemporary debates over a range of representations of these cultural categories.

Cinematic adaptations of the *Ramayana* are especially prepared to contribute to these debates if only because the epic provides the baseline for these concepts. Anupama Chopra (2007) notes that the conventional hero was modeled on Ram, while the villain was pure evil. Chopra explains, "even when Hindi cinema moved into modern settings the actors continued to play archetypes rather than characters. The inspiration remained the great epics, the *Mahabharata* and the *Ramayana*, which are peopled by larger-than-life men and women are concerned with the *dharmic* role of individuals within a society" (113). Many of the films that portray a struggle between good and evil often resemble the *Ramayana*, where the hero is Ram, the heroine is Sita, and the villain is Raavan. K. Moti Gokulsing and Wimal Dissanayake assert the adaptability of the *Ramayana*, which is constantly reconstructed as "stories from the *Ramayana* are [. . .] retold [. . . ,] people learn the difference between right and wrong, develop a high sense of values and understand what constitutes ideal behavior [. . . ; both ideals are . . .] a constant theme of Hinduism and of Indian popular cinema" (43).

The *Ramayana* is such a huge part of the Indian society that often the names of the protagonists are used as a shorthand for the forces of good and evil. For example, *Ram Lakhan*, released in 1989, uses the names to show the significance of *Ramayana* and comment on how the epic is updated. The audience that has an idea of the source text understands the storyline and expects good to win over evil. Another notable example of the epic being a part of the Indian collective consciousness is *Hum Saath Saath Hain* (We Stand United), released in 1999, which has a storyline similar to the *Ramayana*. These characters tend to lean into traditional understandings of these epic heroes, even as more contemporary adaptations, like those being more specifically examined, tend to liberate them from these rather flat and unsophisticated representations.

In an interview with Alex Dueben (2016), Nina Paley, the creator of *Sita Sings the Blues*, was asked what was it about the story and Sita that made her want to tell this story. Paley answered that she liked the "ambiguity of the characters, where it seemed at first that they're either really good or really bad, but they actually have contradictions and they behave mysteriously in a way that seemed very, very real" (Dueben). She is an example of the reader/audience who finds ambiguity in a text that might be missed on the first reading/viewing. Paley also comments that she likes tension that arises from the fact that the original story asserts the greatness and goodness of Rama, yet he banishes Sita, and (despite being "this perfect man") behaves in imperfect ways. For Ram, it was more important to be an ideal monarch even if that meant mistreating Sita. These two things create an ambiguity that is not always explored. Paley wanted to correct that. In so doing, she follows the same impulse on view in Mani Ratnam's *Raavan*. Ratnam also admits in an interview on the DVD that he sees the two male protagonists as two sides of a coin: the right and the wrong side. Ratnam permits that if we, as audience, "shift our position and view from the character's point of view, then the way we look at it changes" (*Raavan*). The change will depend on the viewer.

The same potential change occurs in relation to the heroes of adaptations. The concept of the hero has obviously changed from the early Hindi films to contemporary times. In earlier films, the male protagonist could do no wrong. Whatever he did was justified for the greater good. The villain, on the other hand, would be completely corruptible. By the end of the film, he would be taken away by the authorities and punished. The virtuous hero would not be permitted to kill even the villain. The criminal mastermind was the only character deserving of death. However, *Raavan* complicates the binary of good and evil. Film criminals have various motivations: creating an empire, megalomania, riches, and ambition. These traits do not yield entirely villainous characters, though; they may only have a darker side. This point is explored in an adaptation like *Raavan*, where the filmmakers problematize gender roles so that the male protagonists and antagonists are given power and justification for everything that they do, be it murder, kidnapping, lies, and manipulation.

Similar to the character of Raavan, one of the male shadow puppets in *Sita Sings* observes that Raavan is a villain who does not rape Sita; Raavan informs Sita, "If you do not come willingly, I will not touch you. I will not force you in my house, I will not force myself on you" (*Sita Sings the Blues*). This suggests that Raavan is a villain, but a villain who still shows some restraint. Ram, though, in *Ramayana* and in *Sita Sings the Blues*, is unconvinced of Sita's chastity and loyalty. He orders her to go through fire to prove her purity. Somewhat surprisingly, one of the male puppets in *Sita Sings* claims that Ram banishes Sita only to gain the respect of his subjects. Despite Ram's knowing of her love and devotion, he chooses his subjects instead of believing Sita's protests. Ram is heartbroken and distressed, but he suspects that Sita had a relationship with Raavan. The depiction complicates what is often seen as a clear good or a clear evil. Ram's action is both good and evil.

The blurring of the binary good and evil is even more evident in Mani Ratnam's *Raavan*. The film's characters are entirely morally ambiguous. *Raavan* not only portrays the villain, Beera (Abhishek Bachchan), the Raavan character, as sympathetic but also gives more voice and agency to Ragini (Aishwarya Rai Bachchan), the Sita character, who is always powerless and held as a paragon of marital values and morals, a change that reflects the society's demand to give a voice to the marginal and the oppressed. Possibly to avoid controversy, Ratnam did not name the characters as Ram, Sita, and Raavan. Malashri Lal suggests that the name Sita "itself was sacred, an utterance which denoted a natural veneration, the context for which had to be suitably pious" (59). However, despite not naming the characters, it is still obvious to an audience who knows the text what each character represents. For Linda Hutcheon (2006), "for an adaptation to be successful in its own right, it must be so for both knowing and unknowing audiences," where knowledge of the text is known/unknown to the audience (121). The knowing audience functions a bit differently in India, where they might have a general idea of the story line, including the gender roles but not all the details. This "knowing audience" connects the central protagonists of the movie to the epic: Beera, the tribal leader is Raavan; Dev Pratap Sharma, the police superintendent is Ram; his wife and an accomplished classical dancer, Ragini, is Sita; Sanjeevani Kumar (Govinda), the forest guard, is Hanuman; and Inspector Hemant (Nikhil Dwivedi), who is Sharma's partner and the deputy superintendent of police, is Laxman.

A short summary of the film shows how the story corresponds to the epic as well as how it blurs the straightforward division of good and evil. The film sets up a binary between Beera, the bandit, and the police officers, led by Dev. As Beera is a tribal leader and a marginal figure, he is seen as a terrorist who runs a parallel government. The movie justifies Beera's actions as the audience uncovers his motivations and background through the perspective of Ragini, whom Beera abducts. Beera and Dev are the grey characters in this adaptation. The film starts with a straightforward binary that Beera is evil as he is terrorizing the indigenous population, and his followers have also killed policemen and destroyed government property. Dev is tasked with capturing

Beera, with the help of Hemant and Sanjeevani. Beera abducts Ragini and decides that she will die in fourteen hours, referring to the fourteen years that Ram spent in the forest with Sita and Laxman. However, Ragini is allowed to live and see how Beera and his followers live in the forests. Through Ragini's perspective, the audience sees that Beera is justified in his actions. Ragini is freed, and Dev interrogates Ragini, similar to the exchange between Ram and Sita, after Sita is freed from Raavan's clutches. Ragini returns to Beera, but Dev follows her to apprehend and kill her. The film brings forward the idea that there is good in evil as shown through Beera, and evil in good as shown in Dev's behavior towards Ragini. Although this idea was only indirectly present, it is more focused in the film. Beera and Dev are never simply good and evil.

This change is just one of the changes that fit Robert Stam's understanding of transtextual subversion, "when a recombinant text challenges the socially retrograde premises of preexisting hypotexts or genres, or calls attention to repressed but potentially subversive features of preexisting texts" (243). The film becomes a recombinant text that challenges the premise that the world can only be good or evil, how women are wrong, and how men are right. Ragini trusts Dev completely, but once she understands Beera's actions and the motivations behind those actions, she comes to see the world as something other than good or evil.

When Dev and Ragini are returning on a train, Dev orders Ragini to take a polygraph test after she tells him that nothing happened between her and Beera. Ragini says that she wants to die after hearing his suggestion. Dev informs her that Beera had said that Ragini was impure. She gets off the train and meets Beera, asking him what he told Dev. Beera had said that he can kill and save lives for Ragini. This shows Beera's purity despite the government labeling him a criminal. He does not lay a finger on her; neither does he rape her. Beera even refuses to manipulate Ragini. Later when Dev follows her, Ragini realizes that Dev had incited her so that she would lead him to Beera. Ragini tries to save Beera by getting in front of him, but she fails. Dev is ready to do anything for the greater good, even capturing a dangerous criminal who is terrorizing a region, which makes him like Ram, who abandoned Sita and asked her to go through the trial by fire. Dev is shown as slightly evil as he goes to great lengths to capture Beera. Beera is shown to be kind and compassionate, and Ragini falls in love with her abductor. The film is more than willing to explore the epic's repressed ides of good and evil, and, more especially, the idea that these two traits can coexist.

The recent adaptations are just as quick to renegotiate traditional gender constructs. Both *Main Hoon Na* and *Sita Sings the Blues*, for instance, focus on how the role of women has changed since *Ramayana*. The films explore new possibilities and, especially in the latter, how it is important to also consider this patriarchal epic from Sita's perspective. Farah Khan's *Main Hoon Na* features a nontraditional student, army major Ram Prasad Sharma (Shah Rukh Khan), returning to college as an undercover agent. His mission is to guard his general's daughter, Sanjana (Amrita Rao), from the threats of a radical militant, Major Raghavan (Suniel Shetty). The film references the *Ramayana* in the naming of the central male characters and the villain and alludes to other texts in its songs and dialogues. Ram is also on a quest to search for his brother, Lakhman 'Lucky' Sharma (Zayed Khan). Ram was his father's illegitimate son, and Lucky's mother, Madhu (Kirron Kher), had left her husband when she got to know about his affair. Here, a reversal occurs where the wife abandons her husband.[3]

Lucky's girlfriend Sanjana, also called Sanju, who is in charge of Ram's protection, becomes an important female character in *Main Hoon Na*. She is a tomboy who has a grungy appearance before she ultimately transforms into a lady under Chandni's care. Chandni (Sushmita Sen) is the other Sita-like character and Ram's girlfriend. After Sanju's transformation, Lucky realizes that he is in love with her. This newly professed love injects an element of queer sexuality into the story, but the film does what it can to temper this aspect. The plot suggests that Lucky is interested in Sanjana, only after she dons the clothes and hairstyle of a woman. The story further suggests that Lucky would not have accepted her without these changes. Using the trope of the boyish woman changing into a traditional female role has been criticized recently, but it remains a regular part of Bollywood. The trope appears regularly enough that it is worth investigating rather than simply rejecting when it appears. As it relates to *Main Hoon Na*, the trope is turned in an unexpected way when Sanjana confronts Lucky to tell him that her transformation is fake and temporary. She contrasts Lucky with Percy (Rajeev Punjabi), their common friend who has feelings for Sanjana despite her nontraditional appearance. Lucky is understandably upset, but they both get together at the prom-night dance sequence, signaling a happy ending for this couple.

Sanjana's clothing is more than a mere fashion statement. The film presumes that she dresses up and behaves like a tomboy because of her strained relationship with her father, General Bakshi (Kabir Bedi), who had wanted a son who, like him, would join the army. Sanjana's transformation can be seen as similar to what Surpanakha, Raavan's sister, would have gone through in the *Ramayana*. Surpanakha is described as ugly, unnatural, and monstrous, but she is infatuated with Ram. Lakshman was also married, but he had left his wife, Urmila, behind to be with his brother. Lakshman follows his elder brother without thinking of the trauma it causes his wife. Urmila, who was Sita's younger sister, wanted to follow her husband into exile, but Lakshman reasons that her welfare will be a concern for him. He admits that he will not be able to devote himself to the care of Ram and Sita. In this film adaptation, there is a sisterly bond shown between Chandni (Sushmita Sen) and Sanjana. Sanjana, therefore, is transformed from Surpanakha to Urmila, under the care of Chandni/Sita. Sanjana, unlike Urmila and Surpanakha, is more independent and capable of demanding the love that she wants and deserves from both her boyfriend and her father. Sanjana has been changed to meet contemporary audience expectations. Sanjana's friendship with Chandni also shows that two strong independent women can be friends instead of being competitors.

In the epic, Surpanakha complains to Raavan about her disfigurement at the hands of Ram and suggests the kidnapping of Sita. If Sanjana corresponds to Surpanakha, then she is much more deferential to Chandni, who is her college teacher, and accepts her transformation under Chandni's care and Ram's insistence. Surpanakha does not transform into Urmila in the *Ramayana*, but Sanjana does. This transformation, though, reinforces expectations of female beauty and behavior. Sanjana knows that the new feminine person is not her real identity. This realization keeps the representation from being regressive. Sanjana appreciates the limits of some changes, and while she is willing to test those limits, she returns to some sense of an original self. The change also acts as a catalyst whereby Lucky confront his feelings for Sanjana and his social expectations; he grows up as an individual.

Main Hoon Na shows a transformation in the character of Surpanakha, but in *Ramayana*, Sita is shown as almost saintly. Sita is stripped of sexual desires. She is little more than a dutiful wife. Her one transgression is the mere suspicion that she has had some kind of a relationship with her abductor, Raavan. Chandni's modern-day Sita is much sexualized. Part of this sexualization follows the decision to cast Sushmita Sen in the role of Chandni. Sen has been a trailblazer in social and cultural changes. She adopted a girl when she was only twenty-five and single. She adopted a second child when she was thirty-five and still unmarried. Contrary to what cultural projections might presume about her, she is an open feminist in a country whose celebrities still shy from that label. These personal traits inject Sen's performance in interesting ways. Chandni is a college professor that teaches chemistry. She is considered to be hot and sexy by the students and the teachers. Her clothes also parody the fact that Bollywood actresses wear flimsy thin clothes, including chiffon sarees, in freezing temperatures, as seen in songs and to sexualize the actress. The hero, on the other hand, will usually be dressed in warm clothes. Chandni is shown as independent, outspoken, and extremely sexualized in the film, a drastic change from the original demure and submissive Sita.

Chandni also acts as Ram's partner, and later, when she learns of his true identity, as an army major, she starts seeing him as an equal, rather than as her overgrown, infatuated student. Chandni fulfills the traditional roles expected of a Sita-like character, but she is more independent, individualistic, and on an equal footing with Ram than the original Sita. She is shown as more sexually and fashionably appealing than most any other representation of Sita. The interesting thing about Chandni is that, despite her Sita-like qualities, she is not named Sita. Presumably, this choice means to avoid controversy, but the similarities are there for anyone who wants to see them. Those who do see them certainly see a modernized Sita, who has been transformed in terms of her sexuality.

Nina Paley's *Sita Sings the Blues* updates Sita in other ways, especially as they relate to Ram's treatment of her. Giving Sita's voice to the *Ramayana* is revolutionary, as it is a patriarchal epic that sees a perfect Ram who is above any reproach. Paley's film adopts four animation styles: one features the autobiographical story of Paley, who was abandoned by her boyfriend; another one features the actual storyline of the epic created in the style of Rajput paintings; a third features the songs that Sita sings; and the last one is a discussion of the epic by three shadow puppets with the events created in the style of Indian calendar art. This adaptation is intertextual in incorporating sources other than the *Ramayana*, "compositing maps, excerpted texts, reproductions of paintings and various other graphics" (Scheib). The songs, like those in Hindi films, comment on the actions of the main film, "as Sita intones 'Mean to Me' while her beloved Rama cavalierly dropkicks her into a blazing funeral pyre to test her purity" (Scheib). These songs lend a Bollywood feel where the songs discuss the themes of the *Ramayana* but are dependent on the story. All the different animation styles provide visual cues to the reader to show how the epic is being portrayed and analyzed and the songs add an extra layer of adaptation.

In an interview Paley mentions that the story of the *Ramayana*, Annette Hanshaw's songs, and her own story prove the universality of the epic (Dueben). This is evident in Paley being abandoned and Hanshaw's songs focusing on heterosexual relationships where the man is less than perfect. The songs have a different animation style in which Sita is hypersexualized as a Betty Boop character with exaggerated breasts, tiny waist, and luxurious hair. Ram is also sexualized as a character with a huge wide torso, bulging biceps, and tiny legs. Paley notes that these "extreme poles of masculinity and femininity" are transferred to Ram and Sita, who are viewed as ideal characters (Paley and Lal 126).

The other animation styles conform to traditional portrayals of Sita, be it the Rajput paintings or the Indian calendar art, both of which shows Sita covered in sarees, modestly dressed, and demure, with only a few lines of dialogue. These animation segments focus on the original epic where Ram can do no wrong and where Sita is the perfect wife. It is only in Hanshaw's songs that Sita's voice and perspective are heard. Like Dev Sen's analysis of rural songs that are sung by women, which show Sita's condition, Hanshaw's songs and Paley's adaptations show what Sita went through. Perhaps Sita's narrative could not be accommodated in the main storyline of the paintings and calendar art, and had to be shown only through Hanshaw's songs.

Through the song "Daddy Come Home," Sita sends a message to Ram, via Hanuman, the monkey god, that she wants Ram to rescue her from Raavan. The shadow puppets try to understand Sita's motivation for not going with Hanuman and instead being Raavan's hostage. The female shadow puppet suggests that Sita wants to glorify Ram by forcing Ram, her "man," to rescue her—"He is virtuous and he will kill Raavan"—leading one of the male puppets to conclude that Sita is a "blood-thirsty woman." Such a discussion exemplifies the traditional gender roles of men as protectors who rescue women in distress. Even if Sita had wanted to leave with Hanuman, it would have been inappropriate in traditional cultures, since Hanuman is male, and Sita is still married to Ram. This change, though, highlights Sita's virtue and purity even if it does so in unexpected ways. The point of the film is that Sita's perspective is able to emerge from the traditional narrative.

In all three adaptations, the audience gets to see and understand different perspectives, be it that of Sita in *Sita Sings the Blues* or Beera/Raavan in *Raavan*, or confronting ideals of feminine beauty in *Main Hoon Na*. *Sita Sings the Blues* and *Main Hoon Na* are playful, while *Raavan* is more realistic. No matter their diverse differences, the knowing audience can easily understand their content based on the shared knowledge of the two epics and the common culture. However, with change, the ideal qualities of the characters in the epics are used as a way to educate and uphold tradition, not so much as to emulate the characters. They are guides to live a morally upright life. The audience believes that these characters are perfect but also concede that the perspective of the epic characters might not be the only dominant perspective or that these characters behave in a vacuum. The audience realizes that the characters in the film adaptations reflect the contemporary reality where the epic characters are more human, more believable, more realistic, and definitely more understandable. For the filmgoing audience, the personae in these postmodern film adaptations reflect the traditional epics as well as a change in contemporary gender, whereby women are given more agency and sexual appeal and men are neither strictly good nor evil. Lastly, the filmgoing audience is also colonizing the films, as per Leitch, where they continue the process of adaptation by filling the text with new interpretations, including ideological, social, or something else.

Works Cited

Cartmell, Deborah, and Imelda Whelehan. *Screen Adaptation: Impure Cinema*. Palgrave Macmillan, 2010.

Chopra, Anupama. *The King of Bollywood: Shah Rukh Khan and the Seductive World of Indian Cinema*. Warner Books, 2007.

Desai, Meghnad. "Sita and Some Other Women from the Epics." *In Search of Sita: Revisiting Mythology*, edited by Malashri Lal and Namita Gokhale. Penguin Books and Yatra Books, 2009, pp. 3–9.

Dev Sen, Nabaneeta. "When Women Retell the *Ramayana*." *Manushi: A Journal about Women and Society*, no. 108, 1998, pp. 18–27. manushi.in/docs/906-when-women-Retell-the -ramayan.pdf. Accessed 30 November 2016.

Dueben, Alex. "Nina Paley Talks 'Sita Sings the Blues.'" *Comic Book Resources*, Valnet Property, 29 March 2010. cbr.com/nina-paley-talks-sita-sings-the-blues. Accessed 11 November 2016.

Gokulsing, K. Moti, and Wimal Dissanayake. *Indian Popular Cinema: A Narrative of Cultural Change*. Trentham Books, 2004.

Hum Saath-Saath Hain. Dir. Sooraj R. Barjatya. Perf. Salman Khan, Saif Ali Khan, Mohnish Behl, Tabu, Sonali Bendre, Karisma Kapoor. Rajshri Productions, 1999.

Hutcheon, L. *A Theory of Adaptation*. Routledge, 2006.

Kam, Garrett. *Ramayana in the Arts of Asia*. Select Books, 2000.

Lal Malashri. "Sita: Naming Purity and Protest." *In Search of Sita: Revisiting Mythology*, edited by Malashri Lal and Namita Gokhale. Penguin Books and Yatra Books, 2009, pp. 55–61.

Leitch, Thomas. *Film Adaptation and Its Discontents*. Johns Hopkins University Press, 2009.

Paley, Nina, and Malshri Lal. "Sits Sings the Blues: Nina Paley and Malashri Lal in Conversation." *In Search of Sita: Revisiting Mythology*, edited by Malashri Lal and Namita Gokhale. Penguin Books and Yatra Books, 2009, pp. 124–27.

Pollock, Sheldon. "*Ramayana* and Political Imagination in India." *Journal of Asian Studies*, vol. 52, no. 2, May 1993, pp. 261–297. jstor.org/stable/2059648. Accessed 10 October 2016.

Raavan. Dir. Mani Ratnam. Perf. Vikram, Abhishek Bachchan, Aishwarya Rai. ShowMan Pictures, Madras Talkies, and BlackMan Pictures, 2010.

Ram Lakhan. Dir. Subhahs Ghai. Perf. Anil Kapoor, Jackie Shroff, Raakhee. Mukta Arts, 1989.

Scheib, Ronnie. "Sita Sings the Blues." *Variety*, May 12, 2008, p. 41. o-search.proquest.com.library.uark.edu/docview/236228524?accountid=8361.

Sita Sings the Blues. Dir. Nina Paley. Perf. Sanjiv Jhaveri, Nina Paley, Deepti Gupta, Debargo, Sanyal, Reena Shah, Pooja Kumar, and Aladdin Ullah. 2008. *YouTube*, uploaded by drakar7002, 11 December 2011. youtube.com/watch?annotation_id=annotation_95220 3&feature=iv&src_vid=PfS2p1vFics&v=f8LvBnz7oRA.

Sohrabji, Sunita. "Hindu Groups Protest Screening of 'Sita Sings the Blues.'" *India West*, indiawest.com/news/global_indian/hindu-groups-protest-screening-of-sita-sings-the -blues/article_53873151-30ae-5a17-8121-76c35c817866.html. Accessed 10 August 2018.

Stam, Robert. "Revisionist Adaptation: Transtextuality, Cross-Cultural Dialogism, and Performative Infidelities." *The Oxford Handbook of Adaptation Studies*, edited by Thomas Leitch. Oxford University Press, 2017, pp. 239–50.

Notes

1. In India, mainstream songs are usually from films, but folk songs have a niche audience, particularly in rural populations.

2. The epic leaves open the possibility of both forms, even if they pursue other values.

3. In the epic, Ram abandons Sita because of rumors of her infidelity with Raavan.

"BOTH IN AND OUT OF THE GAME, AND WATCHING AND WONDERING AT IT"

Whitmanic Currents and Complications in *He Got Game* and "I, Too"

ZOE BURSZTAJN-ILLINGWORTH

Visualizing America through Montage: Introducing *He Got Game*

Spike Lee's *He Got Game* (1998) opens with a crane shot over a sprawling golden wheat field in the Midwest. The sustained notes of a lone trumpet from the beginning of Aaron Copland's orchestral score based on the American folk legend "John Henry," plays on the soundtrack. Eventually, a grain silo and a barn appear just above the sloping fields and shrubby trees. A musical tension emerges as wind instruments begin to complement the trumpet. The image of a blond, white, teenage boy dressed in a white shirt replaces the rural landscape. He dribbles a basketball in a slow-motion medium shot set against the white buildings that are now more prominently featured. The young player bends his knees to shoot. The string instruments enter the soundscape. The camera tilts upward as the player jumps to shoot. The lens follows his hand as it arcs to release the ball. The ball briefly leaves the frame as it travels toward the rim. The camera stays with player as he returns to the ground. The ball, still traveling in the same slow motion that has marked the sequence, hits its mark and swishes through the net. The player gracefully steps to retrieve it.

The initial sequence serves as a succinct example of "the Whitman montage tradition," a form first theorized and put into practice by Sergei Eisenstein. The montage serves as something of a clue for how Lee will shape the homage to basketball that exists throughout the film. Quite simply, the Whitman montage tradition informs more than just the opening sequence.

Other montages in Lee's oeuvre follow a similar poetics, one that crisply captures the poetic catalogs that characterize Walt Whitman's poetry. Before discussing the particulars of this catalog, a fuller discussion of the full opening montage in *He Got Game* is in order.

The opening sequence gives way to other images to form an opening montage that forms the first three minutes of *He Got Game*. The opening sequence cuts to a new image once the young player moves to retrieve his ball. A long shot of a Black man dressed in gray playing basketball is set in front of a row of pine trees and a small-town general store advertising Coca-Cola. The opening credits for the film begin to roll. The name of Lee's production company, Forty Acres and a Mule, scrawled in an orange, graffiti-like font, appears as the man takes aim on a rim in what appears to be a small northern town. The rhythm of the montage speeds up and the duration of shots decreases after the production credit. Lee cuts to a low-angle shot and sets a static camera on the sandy ground of a Southwest landscape. A water tank, an agave plant, and a satellite dish fill negative space. A third player dribbles up to the net, shoots, and lands a layup. A fourth player in a fourth part of the country replaces this image in a silhouette of a male figure with a shaved head, shooting baskets against a sublime pink and purple sunset. Denzel Washington's credit enters the shot from both sides of the screen in a wipe. The ball arcs into the basket. The strings in the score reach another crescendo.

The musical crescendo parallels a shift in visual focus from relatively long shots of men shooting hoops to a series of frontal portraits in medium shot of both white and Black men holding basketballs. The film's title, *He Got Game*, rolls over a slow-motion image of a Black player shooting a jump shot and scoring in front of a small white church at golden hour. We see a series of brief shots, from varying angles, of both men and women playing basketball alone or with others, in schoolyards, parks, and in more rural settings. A brief, static shot of a basketball backboard that holds a rusted rim without a net fills the frame for a moment as Aaron Copland's "John Henry" continues to pick up tempo. Lee's cuts increase frequency to match the soundtrack. A series of fast cuts present one-on-one basketball games with frontal portraits of white and Black men holding basketballs. Eventually, the camera finds a court in Lee's native Brooklyn. The camera frames in long shot the image of a child playing basketball, dwarfed in scale by the Manhattan skyline behind him. Another series of shots follows, interspersing other inter-city courts with portraits of players. One set of players moves behind cage-link fences. Another man plays on a court in front of the Brooklyn bridge at dawn. The credit for Public Enemy, whose music provides the soundtrack for *He Got*

Game alongside Copland's score, appears. The graphic brings together the images and music. Lee nestles two shots—first, a high-angle shot of Nike-clad feet dribbling a basketball on a sunny day and, then, a long shot of the game taking place in what looks like L.A.—between the long shot of the man dribbling on the Brooklyn Bridge and a close-up of the player. The man's face is neutral, inscrutable even.

In the montage's final minute, there continue to be shots of solo and group basketball being played across a variety of urban and rural settings. Portraits of Black men holding basketballs or of a court at the corner of Division and Sedgwick in Chicago cycle through the opening. Another cut carries a now-panning camera as it moves down a building to reveal a bronze statue of Michael Jordan outside of Chicago's United Center. The camera pauses on the statue to provide a series of closer looks at it. One extreme closeup captures Jordan's name on the sculpture's base. Another shows the sculpture from behind. A third frames the bronze basketball held in Jordan's hand. The final shot returns to more-pedestrian settings. A slow-motion image captures a long shot of young women, white and Black alike, playing basketball against a wall of bright graffiti. The shot begins as a tracking shot of one young woman scoring before it cuts to a passing train. Spike Lee's credit for directing and writing the film appears, and the camera tilts downward to a group of young Black men playing basketball in real time. Lee's poetry gives way to his narrative.

Lee fills his opening montage with a mix of diverse bodies, American landscapes, and portraits. The common thread is solely basketball. One could find any number of ways to distinguish this group from one another, but Lee prefers to collect them as one. In so doing Lee displays a particular poetics that is entirely informed by its descriptive and associative concerns. Unlike the film's diegesis that focuses on a severely damaged father-and-son relationship, the opening montage voices a broader poetics of basketball as it connects America's diverse landscape and citizens. *He Got Game*'s opening montage emphasizes presence and absence, legibility and illegibility, in this grand poetics of America's landscape and national identity as it is shared through basketball. Lee continues to follow this logic as he moves from the opening montage to the narrative subjects at the center of his film, Jake Shuttlesworth (Denzel Washington) and Jesus Shuttlesworth (Ray Allen), a father and son separated in most every way save their ability to play basketball. Lee's introduction of these two characters foreshadows this trait. Both men are playing basketball, but it is clear that they are not playing in the same space. Lee cross-cuts between Jesus playing basketball in his Coney Island neighborhood and Jake playing under intense surveillance of a guard at Attica Correctional Facility. Lee's cross cutting centers narrative concerns over conceptual or poetic ones.

He Got Game's narrative presents a seemingly straightforward father-and-son story, which does not immediately reconcile with the opening montage of American national identity as it is shaped by a sport that mediates race, place, and the body. The film's narrative appears focused on individual characters navigating ethical dilemmas involving the sport and attempting to repair a relationship broken by domestic violence and incarceration. Unlike this opening montage's insistence on present moments in juxtaposition with one another, Lee's editorial style in the bulk of *He Got Game* tends to rely heavily on flashbacks to dramatize early moments of trauma, which include Jake's accidental killing of his wife and Jesus's mother, and that imply some of the ways these traumatic memories might continue to affect these characters' perception of themselves and each other. In contrast to the film's character-driven diegesis, as well as its flashback and cross-cutting heavy editorial style, the opening montage suggests a way to unite with one another, namely, through basketball. Lee's montage represents a capacious, democratic vision of basketball—as purely American, equalizing the heartland and the metropolis, people of different races and genders, and, perhaps most of all, the individual.

The self-enclosed and non-narrative montage form of *He Got Game*'s opening credits forms a filmic poem that glorifies the human body, suspends linear time, evades narrative, and unifies the American landscape. Lee's poem both echoes *and* critiques the project of Walt Whitman's poetry and, moreover, what Whitman's poetry signifies in the American consciousness. Because of the marked influence of Whitman's poetry on Sergei Eisenstein's conceptualization of non-narrative montage (Eisenstein 231), the opening montage of *He Got Game* can be understood as renovating a film form, Eisenstein's "intellectual montage" that is based on a poetic form, the catalog or list (Grant 265). Therefore, Lee's use of portraiture and frontality, particularly in shots of African American men, uses embodiment and the legibility (or illegibility) of the face to challenge the spectral nature of Black presence in this Whitmanic vision.

Whitman's Vision: Democracy, Expansion, and Formal Innovation

To appreciate the echo and critique of the Whitmanic tradition herein described, one must first trace the lineage of Whitman's presence in American cinema, which begins in Whitman's vision of American unification and democratic individuality in *Leaves of Grass*. Twentieth-century scholars, poets, and filmmakers alike have continued a critical dialogue with Whitman's poetics and politics. In film theory Sergei Eisenstein's notion of the Whitman montage conception contrasts narrative montage, a mode more connected with Charles Dickens's novels and D. W. Griffith's films (Grant 231), and speaks to the role that Whitman's poetics and political ideas have played in the theory and practice of film. By considering how Whitman's poetics influenced Eisenstein's montage theory, one can value the way that Eisenstein's Whitman montage tradition, coupled with his mode of "intellectual montage," resembles a poetic catalog (Grant 265) and provides the form for Spike Lee's critique of Whitman's model of democracy and all-encompassing national identity in the opening montage of *He Got Game*.

The dominant critical view of the connection between Whitman's poetry and his politics tends to cast him as the foremost poet of American democracy. Such a view celebrates Whitman for promoting the centrality of democracy to American identity and theorizing a particular kind of "democratic individuality" in both his poetry and political prose (Kateb 19). Even in the first few lines of a short Whitman poem, "I Hear America Singing," from the 1867 edition of *Leaves of Grass*, one may glean the poet's individually expressive yet unified vision for his country: "I hear America singing, the varied carols I hear; / Those of mechanics—each one singing his, as it should be, blithe and strong; / The carpenter singing his as he measures his plank or beam." Later in the poem, Whitman makes clear that these "diverse carols" include not only Americans working individually to build a nation but distinct voices individually expressing themselves: "Each singing what belongs to her, and to none else." Furthermore, one of the most readily apparent poetic features of "Song of Myself," Whitman's use of poetic catalogs (lists using anaphora and other forms of repetition), equalizes the vast geographic regions of America through repetition and, on a formal level, creates an associative, rhetorical link across varying lines. For instance, in a few characteristic lines from the 1891 version of "Song of Myself," the speaker of the poem posits himself as: "At home in the fleet of ice-boats, sailing with the rest and tacking; / At home on the hills of Vermont, or in the woods of Maine, or the Texan ranch." While Whitman celebrates America's diversity and grandeur, one also notes the receptivity and expansiveness of Whitman's poetic persona, marked by the speaker's deep connection to nature rather than to one particular place (Kateb 20). This sense of presence in place and nature dovetails with Whitman's emphasis on the body, physicality, and eroticism in "Song of Myself," which tends to be a feature of his poetry frequently remarked upon in critical introductions to his work.

In terms of form, Whitman's poetry is generally considered to have innovated American poetry. The poet's mode of address, his use of the aforementioned poetic catalogs, and his pioneering use of free verse in *Leaves of Grass* all break from accepted practice. Whitman's mode of address, in particular, his use of a capacious "you" in "Song of Myself"—a "you" that can reflect both the intimacy of erotic embrace and the temporal distance of his future readers—is often credited with creating a sense of democracy between the poem's "I," the poet/speaker, and the reader, addressed in the "you" (Folsom 329). Whitman's use of free verse paired with his use of catalogs, a listlike series of images linked by associative meaning, in *Leaves of Grass* can be viewed as critical to Sergei Eisenstein's theorization of montage in film.

Formal Crosscurrents: Whitman, Eisenstein, and Montage

As Barry Grant argues in "Whitman and Eisenstein," Whitman's use of catalogs can be read through the lens of Sergei Eisenstein's form of "intellectual montage," as seen in *Battleship Potemkin* (1925) and *October* (1928). In these films Eisenstein juxtaposes a series of images in such a way that viewers might conjure an abstract from them (266–67). Eisenstein's formulation of "intellectual montage" in *Film Form* describes a film sequence composed of "montage phrases," shots, in "conflict-juxtaposition" with one another, which ultimately produce an interpretation that is conceptual, as opposed to ultimately psychological or emotional, adding up to an "intellectual overtone" (82). The examples of intellectual montage that Grant and Eisenstein himself give are from Eisenstein's *October*. Eisenstein points his reader to a sequence in the film when "pieces" or shots "were assembled in accordance with a descending intellectual-scale, pulling back the concept of God to its origins (82);" Grant describes a sequence from *October* as "intellectual montage" that juxtaposes various shots of Kerensky playing chess, with shots of a statue of Napoleon, and shots of Kerensky's soldiers, leading the viewer to the conclusion "that Kerensky [. . .] considers the soldiers as nothing more than dehumanized objects" (265). In both cases "intellectual montage" assembles a series of varying images with one another to cultivate an abstract concept that questions governance and divine authority rather than further the narrative or reveal a character's psychology. Similarly, in the opening montage of *He Got Game*, Lee seems to juxtapose images to express the idea that basketball unifies the expansive American landscape and to suggest the partial legibility of Black presence within it.

While Eisenstein may have been interested in Whitman's poetic form, even considering it in the context of his own montage techniques, Grant concludes his essay with a gesture toward the political and historical differences that inform the visions of these two innovators: "The difference was [. . .] largely determined by the artists' respective political realities. Eisenstein was always more conscious of the need for unity, for the common embrace of socialist principles: whereas Whitman embraced the great democratic concept of diversity" (270). Grant wants to account for the differences between these two artists through their separation of time. By comparing Eisenstein's ideas to those captured in Langston Hughes's poem "I, Too," a response to Whitman's "I Hear America Singing," one finds a reason to suspect that there is a more meaningful reason for Eisenstein's divergence from Whitman. Scholarly critiques of Whitman's racial politics, the very idea of Whitman's "democratic concept of diversity" that Grant highlights, further obscure the racial inequalities that riddle Whitman's model of American "democracy."

It is crucial not to overlook the political tenor of Eisenstein's reference to Whitman in "Dickens, Griffith and Film Today," which is fundamentally connected to the history of representations of African Americans in American cinema. Most of Eisenstein's essay argues for the influence of the Dickensian novel on D. W. Griffith 's cinematic techniques for storytelling. Eisenstein finds in Griffith and Dickens a desire to heighten emotional and dramatic tension. This desire motivates a number of editorial and cinematographic decisions, literary descriptions, and narrative structures. In short, the majority of Eisenstein's comparison of literature and early American cinema remains tied to the novel. However, Eisenstein briefly gestures toward Whitman's poetic montage as something different from what one finds in Griffith and Dickens: "I must regretfully put aside Walt Whitman's huge montage conception. It must be stated that Griffith did not continue the Whitman montage tradition (in spite of the Whitman lines on "out of the cradle endlessly rocking," which served Griffith unsuccessfully as a refrain shot for his *Intolerance* (231). While Eisenstein does not go on to explain "the Whitman *montage tradition*" and merely points to Griffith's inability to successfully employ it in a refrain shot, he does recognize some notion of montage in Whitman. He refers to that notion as "huge," even, which suggests some vastness within Whitman's poetic project.

Yet the fact that Griffith is, according to Eisenstein, unable to accomplish the Whitmanic mode of repetition from Whitman's "A Word out of the Sea" in a "refrain shot" from *Intolerance* (1916) implies two things—one formal and one political—about the differences between Whitman's and Griffith's projects. Regarding the formal, Eisenstein seems alert to a poetic, which is to say non-narrative insistence in Whitman's *"montage tradition."* He is further ready to mark this tradition as something antithetical to Griffith's novelistic, sentimental aesthetics. Regarding the political, Eisenstein appreciates that with *Intolerance*, a film made in response to the vast criticism of *Birth of a Nation*'s (1915) racist representation of African Americans and its romanization of the Ku Klux Klan, does not align with Whitman's poetics or his politics of American unification and equalization (Mcgee). *Intolerance* may approximate some line from *Leaves of Grass* in its intertitles, but the film does not, in Eisenstein's estimation, embody the Whitmanic tradition. The recurring image of a witchy-looking Lillian Gish rocking a cradle fails to unify the four short narratives that compose *Intolerance*, and, worse, demonstrates Griffith's failure to formally integrate Whitman's poetic form into his filmmaking (Price 116–17).[1]

Responses to Whitman's Racial Politics and Langston Hughes's "I, Too"

The question arises in the midst of such a critique of whether Whitman's politics of national unification through democratic individualism actually emerges, and, if it does, whether it represents African American experiences. Ivy G. Wilson marks in his recent introduction to *Whitman Noir: Black America and the Good Gray Poet* Whitman's poetry with a "centrality (if often phantom-like quality) of African America to Whitman's imagination and of Whitman's importance to African American literature" (ix). This "phantom-like quality" points to the fact that African Americans are mentioned in poems like "Song of Myself," but that the fullness of African American experience remains obscured by other experiences. Ed Folsom, whose remarks on the racial politics of Whitman's poetry take a more mixed stance with the disclaimer that "there is no easy space to inhabit in American history" (339), still gestures toward some of the issues with the racial politics of Whitman's all-encompassing democratic vision when he states that in the 1855 version of *Leaves of Grass*, "chattel slavery" is used "as a cultural metaphor for the various kinds of enslavement—religious, economic, moral—from which all readers must craft an escape" (338). By using "chattel slavery" as a metaphor for various ways in which individual freedom may become socially restricted, the particularities of African American experiences of "chattel slavery" are obscured by their metaphorical function.[2] One can see how the "ankle-chain of the slave" serves this purpose in the 1860 version of "Chants Democratic," later titled "A Song for Occupations": "What is called right and what is called wrong—what you behold or touch, or what causes your anger or wonder,

/ The ankle-chain of the slave, the bed of the bed-house, the cards of the gambler, the plates of the forger" (Walt Whitman Archive). In this catalog, the "ankle-chain" of an enslaved person gains an equivalency to economic inequality, "the bed of the bed-house," and even the loss of freedom tied to gambling addiction: "the cards of the gambler."

Though Whitman supported the Free-Soil Party, which called for the prohibition of slavery in the newly acquired western territories, his prose and personal writings reveal racist representations of Blackness (Klammer 237). Furthermore, most advocates of the Free-Soil Party opposed slavery not for reasons of the inhuman treatment of African Americans but "because they felt that white laborers should not have to compete with—nor be degraded by—the presence of Black slaves in the new territories" (Klammer 237). Whitman's post–Civil War views on race, that African Americans "were innately inferior to whites and were bound to disappear," were certainly at odds with the fact that many early fans of his poetry were abolitionists and later African American writers (Drews and Hutchinson 568). Paul Outka sums up these contradictions well when he writes in his aptly titled "Whitman and Race (He's Queer, He's Unclear, Get Used to It)": "The same man who called African Americans 'baboons' was one of Sojourner Truth's favorite poets" (297).

It is exactly the dialectic of these contradictions—unveiling the fact that Whitman's poetics of democratic individualism and national unification do not fully *see* the uniqueness of African American experience—that makes Langston Hughes's poem "I, Too" a reparative response to Whitman's poetry and a precursor to Lee's use of the Whitman montage tradition in the opening of *He Got Game*. Langston Hughes's poem "I, Too," published in 1926 in Hughes's first collection of poetry, *The Weary Blues*, clearly responds to Whitman's "I Hear America Singing" from the 1860 version of *Leaves of Grass*, but the tone of this response remains in question:

> *I, too, sing America.*
> *I am the darker brother.*
> *They send me to eat in the kitchen*
> *When company comes,*
> *But I laugh,*
> *And eat well,*
> *And grow strong.*
>
> *Tomorrow,*
> *I'll be at the table*

When company comes.
Nobody'll dare
Say to me,
"Eat in the kitchen,"
Then.

Besides,
They'll see how beautiful I am
And be ashamed—

I, too, am America. (46)

The poem's tone, especially in the third verse paragraph, can be taken as either an optimistic affirmation of future transformation toward racial equality in America or as a more direct challenge to white America in its current state. Donald Gibson argues the latter, that "I, Too" mirrors Whitman's faith in the wherewithal and potential of American democracy to resolve distinctions in American society: "Hughes's commitment to the American ideal was deeply felt and abiding. He held onto it despite his acute awareness of the inequities of democracy, and he seemed to feel that in time justice would prevail . . . 'I, Too' is testimony to his faith" (67–68). However, George Hutchinson's analysis of the poem, though he describes Hughes as an "heir" to Whitman, puts forth a more radical reading that in the American family that Hughes's "darker brother" belongs to, the speaker still voices a sense of protest in the penultimate verse paragraph, "They'll see how beautiful I am / And be ashamed" (Hutchinson).

Although I agree that Hughes responds to Whitman's optimistic vision of American democracy in this poem and that, given Hughes's noted admiration of Whitman, it is reasonable to read "I, Too" as representing American society's potential for equality, I think that it would be a mistake to overlook the poem's elements of direct confrontation and negative affect.[3] While the speaker still "sing[s] America," this song should also be viewed as one of self-definition and distinction. The "I" in "I, Too" is not the same Whitmanic "I," which, even given the original title, "Poem of Walt Whitman, an American," in the 1856 version of *Leaves of Grass*, seeks to abolish distinctions by containing the united, yet contradictory nature of American society within an embodied self: "Do I contradict myself? / Very well, then, I contradict myself / I am large, I contain multitudes" (103). Rather, the speaker of Hughes's poem, though also a public persona as clarified in the final line—"I, too, am America"—is defined in distinction to white America and, particularly, the race and class hierarchies that white America enacts: "They send me to eat in the kitchen / when company comes" (46).

A key turning point, as to whether one reads the poem as emulating or complicating Whitman's exalted view of American democracy, is how the reader understands the speaker's laughter. Laughter does not have to signify acceptance of the absurdity of inequality and mistreatment. Rather, laughter can stand as protest, especially if it leads a Black self to "eat well / And grow strong," which is necessarily a political act; as Black activist and poet Audre Lorde writes in "A Burst of Light: Living with Cancer," an essay paralleling her battle with liver cancer to Black resistance to white supremacy: "Caring for myself is not self-indulgence, it is self-preservation, and that is an act of political warfare" (131). Other lines in "I, Too"—such as "Nobody'll dare / Say to me, / "Eat in the kitchen," / Then"—also signify through diction, "dare," and the line break that isolates "Then" that this potentiality of inclusion hinges on confrontation. Moreover, the recognition of Black America as "beautiful," and worthy of equality, would cause white America to "be ashamed," a state that, according to the *Oxford English Dictionary*, necessarily admits guilt or recognizes that "one's actions . . . are in any way not to one's credit" (*OED* online). The speaker's "laugh[ter]"—if taken as protest, voicing his significance in the face of marginalization—is what empowers the speaker, leading him to claim his space at the "table" and will, in a potential "tomorrow," lead to white America's acknowledgment of not only the Black speaker's existence, which he already affirms in the present-tense "I, too, am America," but their new realization of his "beaut[y]."

My reading of Hughes's "I, Too" and its simultaneous homage and challenge to Whitman's vision of a unified and democratic America emphasizes the resistance to white supremacy that African Americans display by leading individually enriching lives, "grow[ing] strong / And eat[ing]." Thus, white America must acknowledge that such lives are "beautiful." In this way, Hughes's project of confrontation and inclusion provides a transition into Spike Lee's use of the varied American landscape, frontality, and portraiture in the opening of *He Got Game*.

The Opening of *He Got Game* in Light of the "Whitman *Montage Tradition*"

In the beginning of this essay, I describe the opening montage of *He Got Game* but refrain from interpreting it without the frame of Eisenstein's Whitman montage tradition, the link between Eisensteinian montage theory and Whitman's poetic form, critical questions of the role that race plays in

Whitman's poetry and notions of democracy, and how Hughes's "I, Too" poses a challenge to Whitman's supposedly all-encompassing vision. With this frame in mind, I turn to the opening montage of *He Got Game* for how Lee's revision of Eisenstein's Whitman montage tradition echoes Whitman's poetic form but demonstrates the illegibility of Black experience within his poetic and democratic vision.

The first shots in *He Got Game*, a crane shot over wheat fields in the American heartland that cuts to a medium shot of a white, blond teenage boy shooting hoops in slow motion, notably flouts the viewer's expectations of Black and cosmopolitan representation in a Spike Lee film starring Denzel Washington and Ray Allen, primarily set on Coney Island. However, like Whitman's project in "Song of Myself" that draws together disparate Americas through the glory and expansiveness of the speaker as poet's body—"My respiration and inspiration, the beating of my heart, the passing of blood and air through my lungs"—the diverse bodies in motion (and their shared, yet different Americas) that Lee represents are unified through basketball (24). The cinematography in this opening sequence also suggests a Whitmanic (and broadly, poetic) power of observation as both anticipation and vision. Though the camera tilts to follow the arch of the basketball player's shot, it allows the ball to almost completely leave the frame before the player makes the shot and the ball goes into the basket. This camerawork mirrors the perception and anticipation of waiting for the ball to arc into the basket. Like the line from "Song of Myself"—"Both in and out of the game, and watching and wondering at it"—the camera follows the ball when it is in the player's hands but leaves the viewer space to "wonder" at whether or not the shot will be made (27). This moment between when the ball is in the player's hands and when it enters the basket personifies the power of film to confine the senses according to their natural weight, which Stanley Cavell discusses in "Photograph and Screen": "Cinema discovered the possibility of the medium not to call attention to them, but rather to let the world happen, to let its parts draw attention to themselves according to their natural weight" (334–35).

Aside from the Whitmanic powers of visionary observation, receptivity, and wonder that the cinematography in the opening of *He Got Game* displays, a particularly notable characteristic of this sequence is the use of the graffiti-like font over an array of landscapes, which keeps the city present throughout images of rural landscapes. Whitman, too, despite his vast representation of the American landscape in "Song of Myself," remains a poet of New York in "Mannahatta," "Broadway Pageant," and "Crossing Brooklyn Ferry," all from *Leaves of Grass*.[4] Even with a moment of *He Got Game*'s diegesis occurring on Coney Island, the opening sequence's more lyrical landscape begins in a farm setting with a white basketball player as the subject. The next two shots shift to two very different small-town landscapes. The first is a medium long shot outside of a small-town general store in the North. The second is a low-angle shot in which the player runs into the frame in a Southwest landscape. Both of the basketball players in these shots are Black. The diversity of the basketball players coupled with the diversity of place seems to signify not only that America is vast and diverse but that people of color inhabit all of these distinct places across the country. The next shot in this sequence also signifies a shift in place and temporality through color with a shot of the silhouetted form of a basketball player in profile against a purple-blue sunset in front of the ocean. The drastic shifts in mise-en-scène, color, and camera angle create a strong sense that basketball ties together the disparate pieces of the American landscape and the cultural differences that place signifies; basketball, like lyric poetry as a form and Whitman's aspirations to poetic immortality in the last lines of "Song of Myself"—"Failing to fetch me at first, keep encouraged, / Missing me one place, search another, / I stop somewhere waiting for you"—is constant and almost atemporal, existing in the present and the future (104).

For viewers of *He Got Game* considering the way in which the film's visual form enacts and complicates poetic methods of representing American national identity, Lee's comments on Copland's music may read differently. Lee seems to echo the Whitmanic sentiments of his images in the 1998 liner notes to the soundtrack of *He Got Game* in regard to the music of Aaron Copland, whose orchestral composition "John Henry" provides the score for the opening credits: "When I listen to [Copland's] music I hear America, and basketball is America. It's played on the sides of barns in Indiana [and] wheat fields in Kansas. Hoops is played on the asphalt courts of Philly, Chicago and also Brooklyn" (Sterrit 152). Lee's statement "I hear America . . ." is familiar to readers of Whitman's "I Hear America Singing," but also, because "basketball is America," his words recall Hughes's "I, Too" in that these works pose a new, challenging relationship related to embodiment and the contradictory nature of America. Lee views basketball as tying together the disparate and vast American landscape, a purpose that Whitman catalogs formally serve in *Leaves of Grass*. As in the last line of "I, Too"—"I, too, am America"—in which the speaker, "the darker brother," becomes a synecdoche for the contradictory (oft hypocritical) nature of American democracy, for Lee, basketball serves as a similar synecdoche for America's unachieved (yet potential) capaciousness and inclusivity.

George Kateb's description of Whitman's notion of democracy as "democratic individuality" could also characterize the opening montage of *He*

Got Game's use of frontality and portraiture (19). Lee's use of frontality and portraiture is not limited to depictions of African American men in the opening credits of *He Got Game*. There is a distinct sequence of three shots of white men (both children and adults) that occurs in time with Copland's composition, all holding basketballs in their hands and facing the camera. But the last shot in this sequence is of a young Black man holding the basketball toward the camera. This shot places the basketball in the foreground and the man in the background, as though the basketball extends forward an invitation into the game. The man's face becomes only partially legible as the sun behind him creates a halolike effect. This partial legibility of the human face, in the name of basketball, is repeated in another shot later in the opening of the film, but this time in a close-up.

bell hooks discusses the centrality of portraiture in African American art in "Art on My Mind," a personal critical essay published three years before the release of *He Got Game*, about the perception of visual art in the lives of African Americans. hooks believes that its realism detracts from the decolonization of the imagination: "in segregated school settings, the attitude toward art was that it had primary value only when it documented the world as is. Hence the heavy-handed emphasis on portraiture in Black life that continues to the present day" (4).[6] Lee integrates this tradition of African American portraiture into the opening of *He Got Game*, seemingly to express Black presence within a larger portrait of America united by basketball and painted in broad strokes.

However, the frontality of these shots combined with the only partial legibility of these men's faces and figures communicates an intimacy (from the frontality) that functions without the openness of full disclosure. In these shots Lee's representation of distance and boundary even within the intimacy of frontal portraiture runs counter to the total openness and receptivity espoused in the first lines of 1891's "Song of Myself:" "I celebrate myself, and sing myself, / And what I assume you shall assume, / For every atom belonging to me as good belongs to you." And, notably, the basketball, which for Lee is the great unifier of the disparate American landscape, creates this partial legibility. In this way Lee's participation in the Whitman montage tradition takes a more critical and complex approach to Whitman's project of unifying America's place and culture through the body. In fact, despite Lee's statement "Basketball is America," neither of these images of African American men in full frontality portrays a sense of the desired inclusion that Hughes's speaker in "I, Too" voices in the poem's last line, "I, too, am America." The aesthetics of the opening of *He Got Game* suggests, then, that for Lee, though African Americans *are* certainly Americans, there is a way in which

Black America remains obscured within the unifying project of Whitmanic poetics and democracy.

As already mentioned, the majority of *He Got Game*'s style of editing—full of flashbacks, voiceover narration, and cross cutting—and narrative structure lean toward highlighting the personal struggles of its two protagonists, a father, Jake, and his son, Jesus. Unlike the interplay between collectivity and individuation that characterizes Whitman's democratic vision and the cumulative nature of montage and poetic catalogs, the narrative of *He Got Game* highlights the individual agency of its protagonists. Jake's furlough from prison in order to convince his son to attend Big State in exchange for a reduced sentence drives the film's narrative and culminates in a dramatic one-on-one basketball game with his son, Jesus. Jesus ultimately wins the game. He is free to choose any school he likes. His father is handcuffed in front of him. However, Jesus ultimately *does* choose Big State. But this is explicitly *not* because his father told him to and *not* in order to secure his father's release from prison. Jesus's individualistic decision to attend Big State is the narrative climax of *He Got Game*. However, the opening montage of *He Got Game* primes the viewer to understand a narrative focused on the lives of two individuals as representing part of a collective vision of Black presence in the American landscape. During a series of frontal interviews with members of the Lincoln High basketball team, Jesus says, "Basketball is poetry in motion," in direct address to the camera. It is telling in connection to the opening montage and the Whitman montage tradition that the individuation of group members through frontal interviews, making legible individual experiences within the collective of the basketball team is the moment when poetry is explicitly mentioned in the film's narrative.

Seeing the opening montage through the lens of Eisenstein's explicit notion of a Whitman montage tradition and the formal similarity between Whitman's use of poetic catalogs and Eisenstein's "intellectual montage" highlights how African American experience has been rendered illegible within an all-encompassing vision of American unification. Visions of American unification—connecting the redwoods of California with the rocky shores of Maine—typify Whitman's use of catalogs in *Leaves of Grass* and the mode of democracy espoused throughout his writing. Langston Hughes's poem "I, Too" explicitly responds to the erasure of Black experience within Whitman's vision and promotes a similar mode of confronting illegibility with Black presence. Lee's use of non-narrative montage performs something central. The poetic montage refuses to be subsumed by the narrative. The montage means to stand outside of the central narrative. It might be that other Lee montages also intend to bring a narrative into a poetic vision. The opening montage of Lee's first feature-length film, *She's Gotta Have It* (1986), and the concluding montage that caps off his recent film, *BlacKkKlansman* (2018), both fit the structure of a poetic montage frame that contains a film structured around the individual decisions of a protagonist who is Black.[7] What would re-evaluating these montages through Eisenstein's notion of the Whitman montage tradition tell us about Lee's vision of African American presence or legibility in contemporary America? In *He Got Game*, the montage insists on an unmistakable Black presence that is equal part of any harmony America may sing.

Works Cited

"ashamed, adj." *OED* Online. Oxford University Press, March 2017. Accessed 15 May 2017.

Brazee, Christopher. "Walt Whitman Residence." NYC LGBT Historic Sites Project, 2016. nyclgbtsites.org/site/walt-whitman-residence/.

Cavell, Stanley. "Photography and Screen." *Film Theory and Criticism Introductory Readings*, edited by Leo Braudy and Marshall Cohen. 5th ed. Oxford: Oxford UP, 1999. pp. 334–35.

Drews, David, and Hutchinson, George. "Racial Attitudes." *Walt Whitman: An Encyclopedia*, edited by J. R. LeMaster and Donald D. Kummings, Garland, 1998. 567–69.

Eisenstein, Sergei. *Film Form: Essays in Film Theory*, edited and translated by Jay Leyda. New York: Harcourt Brace, 1949.

Folsom, Ed. "Walt Whitman's Invention of a Democratic Poetry." *The Cambridge History of American Poetry*, edited by Stephen Burt and Alfred Bendixen. Cambridge: Cambridge UP, 2014. pp. 329–59.

Gibson, Donald B. "The Good Black Poet and the Good Gray Poet: The Poetry of Hughes and Whitman." *Langston Hughes: Black Genius: A Critical Evaluation*, edited by Therman B. O'Daniel. New York: William Morrow, 1971. pp. 65–80.

Grant, Barry K. "Whitman and Eisenstein." *Literature/Film Quarterly*, vol. 4, no. 3, 1976, pp. 264–70.

Hartman, Saidiya V. *Scenes of Subjection: Terror, Slavery, and Self-Making in Nineteenth-Century America*. New York: Oxford U P, 1997.

hooks, bell. "Art on My Mind." *Art on My Mind: Visual Politics*. New York: New Press, 1995. pp. 1–9.

Hughes, Langston. "I, Too." *The Collected Poems of Langston Hughes*, ed. Arnold Rampersad and David Roessel. New York: Alfred A. Knopf, 1995. p. 46.

Hutchinson, George B. "Langston Hughes and the 'Other' Whitman." *Poetry Criticism*, ed. Timothy J. Sisler. Vol. 53. Detroit: Gale, 2004.

Kateb, George. "Whitman and the Culture of Democracy." *A Political Companion to Walt Whitman*, edited by John Seery. Lexington: U of Kentucky P, 2011. pp. 19–46.

Klammer, Martin. "Free Soil Party." *Walt Whitman: An Encyclopedia*, edited by J. R. LeMaster and Donald D. Kummings, Garland, 1998. p. 237.

Lorde, Audre. *A Burst of Light and Other Essays*. Mineola, NY: Ixia Press, 1988. pp. 40–143.

Mcgee, Scott. "*Intolerance*." Turner Classic Movies. Accessed 12 May 2017.

Outka, Paul. "Whitman and Race ('He's Queer, He's Unclear, Get Used to It')." *Journal of American Studies*, vol. 36, no. 2, 2002, pp. 293–318

Price, Kenneth M. *To Walt Whitman, America*. Durham: U of North Carolina P, 2004.

Solnit, Rebecca, and Joshua Jelly-Schapiro. *Nonstop Metropolis: A New York City Atlas*. Vol. 3. Berkeley: U of California P, 2016.

Sterrit, David. *Spike Lee's America*. Cambridge, UK: Polity Press. 2013.

Whitman, Walt. *Leaves of Grass, 1860: The 150th Anniversary Facsimile Edition*. Ed. Jason Stacy. Iowa City: U of Iowa P, 2009.

Whitman, Walt. *Leaves of Grass*. 1855, Walt Whitman Archive, whitmanarchive.org/published/LG/1855/whole.html.

Whitman, Walt. *Leaves of Grass*. 1860, Walt Whitman Archive. whitmanarchive.org/published/LG/1860/whole.html.

Whitman, Walt. *Leaves of Grass*. 1867, Walt Whitman Archive. whitmanarchive.org/published/LG/1867/index.html.

Whitman, Walt. *Leaves of Grass*. 1891, Walt Whitman Archive. whitmanarchive.org/published/LG/1891/index.html.

Whitman, Walt. *Walt Whitman: Selected Poems, 1855–1892*. Ed. Gary Schmidgall. New York: St. Martin's, 1999.

Wilson, Ivy G. "Looking with a Queer Smile: Whitman's Gaze and Black America." *Whitman Noir: Black America and the Good Gray Poet*. Iowa City: U of Iowa P, 2014. pp. vii–xix.

Notes

1. Whitman scholar Kenneth Price's interesting discussion of *Intolerance* and Whitman's relationship to Griffith (as well as other citations of Whitman's poetry and persona on screen) mentions that the filmmaker was an admirer of Whitman's poetry, even stating that Griffith once said that he "would rather have written one page of *Leaves of Grass* than to have made all the movies for which he received world acclaim" (115). However, the major similarities that Price sees between Griffith's vision and Whitman's poetics—epic scale, attention to detail, and interest in "the gritty materiality of life"—remain unanchored to visual or poetic form (116). It is my view that, formally speaking, Whitman's poetic style, his catalogs and modes of repetition, in *Leaves of Grass* much more closely resembles Soviet filmmaking than early American cinema, setting aside Sheeler and Strand's *Manhatta* (1926). For further discussion of the relationship between Whitman and the visual form of Soviet cinema, see Barry Grant's "Whitman and Eisenstein" and Ben Singer's "Connoisseurs of Chaos: Whitman, Vertov, and the 'Poetic Survey.'"

2. In *Scenes of Subjection: Terror, Slavery, and Self-Making*, Saidiya Hartman describes the phenomenon of "fungibility" in white abolitionist writers before the Civil War as they attempt to empathize with the experiences of enslaved people but instead highlight how the particularity of Black experience is made transferable within the universality claimed by whiteness (21). Arguably, Whitman's use of chattel slavery as a metaphorical function might also fall under this fungible use of Black bodies and experiences.

3. Hutchinson notes Hughes's admiration of Whitman by pointing out that Hughes assembled three different anthologies of Whitman's poetry and also describes an anecdote

in which Hughes, on a ship from New York to Europe and Africa, threw overboard all of his books except for *Leaves of Grass*, which he couldn't bear to discard.

4. While it is true that the versions of New York inscribed in Lee's filmmaking and Whitman's poetry are temporally separated by a over a century, geographically, their sites of production are closer than one might imagine. Both artists produced their most critically acclaimed works, *Leaves of Grass* (1855) and *Do the Right Thing* (1989) respectively, mere blocks away from each other in Fort Greene, Brooklyn (Solnit and Schapiro 156). Lee's production company, Forty Acres and a Mule, which produced *He Got Game*, is located one mile from the building at 99 Ryerson Street, where Walt Whitman completed the first version of *Leaves of Grass* in 1855 (Brazee).

6. hooks goes on to critique the role of television and film in Black life: "Television and cinema may fast be destroying any faint desire that black folks might have to . . . identify with art." Given this stance, it is unsurprising that hooks has also outspokenly criticized Spike Lee's representation of Black women in *She's Gotta Have It* (1986) and *Crooklyn* (1994).

7. *She's Gotta Have It* (1986) begins with a Zora Neale Hurston quote from *Their Eyes Were Watching God* and a montage of still photographs of life in Brooklyn. *BlacKkKlansman* (2018) concludes with a montage of newsreel footage of Donald Trump, the Unite the Right Rally in Charlottesville, Heather Heyer, the victim of the far-right terrorist attack in Charlottesville, and, ultimately, an image of the American flag upside down and in black and white.

WOLF TOTEM BY JEAN-JACQUES ANNAUD

Turning a Chinese Novel into a Transnational Film

CAROLINE EADES

WITH *WOLF TOTEM*, PUBLISHED IN CHINA IN 2004, JIANG RONG DEPICTS HIS FORCED EXILE TO Mongolia as one of the many students sent "Up to the Mountains and Down to the Countryside" during the Cultural Revolution (1966–1976). The auto-biographical account provides a pretense for the author to comment on a range of current political debates in China regarding ethnic diversity and national identity meant to promote "a greater community of *us*" (Xinjian 102). The novel was an unprecedented commercial success in China, with more than twenty million copies sold. The book fared well internationally, too, including in France, where it was soon translated by Yan Hansheng and Lisa Carducci. Reviewers accounted for the appeal of Rong's story through the powerful political metaphor found in the image of the wolf. The specific allegory Rong draws speaks most directly to the resistance of Mongolian people to the Maoist agricultural and social upheaval led by the Chinese Han, which resulted in the destruction of grasslands and the sedentarization of nomads. This specific allegory is not so unequivocal that it prevented others from pulling from this tale an array of interpretations able to address a number of more recent philosophical, environmental, and anthropological debates. More generally, readers regularly connect to the novel's message of "freedom, democracy," and hope for China to become a people of "civilized wolves" (Callahan 117).

Amidst this broad appeal, it is not surprising that Jean-Jacques Annaud decided to adapt Rong's novel to film. A bit more surprising is the way some faulted *Wolf Totem* (2015) for emphasizing adventure and romance for the sake of an all-too-explicit metaphor that references tales and myths based on the figure of the wolf. The headline of a review of Annaud's film in the state-controlled newspaper *China Daily*, "*Wolf Totem* celebrates love for nature," betrays the attempt of government officials to present the novel, and its filmic adaptation, as an autobiography based on historical approximations imbued with nostalgic overtones. On the surface Annaud's film offers a bucolic and rather fatalist depiction of Mongolian tradition and environment in the 1960s; however, when placed within the general frame of Annaud's oeuvre and world vision, it appears that *Wolf Totem* draws its plot from Rong's novel while still linking itself to Annaud's previous films. Those who know Annaud's canon might recognize his usual idiosyncratic narratives and visual components that serve specific settings, genres, characters, and references, as well as his own political views. I argue that the very fact that Annaud is an Other, more specifically a French filmmaker, influenced his treatment of Rong's descriptions of environmental, economic, and political questions, first with his own stylistic and thematic mannerisms as a filmmaker, second with typical French representations of Chinese people and mores, and finally with a specific use of moving images to comment on the current regime in China from the perspective of the Western world. Annaud's strong commitment to film as at once the product of an individual and of collective imaginary calls for the right of everyone, director and viewer alike, to be allowed to look at reality from an independent, informed, and critical perspective.

A Film among Others

Since the beginning of his career, Annaud has chosen to address significant ideological and societal issues. Annaud's first two films possess a harsh, almost disenchanted tone that gives way to a more optimistic outlook in later movies. For instance, Annaud follows his scathing denunciation of French colonization in *Black and White in Color* (1976) and the satire of nepotism and corruption in French provincial cities in *Coup de tête* (1979), to consider a variety of international concerns and attitudes in later projects. He examines the Chinese invasion of Tibet in *Seven Years in Tibet* (1997), conflicts in the Middle East in *Wings of Courage* (1995) and *Day of the Falcon* (2011), and environmental issues in the Great North (*The Bear*, 1988) and the tropical jungle (*Two Brothers*, 2004). Each of these films carries a clear activist message advocating for the defense of nature and criticizing violence, oppression, and intolerance, but some do so with compassion and forgiveness. One even finds an undeniable romantic or whimsical atmosphere in *The Lover* (1992), *Quest for Fire* (1981), and *His Majesty Minor* (2007). His filmography also includes a historical trend ranging from prehistory (*Quest for Fire*) and archaic times (*His Majesty Minor*) to medieval times (*The Name of the Rose*, 1986), to

World War II battles with *Enemy at the Gates* (2001). Annaud's legacy is more
thematically and tonally diverse than is sometimes recognized. *Wolf Totem*
is therefore not an exception in an ensemble of films that combines epic
features, environmental concerns, romantic undertones, and a humanistic
message supporting diversity, freedom, and individual resilience across the
centuries. The film definitely adheres to Annaud's recurring interests.

One feature of Annaud's filming style that contributes to the homogeneity
of his oeuvre is his predilection for shooting on location. Since his first feature film, *Black and White in Color*, location shooting can be considered not
only as a technical characteristic warranted by the screenplay or an aesthetic
trait defining Annaud's style but also as a political gesture pointing toward the
geographical and social context of the film's production. For instance, the fact
that *Black and White* was shot in Côte d'Ivoire and not in Cameroon, where
the action takes place, adds another level to the colonial references present
in the plot by raising awareness about neocolonialist situations today. Early
on in his career, Annaud was confronted by a persistent and valid question:
does the shooting of a French film in former colonies, as a commercial and
artistic endeavor, reflect, support, or challenge the current relations between
them and the postcolonial regimes? Annaud's decision to shoot his films on
location does not answer this question but emphasizes its relevance today.

Regardless of the broader significance, one can see how *The Lover* ben-
efited from Vietnam's decision to open its frontiers in 1992 and allow three
French productions on the recent colonial past to be shot in the country:
Indochine (1992) by Régis Wargnier and *Diên Biên Phu* (1992) by Pierre
Schoendoerffer, in addition to Annaud's film. The Chinese government, however, refused to let Annaud film *Seven Years in Tibet* on its territory (it was
shot in Argentina) in 1976, before allowing him twenty years later to spend
more than a year in Mongolia shooting *Wolf Totem*. This film therefore is a
defining testament to Annaud's long engagement and particular resilience
with respect to the premises and consequences of making a film in a challenging environment. He proves with *Wolf Totem* that it is always possible
to overcome technical difficulties; one must adopt more subtle strategies
to overcome political obstacles, and such maneuvering is not for everyone.
Several directors before Annaud, including Peter Jackson, backed away from
adapting Rong's novel, which they found too challenging. For Annaud, the
main difficulty was to avoid making the same error he had made in *Seven
Years in Tibet* by criticizing the Chinese Communist Party's diktats: with
Wolf Totem, he endorsed the Spirit of the Wolf.

In other terms, since the beginning of his career, Annaud has situated
his practice as a filmmaker in the historical moment of its production with

the somehow overoptimistic yet deliberate hope of overcoming technical, military, and political hurdles to promote understanding, peace, and cooperation. In doing so he has attempted to add a politically committed dimension to transnational coproductions beyond strictly financial and commercial objectives. *Wolf Totem* offers another example of Annaud's resilience when problems surface as to whether he has to modify initial plans or wait for a second chance to implement his project. A realistic yet obstinate approach is part of his unrelenting commitment to cinema as an art without frontiers, whether geopolitical or imaginary, technical or aesthetic. Not only is *Wolf Totem* shot in China, or more specifically a territory occupied by China, it also produces a commentary on the consequences of this occupation, in lieu of the missed opportunity to film in Tibet. Thirty years after starting his career with a satire of French colonization, Annaud offers with *Wolf Totem* a similar distanced yet critical perspective on the present as still being informed by Chinese recent history.

In addition, contrary to some of his compatriots, Annaud has steered away from the lure of heritage cinema. Critics of French postcolonial cinema like Brigitte Rollet (1999) and Naomi Greene (1996) have long suspected heritage films' nostalgic performances to justify colonial abuse and oppression rather than atone for it. A similar perspective can be observed in Chinese cinema with its own series of heritage films on imperial times that commenced in 1991 with the success of Zhang Yimou's *Raise the Red Lantern*. Ironically, the opening credits of Annaud's *Wolf Totem* display the names of two production companies, China Film Co. and Beijing Forbidden City, which hark back to the two main totalitarian regimes in Chinese history: the current Communist regime and the former imperial regime. The nods to these two entities carry a certain bite. Annaud could not avoid the realpolitik of film production. Still, the inclusion of these credits could align with Rong's call for a reconciled nation in the near future of his country. Either way, the choice of Rong's novel can be understood as a political move by Annaud within the context of his usual political and ideological stances.

More generally, the selection of Rong's novel certainly satisfies Annaud's long-standing conception of adaptation as a dialogue between the film and the source text. Annaud regularly selects literary texts that possess narrative and aesthetic qualities able to invite political discussion. The literary source often contains the material—ideas, arguments, questions—that allows readers and critics to engage in a commentary and even a debate. However, using these texts as primary sources for his screenplays does not mean that Annaud endorses the author's views; rather, it allows him to participate in the discussion and offer his own perspective. The filmmaker's contribution as a metadiscourse on the text shifts the question of the film's relation to the literary source away from considerations of "fidelity," accuracy, and transformation. This tendency has led to some sharp rebuke of Annaud's films. For instance, Annaud's perceived ideological ambiguity and distance from the original texts raised criticisms from Marguerite Duras opposed to his adaptation of her novel, *The Lover*; historians irritated by the Nazi past of Heinrich Harrer, the author of *Seven Years in Tibet*; and literary scholars condemning the Célinian undertones of *Black and White in Color*. I argue, however, that Annaud's provocative stance originates not so much from the need to advance his own political agenda as to promote cinema's independence from any ideological, material, financial, and artistic constraints. There is no more reason for him to subject a filmmaker's creative gesture to geographical frontiers or bureaucratic decisions than to the diktat of the written text.

Besides its political commitment, *Wolf Totem* is not an isolated film in terms of subject and location. Annaud's satirical or polemical targets during these past forty years have been quite eclectic, ranging from the corruption of a soccer team in a French provincial town to a biracial love affair in Indochina, from a wacky mythological tale to the atrocities of WWII's battles. Within this corpus *Wolf Totem* constitutes the third element of a triptych started with *Two Brothers* (recounting the story of two tiger cubs in a Southeast Asian forest) and *The Bear* (adapted from *The Grizzly King* by James Oliver Curwood). These three films feature animals as protagonists, and common themes such as the lyrical depiction of vast expanses of natural wilderness that have been and still are invaded, exploited, and destroyed by humans: North American forests, the rain forest in Southeast Asia, and Mongolian grasslands. This choice of settings not only serves to illustrate current environmental issues; it also represents a challenge to the filmmaker's skills and ambition because of the nature of these landscapes: rough terrain, open spaces, harsh weather, wild animals as performers (requiring multiple "actors" and expert trainers). For *Wolf Totem*, Annaud surpassed himself by achieving what no other filmmaker had dared undertake, with hordes of "extras" (200 horses, 25 wolves), lengthy location shooting (four seasons in Mongolia), and state-of-the-art special effects technology that included drones.

What some have criticized as another example of Annaud's megalomania is nonetheless current in a global film industry, whether in Hollywood or Bollywood, that strives to lure record numbers of spectators/consumers with visual effects and production values. Yet what was hailed as an epic adventure for the sake of producing a film could in return be criticized as characteristic of human reckless and destructive behavior toward wildlife. In a cat-and-mouse game between the contents of moving images and the man behind the camera, Annaud acknowledges the presence of the most dangerous elements one can find in nature. These elements range from the cruelest beast to the icy storm in *Wolf Totem*. At the same time, he celebrates the human ability to have mastered these environmental obstacles since the dawn of humanity through patience, resilience, technology, and art. Cinema thus becomes the ultimate victory of humankind: overpowering nature while leaving it intact by reducing formidable landscapes and animals to a two-dimensional image that raises audience awareness. And, indeed, the promotion of *Wolf Totem* through the director's interviews to the press and the release of "making-of" documentaries strove to stress the minimal impact of the film location shooting compared to the global exposure the film could bring to environmental issues in China thanks to its grandiose visual dimension.

There is, however, another layer of commentary in the film that is created neither by the plot nor by production values or spectacular settings. In line with the reception of Rong's book and the author's own comments,[1] the disparity between the vast expanse of Mongolian plains and its lone characters (the cub, the old wolf, Chen Zhen the student from Beijing, Bilig the old Mongolian tribe leader, his daughter-in-law Gasma, and her son Bayar) also serves a direct political purpose beyond allegorical and mythical references about the nation and its identity. Resistance against the authority, the Party, the Han majority, is symbolized by Chen and his Mongolian hosts' conflict with the local Party representative "Director" Bao Shunghi, who is portrayed in typical Annaud fashion. Shunghi is not an evil and radically othered character (at the end of the film, Gasma explains that Bao's family is from Eastern Mongolia), but rather an opponent in a conflict of scale, space, and movement.

From *Black and White in Color* to *Enemy at the Gates*, Annaud has constantly relied on visual aesthetics to convey his political message on power relations between opposite groups (Africans and French colonizers in the colonial context, or Russian and German soldiers during the battle of Stalingrad). Annaud's contrast between close-ups and very long shots, subjective point-of-view shots and documentary-like scenes, endless panning shots and ironic montage brings the relation of these groups into particular focus. As to *Wolf Totem*, in addition to the conventional antithesis between "Nature and Man" to illustrate social and political conflicts, the film heavily plays on the opposition between the color red (on caps, clothing, flags, tractor) associated with the Communist Party, and a yellow/beige hue as the dominant color of fields, skies, clothes, and wolves to describe the Mongolian environment and articulate the conflict between characters and cultures.

The figure of the wolf is another fixture of Annaud's idiosyncratic representations and storytelling mannerisms with political connotations extending
beyond the Chinese context and Rong's novel. Before *Wolf Totem*, Annaud's
filmic bestiary repertoire already included the combination of a wolf and
a frightened horse in *Enemy at the Gates*, as Vassili (Jude Law), the Russian
sniper, remembered his training as a wolf hunter under his grandfather's
guidance. In *Wolf Totem*, Chen's (Feng Shaofeng) first encounter with wolves
while riding in the mountains, as well as the attack on the government's
horses by a pack of wolves during the ice storm, can be considered not only as
a realistic description of wildlife in the grasslands or an adaptation of Rong's
text, but also as a motif in Annaud's work. Besides their ethnographic value,
the wolf and horse scenes continue to build a specific message that becomes
more explicit in *Wolf Totem* once it is set in reference to *Enemy at the Gates*.
Contrary to Vassili, Chen is taught by old Bilig (Basen Zhabu) not only to
avoid the wolf's attack in a peaceful manner but also to gaze at the wolf from
a distance with binoculars. The subjective point of view, the object of the
vision, and the circular masking of the frame recall the shots seen through
the Russian hunter's gun scope, only to emphasize another perspective on
the animal and justify the use of another peaceful instrument of vision, that
of the filmmaker's camera.

Images of China, Images from China

In progressively abstracting Rong's characters and narrative from known
references to the Chinese context and refocusing them on his own practice,
Annaud grounds *Wolf Totem* in other representations of China that belong to
the Western tradition, and more specifically to French history and culture. In
fact, the adaptation of a Chinese text with a Chinese cast in an exotic location
with local administrative, economic, cultural, and environmental concerns
is not what distinguishes this film from other productions by Annaud. With
the exception of *Coup de tête*, a satire of the "Franco-French" chauvinistic
inhabitants of small provincial cities, and films set in the French colonial
empire (*Two Brothers*, *Black and White in Color*, and *The Lover*), *Wolf Totem*
belongs to the majority of Annaud's films such as *His Majesty Minor*, *Enemy
at the Gates*, and *Seven Years in Tibet*, with a plot and characters set in a
foreign country without any direct references to French history, society, or
culture. What *Wolf Totem* shares with these other films and Rong's novel is
a philosophical perspective that consists in portraying humanity's tragic fate

and resilience through love and friendship when confronted with natural disasters and social feuds.

It should be noted, however, that these general and universal themes are usually inflected by a Western perspective in Annaud's films through the choice of English-speaking actors (Jane March in *The Lover*, Brad Pitt in *Seven Years in Tibet*, Antonio Banderas in *Day of the Falcon*, Jude Law in *Enemy at the Gates*, Guy Pearce in *Two Brothers*, Val Kilmer in *Wings of Courage*, Sean Connery in *The Name of the Rose*). His plots also consistently reflect Western issues and historical benchmarks: conquest, colonization, world wars. *Wolf Totem*, on the contrary, does not include any Western character, and if the story relates to the "civilizing" mission, there are only a few allusions to the influence of Western civilization on Chinese and Mongolian life.[2] In fact, these allusions are already present in Rong's novel and include "the power of modern medicine" and means of transportation imported from the West (buses, Jeeps, tractors).[3]

What is more striking in the film is that very few direct references are made to the Cultural Revolution and the Maoist regime responsible for the displacement of students throughout the country and its consequences. Apart from any attempt to retain Rong's ambiguous discourse and obtain the support of Chinese authorities, the absence of contextual information is problematic in a film geared toward an international audience, as the scope of its production suggests, and featuring Annaud's usual themes: power relations and resistance to authority.

It is not uncommon, however, for Annaud to refuse any claim to historical authenticity or documentary objectivity in favor of the right to tell a story from the author's point of view. The emphasis on fiction, storytelling, irony, and/or fantasy contributes to blurring or even distorting historical references. In *Black and White in Color*, for example, the viewers are given several clues that the story takes place in Cameroon (colonized by the Germans, then by the French after World War I, before the British took over), but the lack of explicit geographical information turns the film into a general depiction of colonial situations. The beginning of *The Lover* multiplies visual and verbal information on the location of Marguerite Duras's protagonist in Indochina—the village of Sadek, then Saigon and the Cholon district—before restricting the frame of the story to the confined space of one room. Similarly, the opening of *Wolf Totem* offers precise information on the geographical and historical context: the story starts in Beijing in 1967 at the beginning of the Cultural Revolution. The circumstances of Chen's adventure are not developed further as he reaches the vast expanse of the grasslands and is introduced to the traditional lifestyle of the nomads, before being progressively confined to Bilig's family tent (and his wolf cub to a nearby hole).[4] The film ends with wide views of the land and the sky, where a cloud in the shape of a wolf roams freely. In typical Annaud fashion, the animal apotheosis is accompanied by a note on the future of the human protagonist (who will "devote his life to writing a book on wolves"). There is no mention of the historical context of his return to Beijing and the outcome of the "Up to the Mountains and Down to the Countryside" Movement.

The reason why the film does not dwell on the Han's progressive and organized control of Mongolia as a component of Mao's politics and revolutionary transformation of Chinese economy, society, and culture can be linked to the status of its author as a French filmmaker. Annaud's ideological commitment to humanistic and universal values cannot be separated from a tradition of historical representations that have contributed to building a constantly evolving imaginary about China in the West.[5]

Even if very few French films are set in China or feature Chinese protagonists, there is a tradition of stereotypical representations of Asian populations in French early cinema, from *Fumeur d'opium* (Louis Paglieri, 1912) and Albert Capellani's *Red Lantern* (produced in the US in 1919) to "yellow face" feature films such as *Les Pirates du rail* (Christian-Jaque, 1937), with Lucas Gridoux as General Tsai.[6] Whether played by white actors or Asian immigrants, these characters, and by extension their culture and regime, were systematically depicted as mysterious, shifty, somehow violent, and utterly distrustful.[7] But it should be noted that before 1949 this type of representation was usually associated with any political and social entity that had resisted French colonialism, from the sultanates of North Africa (Tunisia, Morocco, and Algeria) to the empires of Asia (India, Cambodia, and China).[8]

In spite of its location within the confines of China and far away from any French presence, *Wolf Totem*'s story resembles the literary and filmic accounts of administrative and military overpowering of an ethnic community for economic and ideological purposes that characterized the conquest by the French of vast expanses of land populated by seminomads in Africa. Mongolia as a place foreign to the realities of French colonialism thus becomes what Marc Augé calls a "non-place," that is, a "space which cannot be defined as relational, or historical, or concerned with identity" (77–78) and sets Annaud's Western viewers in a comfortable location, remote from their history, yet close to their imaginary.

Annaud's objective is therefore less an indictment of the Cultural Revolution, the Maoist regime, and its current legacy, and more a reflection on stereotypes and prejudice conveyed by representations of another culture.

In France the invasion of the Huns led by Attila, the "scourge of God," across Central Europe in the fifth century until its defeat near Orleans by a Roman coalition in 451 caused a long-lasting anxiety for the return of the "Yellow Peril."[9] So vivid and terrifying was this image, conveyed by history textbooks and popular culture, that when Tatar soldiers from the Idel Ural Legion were sent by Hitler in 1943 to fight in France, local populations took them for descendants of the Huns because of their Mongoloid features.[10]

Annaud's shift away from the stereotypical description of Chinese characters in French culture to address environmental and political issues faced by Mongolian people during the Cultural Revolution paradoxically leads him to share French scholars' new interpretations of historical facts and look at the Mongolian invasion from the perspective of Fernand Braudel's *"longue durée"* and Emmanuel Leroy Ladurie's historical climatology as a consequence of the end of the Roman Climatic Optimum, a period of unusually warm weather in Europe. The cold weather that ensued could account for Asian invasions in the fifth century. In *Wolf Totem* the disruption of traditional nomadic life and long-lasting balance between human beings and natural elements in Mongolia is described as the consequence of political decisions and foreign incursion. But Annaud's film also removes this situation from the Chinese context to allude to French history and provide an updated account of facts and events that challenges a tradition of stereotypical representations in his home country.[11]

In the early 1900s, French films on Chinese landscapes and people as being utterly exotic and different were included in the Gaumont and Pathé catalogues of short documentaries and news from the world, and collected by Albert Kahn for his "Archives de la Planète" (see Amad 2010). Sun Yat-sen's fight against imperial rule then became of particular interest in a country that had to undergo the reigns of three kings and two emperors before the definitive instauration of a republican regime in 1871. In 1933 André Maurois's *The Human Condition* on the repression of Communist activists by the Kuomintang was an immediate commercial and critical success in France.[12] The Maoist Revolution in 1949 raised new hopes among French philosophers and activists at a time when the French Communist Party affiliated with the USSR was losing ground. However, by 1968 the Marxist model had run out of steam in the West, and Red China had become a mysterious and dangerous threat, as predicted by Alain Peyrefitte in his ominous book *Quand la Chine s'éveillera . . . le monde tremblera* (When China wakes up, the world will tremble), published in 1973. Popular anxiety was mostly built on ethnic and ideological stereotypes that were fueled by the fear for the "Yellow Peril" as well as the sidelining of Maoist intellectuals portrayed at the time with derision in two very different films: Jean-Luc Godard's *La Chinoise* (1967) and Jean Yanne's *Les Chinois à Paris* (1974).

Since the 1970s, images produced in France about the Republic of China, its recent access to the liberal market, and its violations of human rights on all territories under its rule, have been provided mostly by news reports and political analysts.[13] Between silence and caricature, Annaud, just as almost all French filmmakers, had to find a third way to describe the current legacy of the Red Revolution: a dictatorial regime, censorship, economic dumping, extreme pollution. The readers of Rong's novel in China possess the daily and personal experience necessary to understand the meaning hidden between the lines of the text. But the film had to address a Western perspective informed by selected and distorted images from China that have been sent abroad for decades by government officials for the sake of Communist propaganda. In order to emphasize their nature as "fictional" or "indirect," Annaud summoned the resources provided by his medium of choice: the presence of an intradiegetic first-person narrator, the objectification of literature in general, and the use of still images isolated from the flow of the main narrative.

From Fiction to Reality

The presence of an intradiegetic narrator in *Wolf Totem* is a characteristic of almost all Annaud's films, whether adaptations of literary texts or not. The first-person narration in *Wolf Totem* is of course a reminder that the screenplay is based on Rong's actual experience and autobiographical writing, but it is also used in Annaud's films not so much to help viewers identify and empathize with the protagonists as to provide an intermediary able to communicate with them while keeping his/her cultural difference.

In *Wolf Totem*, Chen is a young student, a "city-man," who happens to become the educated and literate observer of the conflict between Chinese officials and Mongolian nomads; he is at the same time judge and jury, since he belongs to the former group and strives to assimilate with the latter. As such, he resembles Adso (Christian Slater) in *The Name of the Rose*, whose voiceover as an old man narrates his experience as the young witness of fiery debates between officers of the Inquisition and Benedictine monks. A voiceover in the prologue of *The Lover* cites the beginning of Marguerite Duras's novel where she describes a young girl's ordeal in the "impossible" colonial situation. *Two Brothers* starts with images taken from Aidan McRory's book on his hunting adventures in the tropical jungle. In all cases protagonists are first presented as authors of literary texts and future narrators of their own experiences that are later turned by Annaud into cinematographic images. These characters might take sides in the conflicts and debates that they recall, but their most significant function is to transform their personal knowledge into stories to be read, heard, and seen.

Reception thus represents a key feature in Annaud's choice of literary texts for his screenplays: these texts must have an established readership in order to inform the contents and the context of his own stories. The authors he selected, from Umberto Eco to Marguerite Duras to Jiang Rong, all met with commercial and critical success and could vouch for an actual connection between the storyteller and the public.[14] Annaud added another challenge by using texts that were considered difficult to adapt because of their philosophical or stylistic characteristics, as in the case of Eco's and Duras's novels. And, indeed, Rong's allusions to Chinese internal debates as well as the remote and dangerous setting of the story deterred many other European and Chinese filmmakers from adapting *Wolf Totem*.

The emphasis thus placed on the status of the book, its function, and its reception, within the plot allows Annaud to distance his work from questions related to adaptation. *Two Brothers*' viewers learn about McRory's book through its readers (Raoul and his mother) and effects (excitement and romantic illusions). In *The Name of the Rose*, the focus is on the books' depositaries (the library guardians). *Enemy at the Gates* depicts how Soviet political propaganda built the legend of Vassili Zaitsev through the press, media, and correspondence. Rong's novel is objectified as the future outcome of Chen's activity throughout the film, thus pointing toward an off-screen time and place, that of the publication of an actual book and its context. Viewers are therefore invited to envision the ideological, environmental, and social issues and events that will derive from the facts related in the film, from Tibet's annexation to the 1989 students' demonstration in Tiananmen Square, in which Rong participated many years after his experience in Mongolia.

The inclusion and objectification of literary texts within the film participate in building the status of moving images as both fictional and indexical, that is, as element of a story and trace of an outside reality. Already in *Black and White in Color*, Fresnoy's letter to the director of the Ecole Normale Supérieure served to underline with irony the difference between pseudo-scientific descriptions of African people and documentary-like images of rural Africa. *Two Brothers* produces a similar effect by juxtaposing still images from the hunter's book and moving images of wildlife in the jungle. In *The Name of the Rose*, Baskerville's (Sean Connery) talent as a detective relies on his ability to decipher various clues in his environment, contrary to the monks unable to go beyond the surface of their books and to understand the world around them.

In *Wolf Totem* the pastoral tale involving exotic animals and young adults in the outskirts of the country works toward displacing the reality of Communist China outside of the frame and the film, as a radical Other—formally and politically. As already mentioned, Annaud cannot use the same resources as Rong did, that is, a set of keys and clues that are easily decipherable by the Chinese reader. Rather, he must resort to an imaginary and a discourse that are accessible to viewers familiar with his work, and generally speaking to French nationals within the particular context of Chinese representations in French politics, history, literature, and cinema.

Although *Two Brothers* and *The Bear* are not set in France, both films convey a message meant to strike home in the midst of fierce debates on the reintroduction of wolves and bears in French mountains.[15] *Wolf Totem* completes the triptych, not only by illustrating the situation faced *hic et nunc* in France; it is also revisiting the romantic and sometimes nostalgic tradition of pastoral literature used since the seventeenth century to depict the French countryside. Descriptions of rural space were juxtaposed to references to the metropole before being expanded to include exotic locations in North America, North Africa, and the Indian Ocean by nineteenth-century novelists, from Chateaubriand to Gustave Flaubert, George Sand, and Pierre Loti. In this regard, Chen's adventure away from the busy life of the capital city, where hard work does not always guarantee a comfortable life, resembles the story of literary characters who before him traveled to foreign lands and fell in love with local women. Cultural differences, fear of miscegenation, acts of bravery, and the benevolent father figure present in the Chinese novel are familiar themes in French Romantic literature, not to mention the staples of colonial and postcolonial cinema, from the adventures of French officers in Morocco portrayed in *L'Occident* (Henri Fescourt, 1927) to Lieutenant Le Guen's affair with the Red Princess in *Indochina*.

From a literary perspective, *Wolf Totem* as a film made by a French filmmaker can also be differentiated from the Chinese novel through its connection with the Western tradition of stories, fairy tales, and legends featuring the wolf as a dangerous character.[16] This tradition includes many French references, from Charles Perrault's *Le Petit chaperon rouge (Little Red Riding Hood)*[17] to Christophe Gans's screenplay and film *Le Pacte des loups (Brotherhood of Wolves*, 2001). In the Chinese context, on the contrary, as Xiaojiang notes: "What is surprising about ancient Chinese mythic and allegorical stories is how limited stories about wolves are in ancient ethnic Han writings. Even in fables few have wolves as main characters" (23).

In Annaud's work, however, children's literature and cinema play a significant role and contribute to set the adaptation of Rong's novel at the crossroads of French cultural tradition and the filmmaker's idiosyncratic imaginary. Many of his films depict young characters, refer to popular literary genres for young readers and viewers (exotic adventures, detective stories, animal stories), and use stylistic figures that appeal to a young audience such as point-of-view shots from the perspective of the animal or close-ups and montage that humanize animal faces and movements. Even *The Lover*, perhaps not the best example of such literature, starts with a photograph of the "young girl." These images are explicitly shown as linked to the text in *The Name of the Rose*, where they appear as medieval illuminations, and in *Two Brothers* as colorful drawings in the hunter's book.

In *Wolf Totem* a set of specific images brings an additional clue. They are still shots displaying immobile objects: a section of the Great Wall observed by Chen from the bus taking him to Mongolia, the frozen horses caught in the ice, and Director Bao sitting on a red tractor. The fact that they are related to the young protagonist as future author of a book on his experience in Mongolia during the Cultural Revolution designates them as the illustrations of the book-to-be. However, because they are placed within a film, they stand out as anticinematic in the etymological sense of the term: they introduce a pause in the motion of the narrative and the flow of images and point to an extradiegetic reality, outside of the story being told, that is more specifically the Chinese past from the Qin dynasty (builders of the Great Wall and the Terracotta Army) to the Maoist Revolution (and its propaganda posters advocating economic development).

The lack of movement inherent in these images clearly sets them apart from the flow of moving ones that have a different nature and a different function. Annaud thus makes a clear distinction between his film, as a personal, cultural, and aesthetic product, and other images frozen by a political agenda that renders them fictitious and mendacious (including press images in *Enemy at the Gates* and the photograph of the tiger with a pierced ear in *Two Brothers*). In the case of *Wolf Totem*, the reality of Chinese history is characterized by its irrepresentability: images produced by the Chinese regime must be considered as stereotyped as French literature and cinema, and should not be trusted. To bypass censorship, Annaud could only resort to a handful of pictures that stand out from the rest of the story and its Chinese source because they speak to an outside eye with limited access to Chinese realities. The film's intended viewers—contrary to the novel's initial readers—are from the West and bring their own imaginary about China to the film experience, whether they are international tourists familiar

with images of Chinese historical sites, Annaud's aficionados attuned to his
ideological commitment and stylistic idiosyncrasies, or foreign collectors of
Chinese Revolution paraphernalia (Red Books, caps with the red star, *dazibao*
facsimiles, etc.). For Xianjang, the use of the wolf allegory in Rong's book fits
the definition once proposed by Chen Puqing as having "a double structure:
the surface is one story, called 'the vehicle'; its inner layer contains the author's
'implied meaning'" (quoted by Xiaojiang xv). Annaud proceeded differently
thanks to the ability of his medium to produce both still and moving images,
and inscribe referential statements in the flow of film shots through montage
effects. The implied meaning of the wolf figure is therefore deployed by the
film resources beyond the Chinese reference and the literary text toward an
international audience with a more universal message.

   Wolf Totem is the story of a young protagonist who experienced the Cultural Revolution as a geographical and cultural displacement away from
the city of Beijing, economic hardship, the rule of the Communist Party,
and the Han domination. During his stay among Mongolian nomads, he
became acquainted with the Spirit of the Wolf, a philosophical and political
opening to the diversity of his world and the construction of a new identity
as a Chinese national. Rong's allegory of the wolf, however, looks to Western
eyes like a fairy tale in reverse, *Little Red Riding Hood* turned into the story
of a young Communist unwillingly victimizing a wolf cub.[18] The cultural
specificities and political innuendos that characterize Rong's text were addressed by Annaud in his adaptation to offer Western viewers an engaging
and meaningful transposition of the novel, thus providing access to a literary
work with environmental concerns to a larger audience. In addition to Western references to the myth of the wolf, Annaud conjures all sorts of images,
from historical traditions to literary representations, from his previous films
to children's books, to transform a Chinese novel into a transnational film.
But this emphasis on the power of images to reach an international audience paradoxically stems from the recurring presence of Annaud's specific
themes and stylistic features, film after film, as well as the particular history of
French relations with China. In Rong's footsteps, Annaud thus achieved two
more personal objectives with his film: the reaffirmation of his own aesthetic
choices, whether in the treatment of literary sources (with first-person narration, references to verbal language, and the use of still images) or by his
filmic style (location shooting, production values, symbolic montage); and a
subtle yet urgent call for revisiting official discourses and popular stereotypes
for the sake of truth, resistance to oppression, and freedom both in his own
country and worldwide. As a matter of fact, the combination of a literary
text with a wealth of iconographical resources in Annaud's film allowed for

the emergence of missing images, unseen images, marginal images, those produced by Chinese opponents to the regime and systematically censored by party officials. With *Wolf Totem*, Annaud bravely endorsed a significant responsibility, that of international cinema and its institutions to give global exposure to artists who cannot work freely and are exposed to government diktat and censorship. In short, *Wolf Totem* demonstrates that the successful adaptation of a Chinese novel by a French filmmaker can result in expanding the personal, political, and cultural specificities and commitments of each artist to a global level.

Works Cited

Amad, Paula. *Counter-Archive. Film, the Everyday, and Albert Kahn's "Archives de la Planète."* Columbia UP, 2010.

Augé, Marc. *Non-Places: Introduction to an Anthropology of Supermodernity.* Translated by John Howe. Verso, 1995.

Benali, Abdelkader. *Le Cinéma colonial français au Maghreb.* Paris, Cerf/7ème art, 1998.

Bosséno, Christian. "La bonne conscience du cinéma colonial français." *Hommes et migration,* 1131, April 1990, p. 73.

Braudel, Fernand. *On History.* Translated by Sarah Matthews. U of Chicago P, 1980.

Callahan, William A. *China Dreams: 20 Visions of the Future.* Oxford UP, 2013.

Etiemble, René. *L'Europe chinoise : De la sinophilie à la sinophobie.* Gallimard, 1989.

Fuller, Karla. *Hollywod Goes Oriental: Caucasian Performance in American Film.* Wayne State UP, 2010.

Greene, Naomi. "Empire as Myth and Memory." *Cinema, Colonialism, Postcolonialism. Perspectives from the French and Francophone Worlds,* edited by Dina Sherzer. U of Texas P, 1996, pp. 103–19.

Le Roy Ladurie, Emmanuel. *Times of Feast, Times of Famine: History of Climate since the Year 1000.* Translated by Barbara Bray, Doubleday, 1971.

Moon, Krystyn R. *Yellowface: Creating the Chinese in American Popular Music and Performance, 1850s–1920s.* Rutgers UP, 2005.

Moura, Jean-Marc. "Péril jaune." *Dictionnaire des mythes d'aujourd'hui,* edited by Pierre Brunel. Editions du Rocher, 1999, pp. 616–27.

Peyrefitte, Alain. *Quand la Chine s'éveillera . . . le monde tremblera.* Fayard, 1973.

Rollet, Brigitte. "Identity and Alterity in *Indochine* (Wargnier, 1992). *French Cinema in the 1990s: Continuity and Difference,* edited by Phil Powrie. Oxford UP, 1999, pp. 37–46.

Shi, Zhan. "L'image de la Chine dans la pensée européenne du XVIIIème siècle : De l'apologie à la philosophie pratique." *Annales historiques de la Révolution française,* 347, 2007, pp. 93–111.

Staszak, Jean-François. "Screening the Other: Asian-American in Western Motion Pictures." *Annales de géographie,* vol. 6, 682, 2011, pp. 577–603.

Xiaojiang, Li. *Wolf Totem and the Post-Mao Utopian, A Chinese Perspective on Contemporary Western Scholarship.* Translated by Edward Mansfield Gunn Jr., Brill, 2008.

Xinjian, Xu. "The Chinese Identity in Question: 'Descendants of the Dragon' and 'The Wolf Totem.'" *Revue de Littérature Comparée,* vol. 1, 337, 2011, pp. 93–105.

Notes

1. See Callahan (2013, 115) on Jiang Rong's sixty-four appendices to his novel.

2. Annaud's next production, *Gengis Khan* (Hasi Chaolu, 2018), has also an all-Chinese cast and plot, but Annaud did not direct the film himself.

3. Chen's admiration for the medicine of "the future" and his desperate attempt to get penicillin after Bayar has been bitten by the wolf cub can either be considered by French viewers as an obvious homage to French scientist Louis Pasteur, who invented the first vaccine for rabies, or sound ironic since the virtues of Chinese medicine have now been acknowledged in the West, starting with Alain Peyrefitte, who devoted a whole chapter to the subject in his book (1973).

4. The same spatial dynamics are found in *The Name of the Rose* that takes Adso from the countryside surrounding the abbey to its inner sanctum, and in *Enemy at the Gates* where Vassili leaves the banks of the Volga River to reach the heart of Stalingrad's ruins.

5. Imperial China was first described in France as a model of rational government by Jesuit missionaries and later by Enlightenment philosophers such as Pierre Bayle and Voltaire before being criticized by Montesquieu for its despotism (Shi 2007).

6. On Western actors playing Asian characters, see Jean-François Staszak (2011), Krystyn R. Moon (2005), and Karla Rae Fuller (2010).

7. Examples include Dr. Fu Manchu, Sax Rohmer's character (created in 1912), and James Bond's foe Dr. No.

8. See, for example, Benali (1998) and Bosséno (1990).

9. According to René Etiemble (1989), the expression was first used by Hungarian geographer Ármin Vámbéry in 1904. See Moura (616–627).

10. The Tatars were originally from the east of Mongolia, but the term is used in the West to designate people of Turkish and Slavic origin living in Eastern Europe and Northern Asia.

11. Eastern European nations such as Hungary and Turkey have developed a totally different reading of the Hunnic Empire, since they celebrate it today as a significant and positive component of their heritage.

12. Of all novels awarded the Prix Goncourt since its creation in 1892, *The Human Condition*, with four million books sold in France, comes second only to Marguerite Duras's *The Lover*.

13. With the exception of *Le Palanquin des larmes* (1987) by Jacques Dorfman, an adaptation of the biography of Chow Ching Lie, a Chinese pianist exiled in France since 1965.

14. Aidan McRory might be considered as an exception, unless one sees in him a substitute for the "Anglo-Indian" writer Rudyard Kipling.

15. Environmental advocacy is an integral part of French politics, as in many other Western nations: France has two major "Green" political parties; a specific department, the Ministère de l'Environnement, was created in 1971; and environmental questions are always featured in the programs of candidates to national and local elections.

16. Jiang Rong's rehabilitation of the wolf image is set against the Chinese tradition and historiography that links the animal "with notions of atrocity, brutality and stupidity" (Xinjian 98).

17. Other famous examples include La Fontaine's *Le Loup et l'agneau* (*The wolf and the lamb*, 1668), Alphonse Daudet's *La Chèvre de Monsieur Seguin* (*The goat of Mr. Seguin*, 1869),

Verlaine's poem "Les Loups" (1884), and Serge Reggiani's allegorical song "Les Loups sont entrés dans Paris" (1967), among many others.

18. Zhang Yimou's contribution to the *Lumière and Company* (1995) anthology marking the anniversary of the invention of the Cinematograph looks like a "Vue Lumière" à *rebours*: shot on the Great Wall, it features turn-of-the-century characters morphing into contemporary musicians.

ADAPTATION, AUTHENTICITY, AND ETHICS IN CARL DAVIS'S SCORE TO *THE THIEF OF BAGDAD*

GEOFFREY WILSON

CARL DAVIS IS A LEADING COMPOSER IN THE SILENT FILM REVIVAL MOVEMENT, WRITING NEW scores for films of the silent era (1910–28). Starting in 1980, with his five-hour score to Abel Gance's epic *Napoléon* (1927), Davis has rescored over fifty of these films, including comedies featuring Charlie Chaplin, Harold Lloyd, and Buster Keaton, and feature films like Rupert Julian's *Phantom of the Opera* (1925/9), King Vidor's *The Big Parade* (1925), Erich von Stroheim's *Greed* (1924), and Raoul Walsh's *The Thief of Bagdad* (1924) ("Silent Film Catalogue"). When Davis describes his approach to rescoring these films, he often claims to imitate the practices of music directors in the movie palaces of 1920s New York. In a 2016 interview on creating the score to *Napoléon*, for instance, Davis recalls:

> I had three-and-a-half months from the thumbs-up to the perfor-
> mance. I could only really start working on it in mid-August 1980,
> and I thought well, this is rather similar, [music directors of the time]
> would be putting things together in a week! . . . And I thought . . . do
> what they did, the silent era film composers. They'd obviously inte-
> grate the great pieces of classical music into the score ("Carl Davis on
> Napoleon").

Davis follows his own suggestion. The score for *Napoléon* adapts many pieces by Beethoven, notably from the Third Symphony, which originally bore the subtitle "Bonaparte." Davis also borrows extensively from the music of Mozart, Haydn, and their late eighteenth-century contemporaries. Together, Davis creates a "portrait of the music of the time" ("Carl Davis on Napoleon"). Beyond this, Davis includes patriotic songs and folk music of the emerging French nation, writing several important themes himself when no suitable preexisting music could be found. The success of the score for *Napoléon* suggested a working method for Davis, and many of his later scores follow the same basic procedure.

Despite this well-regarded formula, Davis's claim to "do what they did" deserves scrutiny. While Davis draws on some elements of silent-film practice, there are important differences that reveal his debt to a later tradition of film scoring, one rooted in the works of Max Steiner and Erich Korngold in the 1930s and continuing with Miklós Rózsa, John Williams, and Howard Shore. These differences include Davis's approach to the musical representation of characters through leitmotivs, the relationship of those leitmotivs to the filmic narrative, and his preference for a unified musical style that contrasts with the patchwork preferred by most contemporary music directors. These tendencies are particularly noteworthy in Davis's score for Douglas Fairbanks's spectacular *The Thief of Bagdad*.

One of the most problematic aspects of silent-film music for the modern audience is its frequent use of essentialist, if not outright racist, portrayals of non-Western characters and settings through a series of musical stereotypes. The practice of representing characters with music that marked their national or ethnic identities was imported from the vaudeville tradition and was common in silent films through the early 1930s. If Davis was after an authentic recreation of "what they did" in the 1920s, using such music would be the inevitable consequence of that fidelity. But given how many fundamental aspects of silent film practice Davis ignores in his scores, it is worth examining whether his reliance on orientalism comes from historical style or something else. This chapter examines this question. It begins with a survey of the musical practice of silent cinema through the 1920s. It then provides a comparison of Davis's 1984 score for *The Thief of Bagdad* as it appears in the 2013 Cohen Film Collection DVD to a contemporary score by James C. Bradford, one of the most prolific compilers of adapted scores in the period. Such a comparison identifies some ethical issues Davis's adaptation of *The Thief of Bagdad* score raises even in the face of its undeniable appeal.

Adapted Music in Silent Film

Silent films were likely never silent. A pianist provided musical accompaniment at the first performance of Lumière films at the Salon Indien in Paris on December 28. 1895. Unfortunately, almost nothing is known about precisely what was played (Marks 31). It is not even clear whether the music accompanied the images themselves, aiding, for instance, the suspension of disbelief, or whether the music simply filled the considerable gaps between the reels being changed, leaving the projection itself unaccompanied (Wierzbicki 19–20).[1] What is obvious from the available accounts of early film is that the presentation of films was regularly supported by an orchestra of three to five players or a single pianist, at least when films were presented as part of vaudeville programs. The musical performers had large repertoires of musical "cues," short pieces arranged by topic, that came from the nineteenth-century melodrama tradition and could be used to accent a variety of skits and scenes. In this way, vaudeville orchestras could be said to simply adapt their music repertories to the films they reinforced. Typical cues for early silent films included "hurries" for action scenes, including chases, battles, and struggles; "misteriosos" for suspenseful moments; "adagios" for laments and funeral scenes; and national anthems, patriotic music, folk songs, and other musical cues intended to identify the nationality or ethnicity of the characters and scenes.

Another source of information about musical accompaniment in early film comes from complaints registered in the musical advice columns that begin to appear in trade publications like *Moving Picture World* around 1909. Some columns complained about the meagre skills of theater pianists. Others protested the musical choices made in performance. In general, critics wanted "better" music for film accompaniments—better performances, less popular music, and a more thoughtful pairing of music and film. In "Jackass Music," critic Louis Reeves Harrison writes a scathing satire of incompetent theater musicians in the guise of three characters: Lily Limpwrist, who plays whatever popular rag she pleases no matter what is happening in the film; Freddy Fuzzlehead, even worse than Lily, who "funs" the picture by choosing music to get cheap laughs; and Percy Peashaker, whose obsession with providing musical sound effects destroys the narrative (42–43). This last complaint became a regular one. Reviewers were quick to note the disruptive effect of musicians frequently changing cues simply to match cuts in the image track of the film. For many critics, the best way to improve the musical accompaniment was to take the choice for what to play away from the performers.

Theater musician and columnist Clarence Sinn dedicated several columns to producing "better" music in theatres. He advises musicians to identify the overall theme of the film and to keep the musical cues consistent with that theme, playing to the general requirements of each scene rather than frantically changing cues to catch every action and twist in the plot (1227). Sinn also provides advice on building a collection of suitable music that could be adapted to many situations.

To begin with, you should have a good library, which in these days of cheap music is not difficult. A few marches and waltzes, though these are indispensable, are not sufficient. Long *andantes* such as "Tramerei," [*sic*] "Flower Song," "Angel's Serenade" and the like are useful. . . . Religious music, national airs (of different counties [*sic*]), Oriental music and dances are frequently called for. Popular songs are useful, especially in sentimental pictures and comedies. The titles of these, if well known, frequently carry out the suggestion of the picture, but care should [be] taken that the music is also in keeping with the scene . . . Your library should also include some melodramatic music, such as mysterious, *agitato*, "Hurrys" for combats, storms, fire scenes, etc. There [*sic*] are in constant demand (1227).

As *Moving Picture World*'s main music columnist, Sinn's opinion was widely influential. The industry generally adopted his advice to organize their libraries by cues, including generic topics like andantes, agitatos, hurries, and specific topics that identify the national or ethnic origins of characters.

As time passed, a number of "cue sheets" began to appear, both to ensure some level of quality and to respond to the musical performer's very demanding schedule. Most theaters changed films quickly, turning over their entire repertoire in a matter of days (Anderson, *Music for Silent Films* xviii–xix). In this environment, theater musicians were not always able to preview the film to choose appropriate music. Naturally, musicians working under these circumstances welcomed cue sheets as practical guides to the kind of music they might play and when to switch from one cue to another. Compilation scores, scores assembled from pieces in the theater library, also began to emerge. If one of the scores listed on the cue sheet was unavailable or if it was deemed unsuitable, it was easy enough to substitute another similar piece of music in the library.[2] The below scoresheet illustrates how this process might look to a performer:

Cue sheet for *Frankenstein* (Edison, 1910) with sources in square brackets

At opening: Andante—"Then You'll Remember Me" [M. W. Balfe, *The Bohemian Girl*, 1843]
Till Frankenstein's laboratory: Moderato—"Melody in F" [A. Rubenstein, 1852/1882]
Till monster is forming: Increasing agitato

Till monster appears over bed: Dramatic music from "Der Freischütz"
[C. W. von Weber, 1820]
Till father and girl in sitting room: Moderato
Till Frankenstein returns home: Andante—"Annie Laurie" [trad./Scott,
1835]
Till monster enters Frankenstein's sitting room: Dramatic—"Der Freis-
chütz"
Till girl enters with teapot: Andante—"Annie Laurie"
Till monster comes from behind curtains: Dramatic—"Der Freischütz"
Till wedding guests are leaving: Bridal Chorus from "Lohengrin" [R.
Wagner, *Lohengrin*, 1850]
Till monster appears: Dramatic—"Der Freischütz"
Till Frankenstein enters: Agitato
Till monster appears: Dramatic—"Der Freischütz"
Till monster vanishes into mirror: Diminishing Agitato

The level of specificity provided by a scoresheet like this was specific enough
to support the player, but still loose enough to allow for easy substitutions.
Such developments certainly aided musicians confronted with limited time
to view every new film.

Cue sheets emerge as another strategy musicians use to respond to the
quick changes in early film exhibition. A sheet like the one in Figure 1 for
Frankenstein was part of a strategy to standardize musical accompaniment
in theaters across the United States. By suggesting what to play and when,
cue sheets establish a set of aesthetic criteria for silent film scores that many
theaters gradually adopt. One notable switch is the preference for long cues
that play to the general emotion or action of a scene, rather than the once-
standard short cues that change with each passing detail. The one exception
to a preference for longer cues is related to cues associated with specific
characters. When it came to characters, musicians continued to mark their
appearance with some musical repetition, which extended the tradition
of leitmotivs, melodies, or other characteristic musical sounds even after
other early practices were being abandoned. The idea was that these repeti-
tions were one of the best ways to represent a character, object, or idea. The
familiar tune would return each time the character, object, or idea appears
or, oftentimes, is even implied by the narrative. In *Frankenstein*, for example,
the music from *Der Freishütz* functions as a leitmotiv for The Monster,
returning five times in a film lasting just thirteen minutes. The rest of the
cues, whether specific pieces or musical topics, intend to support the general
mood of the scenes.

In the 1910s numerous anthologies of photoplay music appeared to help musicians manage the task of selecting music for their accompaniments. Some of these anthologies gathered existing popular, folk, and light classical music. Others consist of new cues from composers specializing in film music. What all these anthologies share is the practice of classifying music into topics just as Sinn had suggested. J. S. Zamecnik's three-volume collection *Sam Fox Moving Picture Music* (1913), for instance, provides theater pianists with several newly composed cues for hurries, battle scenes, comedies, love scenes, religious music, cowboy music, news reels, misterisosos, and death scenes. It also contains music intended to portray nonwhite/non-Western ethnicities through pieces with titles like "Oriental Veil Dance," "Chinese Music," "Mexican or Spanish Music," "Indian War Dance," and "Zulu or African Dance." The musical clichés contained in cues like these were common in early silent film practice and continued into the talking era, even as alternative approaches also began to emerge.

Joseph Carl Breil's score for *The Birth of a Nation* (1915) laid the foundations for the next decade of silent-film music. The main innovation in Breil's score was the composition of new leitmotivs for most of the important characters. Apart from these leitmotivs, Breil's work was essentially a compilation score, combining adapted eighteenth- and nineteenth-century art music excerpts with arrangements of folk and popular songs. In keeping with the widely recognized racist tone of the film, both the newly composed leitmotivs and the adapted music featured musical clichés that ridiculed both the slaves and the white politicians who help them. Breil's score relied on many of the same basic aesthetics already in practice, even though he changed the scale at which these practices were employed.[3] Breil's efforts establish the viability of these practices across a feature-length film. Suddenly, film scores needed to be much longer than Sinn anticipated. A small army of photoplay composers and publishers scrambled to provide reams of new music. New cue sheets were published at breakneck speed.

Most of the guides for theater musicians published in the 1920s reinforce the aesthetic preferences the previous decade established. These guides continue to promote long cues drawn from a variety of musical styles, musical representations of national/ethnic origin, and the use of a limited number of leitmotivs. The difference is that some desire to have unique accompaniment also begins to appear. George Benyon, for instance, urges his readers "not [to] use too much music composed by one man. Each has a certain style and technique which is noticeable to an almost incredible extent, even among the masses" (viii). Hugo Riesenfeld, music director of the Rivoli, Rialto, and Criterion theaters in New York, insists, "The chief difficulty in score writing or arranging is keeping the music subordinate to the action on the screen. It must never obtrude itself. *The audience must never be conscious of hearing a familiar tune*" (103, emphasis added).[4] The general idea is to create music that disappears into the complete experience of the film.

Ernö Rapée's *Encyclopedia of Music for Pictures* (1925) is a comprehensive guide to scoring practices for all kinds of theatrical presentations. Rapée had worked under Riesenfeld at the Rialto Theatre in New York and then at the Rivoli before being hired to direct music at Capitol Theatre. As music director, he created hundreds of compilation scores. The bulk of the *Encyclopedia*, in fact, is devoted to lists of pieces broken down by category and presumably representative of what the music library of a great theater ought to contain. Rapée's categories encompass both musical topics (agitatos, andantes, hurries, misteriosos, etc.) and categories by racial/national identity. His description of the process of choosing music for feature films highlights the standard practice of larger theaters at the time. Rapée advises,

> Firstly—determine the geographic and national atmosphere of your picture—Secondly—embody everyone [*sic*] of your important characters with a theme. Undoubtedly, there will be a Love theme and most likely there will be a theme for the Villain. If there is a humorous character who makes repeated appearances he will also need to be characterized by a theme of his own (13).

For Rapée, as for most film composers in the twenties, the representation of national or ethnic identity is usually the primary consideration in selecting music. Rapée explains, "If you have a picture playing . . . in China, you will have to find *all* your accompaniment material in existing Chinese music, *both to cover atmospheric situations as well as to endow your characters* [. . . ;] you will of course cover your English character, by English music for the sake of contrast" (13, emphasis added). Turning to Rapée's list of "Chinese-Japanese" music, it is immediately clear that "existing Chinese music" means essentialist representations of the Far East by nineteenth-century European art music composers like Tchaikovsky, Sullivan, and Puccini and a vast quantity of music by photoplay specialists like Irénée Berge, Gaston Borch, William Axt, and Rapée himself (140–46).

The *Encyclopedia* reinforces these ethnic representations by creating an abundance of categories for ethnic/national groups. Entries exist for Abyssinian, African (regrettably listed under "Cannibal"), Algerian, American (with separate sections for "Indian," "Southern," and "Negro"), Arabian, Argentine, Armenian, Australian, and Austrian music under the A's alone (31–86). These ethnic categories determine how to score ethnic characters and scenes. Aside from national anthems and folk songs from the Americas and some European nations, these categories mainly offer photoplay cues, a sample of the thousands of essentialist pieces that had been published in the ten years since *The Birth of a Nation*.[5]

Music for *The Thief of Bagdad*

As the subtitle, "An Arabian Nights Fantasy," makes clear, *The Thief of Bagdad* cobbles together its plot from several of the stories in *One Thousand and One Nights*, a collection that provided Western audiences with a colorful picture of Arabian life. The basics of the tale are well known. King Shahryar, having been betrayed by his wife, protects himself from future infidelities by marrying a new woman each day, then having her killed the following morning. Scheherazade, daughter of the royal vizier, marries Shahryar and saves herself, and all Shahryar's future wives, by telling him a different story each night. Enthralled by the stories, Shahryar allows Scheherazade to live so that she can go on spinning stories. The film positions itself as one of Scheherazade's tales through the opening titles, and Davis's music responds strongly to this suggestion. The daughter of the Caliph of Bagdad (Julanne Johnston) is soon to be married. Three royal suitors, including Cham Shang (Sojin Kamiyama), Prince of Mongolia, travel to the city in hopes of winning her hand. Meanwhile, a local Thief disguises himself as a fourth suitor, Prince Ahmed (Douglas Fairbanks), in order to abduct her. The Princess freely chooses Prince Ahmed, but Cham Shang learns Ahmed's secret and exposes the fraud to the Caliph, who sentences him to death. The Princess helps Ahmed escape, then convinces the Caliph (Brandon Hurst) to send the remaining suitors on a quest for magical objects to prove their worth. The Thief, who has fallen in love with the princess, is sent on a parallel quest to prove himself and earn his happiness. Meanwhile, Cham Shang plans an invasion of Bagdad. His plans are ultimately thwarted by the Thief, who uses a magic chest to summon an army to expel Cham Shang's army. The Thief's reward is the Princess. The two end the film flying away happily on a magic carpet.

Douglas Fairbanks hired Mortimer Wilson to compose an original score for *The Thief*, a rare choice in 1924. Wilson spent months on the set, sketching the musical themes during the shooting of the film. When the film opened in New York on March 18, 1924, the Wilson score was rejected out of hand by the theater director, who thought that a compilation score of music by

James C. Bradford's cue sheet for The Thief of Bagdad (1924)

famous composers would ensure a more successful run ("Thief of Bagdad"). The director hired James Bradford, one of the most prolific score compilers, to create a replacement. That version was the most commonly heard score for the film through the cue sheet that Bradford published shortly after the premiere.[6]

Conforming nicely to the aesthetics laid out by manuals in the 1920s, the Bradford cue sheet calls for three leitmotivs: a theme for the Thief, a theme for the Mongol Prince, and a Love Theme.[7] Bradford sets these leitmotivs in just the way Rapée suggests. The THIEF THEME, adapted from Schroder's "March of the Gnomes," appears six times. The first occurs when the Thief walks away laughing from a robbery. The leitmotiv is heard only five additional times in a film that runs more than 150 minutes. Each cue lasts between one and two minutes so that it is not only the melody transcribed on the cue sheet that is heard but contrasting musical material also.[8] The LOVE THEME, adapted from the second movement of Nikolai Rimsky-Korsakov's *Scheherazade*, first appears when the Thief and his associate plan the abduction of the Princess and runs over four minutes, long even by the measure of a compilation score. This theme repeats twice: once when Prince Ahmed ascends the Princess's balcony and again as the happy couple flies away at the end of the film. The theme for Cham Shang, identified as MONGOL THEME in the cue sheet, is adapted from Irénée Berge's "Patrol of the Boxers," a photoplay cue. It repeats three times: first when the royal suitors depart the palace on their quest, and again at the suitor's camp in the desert. The final occurrence of the MONGOL THEME happens after Cham Shang has ordered the murder, by venomous snake, of a fisherman. Shang uses the magic apple to revive him as a test for saving the Princess, whom he poisons. His theme sounds as the fisherman runs away.

Carl Davis's new score for *The Thief of Bagdad* is, in some ways, "the sort of thing they would do at the time." Davis takes inspiration from the look of the sets and costumes that William Cameron Menzies designed for the film. In a 2016 radio interview, Davis explains,

> It looked to me very inspired, in its design, by *Ballets Russes*; the whole atmosphere had that sort of . . . what I call "Russian Orientalism," so I decided that I would do the sort of thing they did at the time. I chose a composer. It was all going to be what I call Rimsky's [Nikolai Rimsky-Korsakov] greatest hits. Everything famous—lots of *Scheherazade*, and other pieces that people would know. [. . .] It makes use of the biggest orchestra. ("Interview")

The score identifies the geographic setting and the ethnic identity of characters and design cues that reinforce these identities. However, Davis adapts all his music from Rimsky-Korsakov, directly contradicting the stylistic variety stressed by Benyon and Rapée. Davis borrows liberally from three works: the symphonic suite *Scheherazade*, and the suites from the operas *Le Coq d'or* and *Tsar Saltan*. Additional cues borrowed from lesser-known works like *Antar*, *Sadko*, and *The Invisible City of Kitezh*, plus a few original themes by Davis himself, round out the thematic material of the score. The principal leitmotivs are given in the following examples, along with their sources. although the titles are my own.

Principal leitmotivs in Carl Davis's score to *The Thief of Bagdad (1984)*.[9]

SHAHRYAR (Rimsky-Korsakov, *Scheherazade* (1888), i, mm. 1–6)

Thief Themes

HAPPINESS (Rimsky-Korsakov, *Scheherazade*, i, mm. 14–18)

STEALING (Rimsky-Korsakov, *Scheherazade*, ii, mm. 5–25)

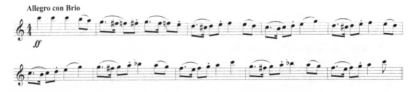

PRINCE AHMED (Rimsky-Korsakov, "Cortège des Noces" from *Le Coq d'or* (1907), 4 bars after r. 229)

THIEF'S ASSOCIATE (Davis, 1984; transcribed by the author)

BAGDAD (Rimsky-Korsakov, *Le Coq d'or*, opening)

PALACE GUARDS (Rimsky-Korsakov, *Le Coq d'or* suite, r. 5)

LOVE (Rimsky-Korsakov, *Scheherazade*, iii, mm. 1–20)

Mongol Themes

CHAM SHANG, Prince of Mongolia (Davis; transcribed by the author)

SLAVE GIRL (Rimsky-Korsakov, *Le Coq d'or*, r. 1)

PRINCE OF THE INDES (Rimsky-Korsakov, *Le Coq d'or*, r. 54)

PRINCE OF PERSIA (Rimsky-Korsakov, *Tsar Saltan* suite, r. 26)

Magic Objects

MAGIC CARPET (Rimsky-Korsakov, *Scheherazade*, iii, at D)

MAGIC APPLE (Davis, transcribed by the author)

SILVER CHEST (Rimsky-Korsakov, *Scheherazade*, ii, 4 after D)

MAGIC CRYSTAL (Rimsky-Korsakov, *Russian Easter Overture* (1888), m. 1–3)

Davis's treatment of leitmotivs in *The Thief of Bagdad* differs greatly from Bradford in both the number and the treatment. The Thief has three associated themes. Cham Shang has a theme. There is also a love theme (coincidentally the same theme that appears in the Bradford cue sheet). Beyond these, there are leitmotivs for the Mongol slave girl (Anna May Wong), the Thief's Associate (Snitz Edwards), each of the royal suitors, the palace guards, the city itself (shared with the Caliph), and each of the magical objects. A total of fifteen primary leitmotivs arise, then, plus one more that will be discussed shortly. Davis adapts nearly all of these melodies from Rimsky-Korsakov, where they function as leitmotivs in operas, symphonic poems, and symphonies. The only newly composed leitmotivs are those for Cham Shang, the magic apple, and the Thief's Associate.

In some cases, the borrowed melodies have no problem shedding their previous associations. The leitmotivs that represent the Golden Cockerel, the Astrologer, and the Queen of Shemakha in *Le Coq d'or* are easily accepted here as BAGDAD/CALIPH, PALACE GUARDS, and SLAVE GIRL. This is surely due to the way that Davis uses the themes. Unlike in Bradford, the themes appear frequently, being heard whenever the characters are on screen and often in place of their speaking voices. As David Neumeyer argues, "nondiegetic music that draws attention to itself . . . moves decisively toward the role of the filmic narrator, tries to set itself up in the role of a voice" (31). By exploiting this tendency, Davis can virtually erase the borrowed music's former meanings.

The set of leitmotivs for the Thief are more complicated. Of these, the most straightforward is PRINCE AHMED, which is first heard in the procession of royal suitors [00:52:04; all timings refer to the Cohen DVD] borrowed from the wedding cortège in *Le Coq d'or*. Davis uses a wedding march to foreshadow the Princess's eventual choice of suitor. Davis also relates the Thief to STEALING, which is first heard when the Thief steals a man's purse in the opening scene [00:02:59]. This leitmotiv adapts music from the second movement of *Scheherazade* and is also associated with the Kalendar Prince, who is portrayed in *One Thousand and One Nights* as a nobleman forced to live disguised as an itinerant mystic. The suggestion is that the Thief's noble character is simply hidden by circumstance. A third theme, HAPPINESS, appears for the first time in the prologue when a mullah tells a tale to a young boy in the desert at night. As he speaks, the moral of the film, "Happiness must be earned," is spelled out by the stars in the heavens. As these words fade into view, the theme enters. Clearly, representing HAPPINESS, this theme's association with Scheherazade's storytelling in Rimsky-Korsakov's symphonic poem cannot be entirely erased in its new filmic context. The problem is that the music itself is a strange fit for the Thief. The high violin melody singing over strummed chords remains, to an extent, Scheherazade's voice; we hear her telling us the tale of the Thief so that the reference to the onscreen character is indirect. When Davis uses this theme to accompany the first appearance of the Thief sleeping by a well, the music does not attach itself completely to the new character in the way that most of the other leitmotivs do. Instead, as we hear the theme continually paired with the Thief's quest for happiness, we also hear the ghost of Scheherazade telling us the story that we are presently witnessing, so that the leitmotiv has two referents, one from the original musical context and the other from the world of this film. Therefore, the Thief requires a second theme, STEALING, that represents him more directly.

Davis thinks of the leitmotivs as short melodies, rather than extended compositions as Bradford does. Although many passages are adapted unaltered from the originals, Davis also arranges long stretches of the music to allow multiple leitmotivs to be played in close succession. Consider the scene in which the Caliph announces the Princess's choice of suitor. Beginning at the title "In the Throne Room" [01:03:35], Davis weaves together leitmotivs for all of the characters present: BAGDAD, PRINCE OF THE INDIES, PRINCE OF PERSIA, CHAM SHANG, PRINCE AHMED, THIEF'S ASSOCIATE, plus a minor theme associated with marriage (not included above) and a theme called SHAHRYAR, to be discussed below. The scene plays for just under three minutes, but it packs fifteen leitmotivs into the underscoring, including two statements of the marriage theme. Here, and in many other passages, Davis's practice is much more closely related to his contemporaries' than with any historical precedent. As a quick comparison, one might consider a scene from Return of the Jedi (1983) in which Luke Skywalker (Mark Hamill) returns to Dagobah to complete his training with Yoda (Frank Oz). Composer John Williams arranges leitmotivs for LUKE, YODA, THE FORCE, DARTH VADER, THE EMPEROR in various transformations, presenting thirteen distinct versions of these melodies in just over six minutes. In both Davis's and Williams's scores, this is possible because the leitmotivs are relatively short melodies and not complete pieces.

Davis's practice alters how a leitmotiv might relate to a character, a point succinctly represented in the Throne Room scene, which assigns its leitmotiv an unexpected function. Labeled SHAHRYAR, this leitmotiv is borrowed from Scheherazade, where it represents the Sultan listening to Scheherazade's tales and reacting to them. This leitmotiv is by far the most frequent melody in Davis's score, appearing in over a quarter of the cues in Appendix B (48 of 168). Interestingly, it is not consistently paired with any character, object, or emotion. It first appears with the studio logo that opens the film. The placement breaks from the practice of a composer from the 1920s. The choice more properly realizes Robert Hatten's sense of inviting a narrative interpretation than a generic cue (Hatten 11–12). In the Throne Room scene, SHAHRYAR occurs twice, once as a soft plucked-string accompaniment to the THIEF'S ASSOCIATE leitmotiv as the Princess's choice is announced, and again immediately after her ring is placed on Prince Ahmed's hand. The second appearance even dominates the score, as it swells in a dramatic orchestral crescendo and a forceful brass presentation of theme that corresponds to the outrage of the other suitors. Whose outrage are we hearing in this scene? One could claim the outrage belongs to Shahryar. In a sense, Davis has introduced a new, purely musical character into the narrative.

Michel Chion has identified the *acousmêtre* as a character in sound film that exists, at least initially, entirely as a sound being (17–30). Often, the *acousmêtre* is a disembodied voice whose transformation into a regular character is complete when the voice is reunited with its physical body on screen. The *acousmêtre* is imbued with magical powers that endure so long as the sound is not mapped onto anything physical in the filmic world. Extending Chion's idea, one could deem the SHAHRYAR leitmotiv, and to a degree the HAPPINESS leitmotiv (which sounds in roughly one-fifth of the cues), to exist as *acousmêtres* in *The Thief of Bagdad*, voices that inhabit the border between filmic and extrafilmic narration (Neumeyer 30). In *Scheherazade*, these two leitmotivs, representing Shahryar and Scheherazade respectively, weave into the movements as a constant reminder of the framing story inside of which all the tales of *One Thousand and One Nights* unfold. In Davis's score, the introduction of SHAHRYAR happens without any reference to the film's characters, occurring before the onscreen action begins and immediately followed by the introduction of HAPPINESS with the mullah's framing story. In this way Davis maps the narrative strategy of *Scheherazade* (and by extension *One Thousand and One Nights*) onto *The Thief of Bagdad* in a fascinating metanarrative. Unlike the other leitmotivs, which either disappear completely into their new diegetic context (the themes for SLAVE GIRL, BAGDAD/CALIPH, etc.) or exist alongside their previous associations to some extent (STEALING, PRINCE AHMED), SHAHRYAR and HAPPINESS occupy a narrative layer that sits between the film's diegesis and the viewer. In Davis's score, we hear Scheherazade telling the story of the Thief, and Shahryar reacting, as characters that occupy this liminal space.

Ethics and the Davis Score

Ethical concerns regularly emerge from any study of early film music if only because so much of the music contains musical stereotypes that now seem unacceptable. While many of the folk songs, patriotic songs, and national anthems that were used for this purpose do not carry particularly negative associations, much of the music created to represent nonwhite, non-European characters certainly does. The resulting stereotypes often reinforce racist and essentialist portrayals that extend well into the soundtracks of twentieth-century films and cartoons. In 2002 the Mont Alto Orchestra adapted Bradford's cue sheet for a release of *The Thief of Bagdad* for Kino. Comparing this adaptation with Davis's score underscores the important differences—as a group committed to an historically informed performance, Mont Alto's score uses many pieces that promote musical stereotypes in an attempt to bring Bradford's conception to modern audiences, making substitutions only when pieces that Bradford recommended were unavailable. The cues are long and the leitmotivs few, so while the score is infused with a general exoticism, it is far less pointed than in the Davis score.

Whatever the ethical issues of authentic silent film re-creations may be, and certain ethical concerns do inevitably arise, Davis's score for *The Thief of Bagdad* does not fit the usual practice. This adaptation breaks from silent film practice. He adapts nearly all his music from a single composer's work, rather than relying on a compilation of many musical styles and voices. He uses short leitmotivs much more frequently than a typical silent film composer, as if he were scoring an action adventure film in the 1980s (which, of course, he was from a certain point of view). The consequence of his method is to concentrate the orientalism of the score around the numerous leitmotivs, replacing the somewhat diffuse orientalism of a compilation score. The *only* element of silent film aesthetics that Davis really preserves is the strong preference for representing national and ethnic identities with music largely by Western composers with little knowledge of the musical traditions of the identities they intend to represent.

Davis's technique is especially dangerous in part because it is wonderfully effective for the modern listener whose expectations of a film score are largely governed by expectations of Hollywood film scoring practices of the last fifty years. By contrast, for all its historical accuracy, the Mont Alto adaptation of the Bradford cue sheet lacks the grandeur and impact of Davis's music. It often seems like mere accompaniment rather than a strong narrative presence. A question emerges: "How should one balance aesthetic concerns with ethical ones?" Interestingly, Davis himself has already provided an answer to this question with his scores for films like *Napoléon* and *The Phantom of the Opera*. Although they share the same tenuous relationship to historical practices as his score for *The Thief of Bagdad*, he handles the representation of national and ethnic identities through patriotic songs and folk music rather than essentialist representations. This simple change in source material makes these scores no less effective but much more appealing to audiences that are increasingly sensitive to musical representations of race, nationality, and culture.

It is easy to dismiss Davis's claims to historical authenticity in these scores as simply playing on the kind of nostalgia that Hollywood film often indulges. From this point of view, fidelity to historical practice is unimportant: so long as the music sounds "old," it can represent a tradition that it resembles only on the surface. Underneath, all the basic strategies that give the music its coherence and meaning are based on the present and not the past. The result is that authenticity becomes something performed for modern audiences in their own frame of reference, rather than something that can be confirmed by historical records. Ironically, this is the same strategy that allowed the musical stereotypes of early film music to represent other ethnicities and cultures so effectively to their audiences. The melodies have surface features that are just unfamiliar enough to strike the ear as foreign without actually stepping outside culturally instilled boundaries. In this way listeners can be presented with a representation of otherness without encountering anything new. The larger point therefore is not just that Davis claims an historical fidelity that is not really there but that he feels compelled to reimagine the past in this way.

In the end, any appeal to authenticity in Carl Davis's silent film scores is ultimately misleading. What he does, very well, is to make silent film much more accessible to modern audiences by creating music that draws on familiar techniques. On some level, Davis acknowledges the impact that sound films have had on his compositional choices for silent film:

> I think that the music for a silent film has to be far more graphic because you must remember that, in a contemporary film, a soundtrack is shared three ways. You may have music under dialogue or sound effects, competing with these so you always have to be careful it will balance out. When dealing with the silent film, you are the complete sound picture. There's nothing else. You have to make the dialogue. Make everyone think they are hearing the people speak, that they're hearing the sound effects" ("Interview with Carl Davis" 2).

In silent film practice, there was no need to make the characters speak—that was the function of the intertitles. Sound effects were reduced to essentials and were never allowed to intrude on the picture. In attempting to compensate for missing soundtrack elements that could be missed only by modern audiences, Davis's scores may be less concerned with doing "what they did" than he realizes.

Appendix A—Cue sheet for James Bradford's score to *The Thief of Bagdad* (1924)

On screen	Title	Composer	Duration
1. Personnel	*Midsummer Night's Dream*	F. Mendelssohn	2 ¾ min.
2. (Title) Douglas Fairbanks in The Thief of Bagdad	*Balhama*	E. Vitalis	1 ¼ min.
3. (Title) A street in Bagdad	*Balhama*	Vitalis	1 ¼ min.
4. (Action) Thief grabs man at well	*Overture comique*	[Béla Kéler]	1 ¼ min.
5. (Action) Thief walks away laughing	THIEF THEME: *Carnival March of the Gnomes*	W. Schroeder	2 min.
6. (Action) Magician with basket	*Orientale* [Op. 7, no. 2] (oboe solo)	N. Amani	1 ½ min.
7. (Action) Woman appears on balcony	"In Minor Mode No. 2" [Op. 165, no. 2]	R. deKoven	1 ¼ min.
8. (Title) Come to Prayer	*Allah*	G. W. Chadwick	¾ min.
9. (Action) Natives rise from knees	Repeat THIEF THEME no. 5		1 ½ min.
10. (Title) Oh True Believers	*Hindoo Song No. 1*	Bemberg	1 ½ min.
11. (Action) Thief appears on steps	*Sakuntala Overture*	Goldmark	1 ¼ min.
12. (Title) Let all these beware	*El Kahira*	Boehnlein	1 ½ min.
13. (Action) Thief enters den	*La source* ballet no. 1	L. Delibes	1 ¼ min.
14. (Title) Open wide the gates	*Cortège du Serdare*	Iwanow	2 ½ min.
15. (Title) Beasts and Scimitars	*Antar*	Rimsky-Korsakov	2 ¾ min.
16. (Action) Slave playing serenade	*Serenade*	Saint-Saens	2 ¼ min.
17. (Action) Princess Awakens	*Dramatic conflict*	Sol P. Levy	1 min.
18. (Action) Knife touches maid	*Indian Misterioso*	Levy	1 ¼ min.
19. (Action) Mongol maid screams	Repeat THIEF THEME no. 5		1 min.
20. (Title) The melody of	LOVE THEME: Young Prince and the Young Princess [*Scheherazade*, iii]	Rimsky-Korsakov	4 ¼ min.
21. (Title) The suitors are at the gates	*Sultanes dormez*	Gabriel-Marie	1 ¾ min.
22. (Title) The Bazaars of the Merchants	Repeat THIEF THEME no. 5		1 min.
23. (Title) Chan Shang [sic], The great Prince of the Mongol	MONGOL THEME: *Patrol of the Boxers*	Irénée Berge	1 ¼ min.

On screen	Title	Composer	Duration
24. (Title) Ahmed, Prince of the Isles	Repeat THIEF THEME no. 5		2 ½ min.
25. (Title) We must make haste to steal her	Moto Perpetuo	Weiss	¾ min.
26. (Action) Thief appears on balcony	Repeat LOVE THEME no. 20		3 ½ min.
27. (Action) Mongol Prince at screen with slave	*Le coq d'or*	Rimsky-Korsakov	¾ min.
28. (Title) In the Throne Room	*March and Procession of Bacchus*	Delibes	2 ¾ min.
29. (Title) He is the thief	*Othello's Remorse*	Baron	1 ¾ min.
30. (Action) Thief and Princess meet	*Moon of my Delight* "Persian Garden"	Lehmann	1 ¾ min.
31. (Action) Thief Arrested	Prelude in G minor	Rachmaninoff	2 ¼ min.
32. (Title) The secret panel	*Dall' Oriente*	Labate	2 min.
33. (Title) Morning	*Orientale*	C. Cui	1 ¾
34. (Title) Come, if thou wouldst still steal her	*Persian March*	Strauss	1 ½ min.
35. (Title) Turned lily white	*In the Mosque* "Caucasian sketches"	Iwanow	1 ½ min.
36. (Action) Procession passes out of gate	Repeat MONGOL THEME no. 23		¾ min.
37. (Action) Flash-back to Priest and Thief	*Sirens*	Gabriel-Marie	1 ½ min.
38. (Title) A day's journey from Bagdad	Repeat MONGOL THEME no. 23		1 ¼ min.
39. (Title) A defile in the mountains	Fantasia from *Die Walküre*	R. Wagner	1 ½ min.
40. (Title) In Bagdad	*Song of India*	Rimsky-Korsakov	1 min.
41. (Title) The first moon—Valley of fire	Fire music from *Die Walküre*	Wagner	1 ½ min.
42. (Title) The second moon	*Yasmina*	Clemandh	1 ½ min.
43. (Title) The third moon—The valley of monsters	Ride from *Die Walküre*	Wagner	1 ¼ min.
44. (Title) The cavern of enchanted trees	Forest Murmurs from *Siegfried*	Wagner	1 ½ min.
45. (Title) The fourth moon	*Scheherazada*	Rimsky-Korsakov	2 min.
46. (Title) The fifth moon—Old man of the sea	*Fingal's Cave*	Mendelssohn	3 min.
47. (Title) The abode of the winged horse	*In the Clouds*	Rapée-Axt	¾ min.
48. (Title) The sixth moon	*Within the Walls of China*	Lively	2 min.
49. (Title) That fisherman	*Gruesome Tales* no. 1	Rapée-Axt	1 ½ min.
50. (Action) Fisherman runs away	repeat MONGOL THEME no. 23		1 ¼ min.
51. (Title) The citadel of the moon	*The bee's wedding*	Mendelssohn	1 ¼ min.

On screen	Title	Composer	Duration
52. (Title) at the end of the sixth moon	*To a mummy* "Egyptien [sic] Impressions"	Crist	1 ¼ min.
53. (Title) A day's journey from Bagdad	*Sultan's Guard*	Seredy	1 ¼ min.
54. (Action) Three princes look into crystal	*Ballet Egyptien* no. 4	Luigini	¾ min.
55. (Title) Spread the magic carpet	Repeat no. 51 *The bee's wedding*		1 ¼ min.
56. (Action) Mongol Prince revives princess	*Ballet Egyptien* no. 3	Luigini	1 min.
57. (Title) Out of the Clouds	Repeat THIEF THEME no. 5		1 ¼ min.
58. (Action) Thief rides away	Intermezzo from *Cleopatra's Night*	Hadley	2 ¼ min.
59. (Action) Thief appears riding across the desert	*Phaeton*	Saint-Saens	2 ½ min.
60. (Action) Mongol Prince on the Bagdad throne	*L'illusion supreme*	Gabriel-Marie	1 min.
61. (Title) Bagdad is in the hands of the Mongols	*The Furious Mob*	J. S. Zamecnik	3 ¼ min.
62. (Action) Mongol slave stops executioner	*The Crusaders*	Zamecnik	1 ¼ min.
63. (Action) Slave speaks to the Thief	repeat No. 51 *the bee's wedding*		2 min.
64. (Title) Priest in Moonlight—Happiness must be earned	repeat LOVE THEME no. 20		1 ¼ min.

Works Cited

Altman, Rick. "The Living Nickelodeon." *The Sounds of Early Cinema*, edited by Richard Abel and Rick Altman. Bloomington: Indiana University Press, 2001. 232–40.

Anderson, Gillian. *Music for Silent Films, 1894–1929: A Guide*. Washington, DC: Library of Congress, 1988.

Anderson, Gillian. "The Thief of Bagdad." Gillian Anderson, conductor. gilliananderson.it/index.php?option=com_k2&view=item&layout=item&id=35&Itemid=29. Accessed 6 June 2018.

Benyon, George. *Musical Presentation of Motion Pictures*. New York: G. Schirmer, 1921.

Bradford, James C. *Douglas Fairbanks in "The Thief of Bagdad": A Fantasy of the Arabian Nights*. New York: Cameo Music, 1924.

Chion, Michel. *The Voice in Cinema*. Edited and translated by Claudia Gorbman. New York: Columbia University Press, 1999.

Davis, Carl. "Carl Davis on Napoléon: 'This Is Fun, This Is Extraordinary!'" *Silent London*, 25 October 2016, silentlondon.co.uk/2016/10/25/carl-davis-on-napoleon-this-is-fun-this-is-extraordinary/. Accessed 8 June 2018.

Davis, Carl. "Interview." By Cléo Thoma and Guy Engels. *YouTube*, 17 March 2016, youtube
    .com/watch?v=cw8-Vpc-2J8&t=5s. Accessed 30 May 2018.

Davis, Carl. "An Interview with Carl Davis." By Luc van den Ven and David Hirsch. *Soundtrack
    Magazine*, vol. 15, no. 58 (1996): 2.

Davis, Carl. *The Thief of Bagdad*. 1984. 3 vols. London: Faber, 2017.

Harrison, Louis Reeves. "Jackass Music (1911)." *Celluloid Symphonies: Texts and Contexts in
    Film Music History*, edited by Julie Hubbert. Berkeley: University of California Press,
    2011. 42–44.

Hatten, Robert S. *Interpreting Musical Gestures, Topics, and Tropes: Mozart, Beethoven,
    Schubert*. Bloomington: Indiana University Press, 2004.

Marks, Martin Miller. *Music and the Silent Film: Contexts and Case Studies, 1895–1924*. Oxford:
    Oxford University Press, 1997.

Neumeyer, David, and James Buehler. *Meaning and Interpretation of Music in Cinema*.
    Bloomington: Indiana University Press, 2015.

Rapée, Erno. *Encyclopedia of Music for Pictures: As Essential as the Picture*. New York: Belwin
    Press, 1925.

Riesenfeld, Hugo. "Music and Motion Pictures" *Celluloid Symphonies: Texts and Contexts
    in Film Music History*, edited by Julie Hubbert. Berkeley: University of California Press,
    2011. 100–105.

Sauer, Rodney, and Susan M. Hall. "The Thief of Bagdad." *The Mont Alto Motion Picture
    Orchestra*, 2002. http://mont-alto.com/recordings/ThiefOfBagdad/ThiefCues.html.
    Accessed 15 June 2018.

"Silent Film Catalogue." Carl Davis Collection, 2018. carldaviscollection.com/silent-film
    -catalogue/. Accessed 6 June 2018.

Sinn, Clarence. "Music for the Picture." *Moving Picture World*, 26 November 1910, 1227.

The Thief of Bagdad. Directed by Raoul Walsh. Music by Carl Davis. Cohen Film Collection,
    2013.

Wierzbicki, James. *Film Music: A History*. New York: Routledge, 2009.

Zamecnik, J. S. *Sam Fox Moving Picture Music*. 3 vols. Cleveland: Sam Fox, 1913.

Notes

1. Three likely scenarios emerge: 1) the pianist adapted some pieces in their repertoire for the performance, cutting some sections and repeating others to cover the required time; 2) the pianist improvised to fill the gaps; or 3) some combination of the two occurred.

2. Cue sheets for individual films are best understood as an approximation of the practice of many theaters, rather than as an accurate historical record of what was heard, which surely varied widely from place to place.

3. For a discussion of the influence of Breil's application, see Anderson, *Music for Silent Films*, xxii–xxix; Marks 156.

4. Riesenfeld's synchronized scores for F. W. Murnau's *Sunrise* (1927) and DeMille's *The King of Kings* (1927) follow this prescription closely.

5. The compilation scores that Rapée and Riesenfeld create did not survive the transition to talking pictures. Starting in 1933 with his landmark score to *King Kong*, Max Steiner

would usher in a new approach to film scoring, one that replaced the aesthetic preference for musical variety with one for stylistic unity. Original scores with relatively little adapted music became the gold standard for film composition, and a whole generation of film composers, including Steiner, Franz Waxman, Erich Korngold, Alfred Newman, and Bernard Herrmann, guaranteed the success of this style.

6. The Bradford cue sheet contains sixty-four cues and features a typical mixture of music by well-known European composers like Rimsky-Korsakov, Wagner, Mendelssohn, and Saint-Saens, less-known Europeans like Jean Gabriel-Marie and Irénée Berge, and numbers from photoplay composers, including Rapée and Zamecnik (Bradford, summarized in Appendix A).

7. Bradford draws all three motifs from photoplay collections.

8. This differs sharply from both Wagner's practice and the practice of Hollywood composers in the 1930s, who use relatively short melodies as leitmotivs.

9. Unlike with a typical cue sheet, Davis organizes his score into forty-five scenes. To read the Davis cue sheet I have created, the musical sources in square brackets behind the leitmotiv indicate passages adapted directly from the Rimsky-Korsakov originals. Davis simply pastes photocopies of the relevant passages (sometimes lightly altered) into the score. When these square brackets are absent, the themes present in each cue are arranged by Davis, who often combines several leitmotivs in counterpoint. For cues without specific themes, I have identified the source of the music; these are often photocopies that are fitted with transitions.

SICARIOS AND THE LATIN AMERICAN ASSASSIN ON FILM

RICHARD VELA

ALTHOUGH *SICARIO* TO MOST AMERICAN FILMGOERS CALLS TO MIND THE 2015 FILM BY THAT name, or its sequel, *Sicario: Day of the Soldado* (2018), the word more specifically refers to a particular type of assassin connected to drug cartels in Colombia and Mexico. Charles Bowen, in an article on a Juárez hit man, writes, "The term 'sicario' goes back to Roman Palestine, where a Jewish sect, the Sicarii used concealed daggers (*sicae*) in their murders of Romans and their supporters" (45). Sicario characters appear mostly in Latin American films and on television. The documentary *El Sicario: Room 164* (2011), for example, presents a masked killer being interviewed in a Texas motel room. In the first season of the Netflix series *Narcos* (2015–17), about Pablo Escobar and the Colombian cartel, the character "Poison" (Jorge A. Jimenez) resembles Jhon Jairo Velasquez, nicknamed "Popeye," who is the subject of his own Netflix series, *Surviving Escobar: Alias J.J.* (2017). The British documentary series *Inside the Real Narcos* (2018–) shows Jason Fox interviewing Popeye, along with other Mexican and Colombian sicarios. Fictional representations include the taciturn Salamanca twin assassins, Leonel (Daniel Moncada) and Marco (Luis Moncada), known as "The Cousins," in AMC's *Breaking Bad* (2008–13) and its prequel, *Better Call Saul* (2015–). The gruff but loyal sicario Pote Galvez (Hemky Madera) appears in both Telemundo's *La Reina del Sur* (2011), and in USA's *The Queen of the South* (2016–). Both shows are based on Arturo Pérez-Reverte's novel *The Queen of the South* (2004). Madera also plays the more amiable Ignacio, a sicario in Showtime's darkly comic series *Weeds* (2005–2012).

In the two recent *Sicario* movies, both scripted by Taylor Sheridan, the sicario is not an outlaw working for the cartels. He is Alejandro Gillick (Benicio del Toro), a lawyer, or, more specifically, a prosecutor, turned vengeful assassin. More importantly, he works for the US government, not a criminal organization, a distinction that seems to establish legitimacy, even as the opening titles of the first film refer back to the original definition for sicarios: "Killers who hunted the Romans who invaded their homeland." Viewed in this light, Alejandro, like the original zealots, pursues the cartels that have invaded his country and caused the death of his wife and daughter. His pursuit also serves the higher purpose of destroying a criminal empire. In fact, Carlos Gallego identifies him as "the main protagonist" of *Sicario* (45). That is even more true in *Sicario: Day of the Soldado*, where Alejandro seems more central to the action that is on a larger scale, more cynical and more complicated, even if he lacks the singularity and focus that shaped him in the first film. Midway through, he shows compassion for a young woman he holds hostage, and at the end of the film he seems ready to mentor a young man from a Texas border town. In fact, young people more clearly become part of the ethical questions raised by the action in the second film. Without making any claims for traditional notions of childhood innocence, it is still possible to argue that they struggle to survive in a world they cannot control. Their situation suggests parallels to several films about children caught in larger violent actions who are then forced into battle or voluntarily become killers.

The connections between border violence, the cartels, and government response, both official and covert, as well as the dilemma of young people caught up in this dynamic, frame the ethical questions examined in this chapter. Drawing on media coverage of drug cartel activity and border violence, Sheridan in effect adapts these narratives to establish complex situations that provoke ethical quandaries and raise the questions of how we can frame an ethical question, how we can reach a conclusion, and whether it is possible to reach a legitimate conclusion without oversimplification and misrepresentation. As such, his films fall generally into the category described by Thomas Leitch in *Film Adaptation and Its Discontents* (2007) as "based on no source text at all but on a true story" (280). More specifically, Leitch mentions "the television series *Law and Order* (1990–), which uses fictionalized versions of contemporary criminal cases to explore the legal and moral issues they raise" (287). Sheridan's scripts, while based in the reality of news stories and current events, become exactly this kind of fictionalized narrative, which he then uses to explore ethical and legal ramifications. In a 2015 interview discussing *Sicario*, Sheridan clearly describes this process as he draws a parallel between America's "using our military to police in Iraq and Afghanistan" and "the carnage of what was taking place in Juarez at the time," which, he points out, "was receiving almost no news coverage at all in America." He goes on to say that he "wrote a screenplay that [. . .] would force people to have a conversation about it" (Beachum). Hence, the flow of events in Iraq and Afghanistan suggested for him the potential for a similar intervention in Mexico and the ethical complications of that intervention.

The Uses and Abuses of a Border Crisis

Common to Sheridan's two *Sicarios* films is the fact that the government goes to unusual lengths to combat the drug cartels, apparently neglecting legal and ethical considerations. In *Sicario*, a questionable team, which James Burridge and John Kavanagh call "a mysterious counter narcotics task force," and Neil Morris simply calls a "paramilitary posse," crosses into Mexico. Their goal is to extradite Guillermo (Edgar Arreola) in an attempt to locate his brother, Manuel Diaz (Bernardo Saracino), who can lead them to his cousin Fausto Alarcón (Julio Cesar Cedillo), the man who is ultimately responsible for the dead bodies that Kate Mercer (Emily Blunt) and her FBI SWAT team discover at the beginning of the film. The second film, *Soldado*, similarly relies on cartel violence to justify American intervention, ultimately raising deeper questions about what amounts to authentic provocation and what constitutes legitimate response. *Soldado* connects the war on drugs with the war on terrorism when it shows Middle Eastern terrorists crossing the border as suicide bombers. Much of the action in *Soldado* recalls Phillip Noyce's adaptation of the Tom Clancy novel *Clear and Present Danger* (1994), where a paramilitary force, prompted by staged events and supported by rogue elements in the US government, illegally begins a covert war against the Colombian drug cartels. In that film, however, we are never unclear about right and wrong. Two obviously duplicitous government officials, CIA Deputy Director of Operations Robert Ritter (Henry Czerny) and National Security Advisor James Cutter (Harris Yulin), initiate the action. Their self-serving agenda is paralleled by that of intelligence analyst Felix Cortez (Joaquim de Almeida), who plays both sides in hopes of taking over the cartel. Jack Ryan (Harrison Ford) is the obvious hero of the film and the embodiment of right thinking and correct ethical choices. At the end of the film, for example, he stands up to the weak and opportunistic President Bennett (Donald Moffat), who advises, "We have to handle this very delicately; otherwise people will get the wrong impression." Ryan's response is "Don't play that game with me. I will not let you dishonor their memories," referring to the American soldiers who died in the Colombian jungle.

In Sheridan's sicario films, the ethical issues are anything but clear. Sheridan admits to favoring uncertain representations: "Let your characters live in the gray. Let the hero do some really bad things. Let the bad guy do some really good things" (Miyamoto). Sheridan performs the same trick in *Hell or High Water* (2016), the movie that came out the year between his sicario films, and tells the story of two brothers, Toby (Chris Pine) and Tanner (Ben Foster), as they embark on a series of bank robberies and then launder the money through an Indian casino in Oklahoma. Toby is careful to hit the banks early, when there are almost no customers, and he takes only the money in the drawer. But as the film develops, we find out, as Peter Sobczynski explains, that their target "is the bank . . . that has recently foreclosed on the family ranch after some shady but legal maneuverings." Toby, a divorced father, wants to pay off the mortgage and put the land in a trust administered by the bank for the benefit of his two sons. The ethical ambiguity of whether Toby is right to take the money is underscored by the fact that several people in the film sympathize with the brothers against the bank in a way that recalls antiestablishment sentiments in Depression era films and films of the late 1960s, when, as Andrew Bergman explains, "with redress to federal benevolence no longer possible and the law a sightless watchman, outlawry again seemed a legitimate stance in society" (173). For example, when Ranger Hamilton (Beau Bridges) asks restaurant customers if they had been there long enough to see anything, one man answers, "Well, long enough to watch the bank getting robbed that's been robbin' me for thirty years." This same level of ethical ambiguity appears in the two *Sicarios* films. What is the difference between corporate crime and individual crime, and what level of wrongdoing justifies committing a crime as a way of making things right? This is a central question in virtually all the films considered in this chapter.

The Land of Wolves

Government forces in both of Sheridan's sicario films use the events on the border to justify disrupting cartel business, even if through unorthodox and often unethical means. Early in *Sicario*, Matt Graver (Josh Brolin) tells Kate Mercer (Emily Blunt) that the goal of their mission is simply "to shake the tree and create chaos." Alejandro tells Kate, "Nothing will make sense to your American ears." By the end of the film, he tells her this is now "the land of wolves," which amounts to a variation on the law of the jungle, and he insists the strong prevail and the weak do not survive, no matter how objectively right either might be. Ultimately it is power, the exercise of violence and force, which distinguishes between right and wrong, rather than some clear ethical standard. The wolves will win. Set in this context, defeating the enemy in a war on terror becomes more important than any other consideration.

In *Sicario*, Matt's willingness to enact casual chaos leads to serious consequences and establishes the general ethical situation. Kate, the FBI leader of
a SWAT team, discovers a house with more than thirty dead bodies sealed
in the walls. She agrees to work with Matt and his CIA task force after Matt
assures her that they will be able to get "the people responsible for this." Such
a goal will require unorthodox measures. From Matt's perspective, to abide
by conventional methods would be to take the chance of letting the drug
lords win; traditional law and order is not effective against the forces of the
cartels, who remain unencumbered by such concerns. Matt admits that he is
willing to employ Alejandro, whose morality clearly follows the logic of the
vigilante, because he needs Alejandro as simply another weapon in the war
against the cartel. What drives Alejandro personally makes no difference.
Results are all that matters. The division between intent and results pervades
and contributes to the moral ambiguity of the film. To what extent are motive and consequence related? Is killing a drug lord for revenge significantly
different from killing him in the process of a legal confrontation? Either
way, he is dead.

While Matt and Alejandro focus only on results, Kate acts as the conscience of the film. Mark Kermode calls her "the movie's one and only moral
touchstone," and José Teodoro explains that Kate, "a heroine caught in a
situation she can't fully comprehend [... is ...] shocked to discover that the
team is operating outside U.S. jurisdiction, ignoring the rules of engagement,
and illegally detaining and torturing prisoners." Kate protests as the team
goes into Mexico to extract a prisoner only to get ensnared in a shootout
on the international Bridge of the Americas. The fact that the incident will
not even "hit the papers in El Paso" only makes the transgression worse to
Kate. Kate's morality directly impedes the team later in the film when she
tries to keep Alejandro from abducting a Mexican police officer. In response
Alejandro shoots her, hitting her bulletproof vest, and knocking her down.
He tells her, "Don't ever point a weapon at me again." Alejandro's real injury
to Kate, however, occurs at the end of the film when he forces her to sign a
document that claims "everything we did was by the book." When she refuses,
he puts a pistol under her chin and tells her it would be suicide not to sign
it. He explains that she "should move to a small town, where the rule of law
still exists." He adds, "You will not survive here. You are not a wolf. And this
is the land of wolves now." A similar confrontation occurs in *A Clear and
Present Danger*, when Ritter calls Ryan "a Boy Scout" who sees "everything
in black and white," to which Ryan answers, "No, no, no! Not in black and
white, Ritter, right and wrong." In some ways Kate is Ryan without authority,
and, because, as A. O. Scott points out, "The action is viewed mostly through

the eyes of Kate Mercer," her presence keeps the ethical issues clearly before the eyes of the audience. Her helplessness signals the defeat of an ethical view that elicits audience sympathy, even as we recognize the success of less ethical characters.

Kate is missing in *Sicario: Day of the Soldado*, so when international terrorists cross the border and seem to threaten ISIS-style violence across the heart of America, there is no voice to raise questions about either the events or the government response. When Matt is asked about "the most valuable commodity cartels move across our borders," he says it is now people not drugs, and when asked what to do about terrorists invading the country, Matt proposes someone make the cartels fight each other. Shortly after, when Alejandro shoots a man in both legs before angrily shooting him dead on the streets of Mexico City, a television reporter in Mexico says the man was killed by a cartel lawyer, thus helping to build the cover story of cartel against cartel. Matt successfully pits one cartel against another thanks to the inaccuracies of the media. Matt's campaign of confusion here recalls his effort to "create chaos" in *Sicario*, but in *Soldado* it becomes a more complicated and costly strategy.

Even without Kate in *Soldado*, Sheridan finds a way to raise a series of ethical issues, namely, through contrasting three main character constructions. The first, of course, includes Matt and Alejandro, with the addition of the secretary of defense, James Riley (Matthew Modine) and CIA operative Cynthia Foards (Catherine Keener). All four characters want to defeat the terrorists, which they link to the power of the cartels. Disrupting cartel power is the solution, because here, as in *Sicario*, no direct ways are available to them. Cynthia's role is virtually the opposite of Kate's role in *Sicario*. Unlike Kate, Cynthia never questions or attempts to restrain. Instead she is a facilitator, who arranges things, pushes, and then rationalizes. Matt's plan to start a war between the cartels means that he will kidnap the daughter of cartel head Carlos Reyes. He explains, "If you want to start a war, kidnap a prince. The king will start it for you." A second narrative focus is the story of the daughter, sixteen-year-old Isabel Reyes (Isabela Moner), a defiant young woman who fights a schoolgirl who was taunting her and then stands up to the principal of her school, who hesitates to do anything, because he knows her father is head of a cartel. The third focus is the developing story of Miguel (Elijah Rodriguez), a fourteen-year-old teenager from McAllen, Texas, who is dissatisfied with his life and poverty, and begins working as a coyote, smuggling people across the border. Near the end of the film, Miguel goes through what amounts to a sicario initiation. In fact, Sheridan seems to build a bridge to a sequel in the very last scene, when veteran sicario Alejandro, a year after

Miguel shot him and left him for dead, confronts the boy and asks, "So you want to be a sicario? Let's talk about your future."

Anthony Lane draws a useful connection between Denis Villeneuve's *Sicario* and Orson Welles's *Touch of Evil* (1958), which, he says, "covered the same land, on the same porous border" (111). Both films reflect a world in which the consequences of actions are usually nearly impossible to predict, and there is a complexity of conflicting ethical claims. Welles himself said that his intention in that film was to say "that in the modern world we have to choose between the law's morality and the morality of simple justice" (Estrin 52). Peter Debruge describes *Sicario* by saying that it is "depicting the brutality with which cartels control the flow of illegal substances across the U.S.-Mexico border, and imagining a no-nonsense response by a shadowy group of American enforcers every bit as corrupt as the criminals they're attempting to extinguish." Establishing the level of corruption in *Sicario: Day of the Soldado* is, however, made somewhat more complicated by Kate's absence and the resulting moral vacuum. Director Stefano Sollima shifts away from depending on a person, such as Kate, who understands morality as conformity to an objective set of rules. According to Sollima, "Without having a character who is a filter between you and the characters, you force yourself and the characters to explain themselves deeper." Richard Whittaker explains, "Sollima portrays that slippery slope as the inevitable risk when law enforcement bends the rules" and "at the end the border between the law and criminality is really subtle." Here, as in Sheridan's other films, the distinction between good and bad, right and wrong, depends less on rules and more on the situation Sheridan presents to his audiences. As Sollima suggests, the audience is drawn into making the ethical evaluation in the absence of a guiding conscience figure like Kate.

Actually, in *Soldado*, objective morality seemingly disappears. The film begins with a controversial set of scenes obviously intended to justify American intervention. The first scenes show a large group of illegal immigrants crossing the border at night. Similar scenes occur in films such as *The Gatekeeper* (2002) and *Machete* (2010), but in those examples, the illegals running across the border are part of anti-immigration commercials developed by characters within the films, and in both films this view is ultimately rejected for a more sympathetic understanding. *Day of the Soldado* provocatively shows members of Middle Eastern terrorist groups invading America through illegal immigration at the southern border. One character runs away, stops, raises his hands shoulder high, and begins chanting. As the soldiers approach him, the militant blows himself up, knocking the soldiers to the ground. The next morning, DEA and ICE officers find three prayer mats at the edge of a cliff. Later at night in Kansas City, three Middle Eastern men get out of a car and walk into a big box store. Shortly afterward, we see explosions when two of them blow themselves up. A blonde woman in the front of the store pulls her daughter to her and moves slowly toward the doors, trying to get past the third terrorist, who has his hand on a button and is chanting. As they approach, he detonates his bomb. All of this happens in the first six minutes of the film, almost exactly the same time that elapsed in the opening of *Sicario* when Kate's team finds the dead bodies and then accidentally explodes IEDs, killing two soldiers. In *Soldado*, the sequence of events leads to a televised warning from Secretary of Defense Riley, who proclaims "our determination to prevent more attacks."

Response to this sequence varies according to political views. Peter Travers in *Rolling Stone* writes, "*Soldado*, intentionally or not, gives credence to the POTUS argument that a zero-tolerance policy against illegal immigrants is meant to protect U.S. citizens from the criminal element [. . .] It plays like Trump-style fear-mongering being used to sell tickets to a Hollywood entertainment." John Nolte, on the other hand, writing for *Breitbart*, says, "As with *Sicario*, we are watching a Hollywood production with the moral courage to tell the truth about just how deadly our southern border is, this poorly guarded frontier we share with a failing and corrupt country; millions of square miles of desert where desperate Mexicans are exploited by godless coyotes who see them only as contraband." Before the presidential election of 2016, Jeff DeWit, Trump's campaign manager in Arizona, claimed, "Now we have ISIS coming over the border. You have problems. There's only one candidate that's going to do anything to fix it, and that's Donald Trump" (Cave). Shortly before the 2018 midterm elections, President Trump, as Tucker Higgins of CNBC reported it, "escalated his attacks on the caravan of migrants making their way to the United States from Central America, calling the situation a national emergency and declaring without evidence that 'Criminals and unknown Middle Easterners are mixed in.'" Todd Bensman, of the Center for Immigration Studies, wrote that the president's claim "is more likely than not true" and stated he "can comfortably support the president's contentions . . . and feel relieved that he has finally acknowledged the threat issue." As the film narrative develops, the Middle Eastern connection in the film is suddenly abandoned and then is discarded completely about midway through the film, when it is discovered that the suicide bombers in Kansas were not illegal aliens at all. Conservative Sonny Bunch complains that "the entirety of the motivating action—namely, the infiltration of terrorists into America via narco-smuggling—is dismissed with a single line of dialogue in an effort to wrap things up." David Sims of the *Atlantic*, summing up from another perspective, comments, "Sheridan is simply jabbing at the hot-button topics of the moment to spur his story along."

Perhaps complicating the issues more, Sheridan has parallel scenes of ethical questioning in both sicario films. In each a prisoner tries to make ethical appeals based on generalizations and assumptions about the person interrogating them. In the final part of *Sicario*, as Christopher Orr sees it, "what began as a critique of violence comes to resemble a stylish exercise in it." Stretching credulity, Alejandro kills a dozen cartel guards and makes his way to the area where drug lord Fausto Alarcón is quietly eating supper with his wife and two sons. Confronted by the armed gunman, Fausto tries a range of ethical appeals to Alejandro's conscience and sense of fair play. He begins, "The people who sent you here, are they any different? Who do you think we learned it from?" When that does not work, he tries a more personal argument: "Your wife, you think she'd be proud of what you've become?" Alejandro's answer is "Don't forget about my daughter," at which point Fausto adds, "*No fue personal*," perhaps recalling his own role in their deaths and echoing the "it's not personal, strictly business" argument from *The Godfather* (1972). Alejandro answers, "For me, it is." Fausto seems to resign himself to his own death, but again misunderstands. He pleads, "Not in front of my boys." Alejandro says, "Time to meet God," and rapidly shoots both boys and Fausto's wife dead. We only see their bodies by the table, but for the first time, Fausto seems wide-eyed and genuinely scared. Alejandro tells him to finish his meal and then inhales slowly and shoots Fausto. This failed attempt to negotiate through the various ethical arguments reveals how Alejandro fits into the scheme of things. He is closer to avenging angel than to judge and jury, so there is no point in presenting defense arguments. At the same time, the argument clearly reveals the ethics of the "land of wolves." In other words, appeals to generalized sets of rules that everyone recognizes to be valid ways to conduct action simply do not apply. The notion of the land of wolves, as Alejandro explained, is that simplified rules of good or bad do not really exist. Winning is all.

A similar kind of ethical argumentation occurs in *Soldado*. Almost immediately after Secretary of Defense Riley promises the "full weight of the United States military" in retaliation for the suicide bombings that they blame on illegal Middle Eastern immigrants, we see soldiers parachute into a remote outpost in the Gulf of Somalia and silently kill several men, taking one captive. Matt visits the man in a narrow room. There is water on the floor, and several large water bottles are nearby. The man, Bashiir (Faysal Ahmed), wears a black hood, and his image strongly resembles those from the infamous Abu Ghraib prison. Noticing that Bashiir looks fretfully at the water bottles, Matt explains that "waterboarding is for when we can't torture. This is Africa. I can do whatever the fuck I want here," but he says he will not need to touch a hair on the man's head. He shows Bashiir's house in an overhead shot on a computer and tells him he will call in a drone strike and destroy the house and anyone in it if he doesn't get the answers he wants. Bashiir protests that the people who carried out the bombing in the US are ISIS, not Somali. Matt says the men got to Mexico by ship, a ship Bashiir's people let pass out of Yemen, and he wants to know who paid to let that happen. He threatens again: "Is that your brother?" he asks, pointing to an image on the screen, "'Cause I don't want to kill the pool boy." Bashiir contends that Matt is just bluffing. He argues, "You American. You have too many rules." The error is the same error Fausto makes in *Sicario*. Bashiir assumes Matt follows a well-established ethical framework. Matt shows his detainee that he does not. He holds Bashiir's head as he calls in the strike: "I want you to watch this." Bashiir sobs as he sees the house explode. He shouts in Somali and tries to get out of the manacles. Matt shows the broken captive a truck on a road and says, "You have a big family, Bashiir. Lots of brothers [. . .] I could do this all day. But sooner or later, I'll get the brother you can't live without." Matt performs a psychological torture that is more sophisticated and crueler than the waterboarding seen in *Sicario*. The shift occurs under the warrant that the ends justify the means. Recalling drone strikes against civilians and the torture of prisoners sets the ethical bar pretty low, but it also marks the more dramatic and confusing ethical shifts that will occur later in the film.

About midway through *Soldado*, the ethical balance and framework of the film seems to change completely. Although the event may seem underplayed to some extent, the moment the government abandons the mission that Matt and Alejandro have begun is significant in terms of the ethical framework of the film. Cynthia, Matt's CIA boss, tells him that what happened in the shootout with the Mexican police is all over TV. This is, of course, parallel to the shootout at the bridge in *Sicario* when they bring back Guillermo, but the result is the opposite. There the story would not even hit the local papers. In *Soldado*, the story is on television news, that there are "54 million Americans with relatives there, and they are all sitting around watching footage of dead Mexican police on Fox News." Cynthia explains that "POTUS doesn't have the stomach for this: He shut us down." She later adds, "He's not worried about winning. He's worried about being fucking impeached because you killed two dozen Mexican police." When Matt tries to argue, she says, "We don't have a position, because we're not supposed to fucking be there. Your objective was to start a war with Mexican cartels, not with the Mexican government." She also informs Matt that his information on the terrorists in Kansas City was wrong. "Two of them were from New Jersey," and, as she says, that "changes the fucking narrative."

The coldblooded result is that Secretary of Defense Riley calls and points out that since the girl Isabel is a witness to the deaths of the policemen, "We can't risk having her fall into the wrong hands." Riley wants Matt to "clean the scene. [...] Your operative included." In other words, both Isabel and Alejandro should die because they know too much. This scene suggests, as we saw in *A Clear and Present Danger*, that when the president worries about creating "the wrong impression," it means that at the highest levels of government only the appearance of correctness is important. The Secretary of Defense and the CIA are willing to sacrifice both Alejandro and Isabel to make sure the operation is "spotless." The move fits the logic of the "land of wolves" ethic that Alejandro conveys to Kate when he suggests she move to a small American town "where the rule of law still exists." The shift at this point of *Soldado* means that Alejandro himself is to become a victim of the simplified emphasis on results. To the government, Alejandro becomes as disposable as the cartel member he has killed, so from some points of view, this is a reversal of everything that seems to have been established so far.

Children at War: From *Day of the Soldado* to *Niños Sicarios*

In fact, a different basis for conduct seems to evolve. Matt and Alejandro, without the urgency to complete a mission with a fairly defined objective, adjust to the complex environment of the second film. What guided actions before now no longer applies, so a new ethic evolves. For example, when Matt is told to get rid of his "operative," Alejandro, his first response sounds chillingly practical: "Do you know how hard he was to make?" Cynthia's response is even more so; she tells him, "I could throw a stick across the river and hit fifty grieving fathers. Make another one." When Matt explains to Alejandro that they need to "get rid" of the girl, Alejandro says simply, "I can't do that." On the one hand, since Matt has been a whatever-it-takes agent in both films, who was quick to make judgments and seemed to have few qualms about doing what it takes, we might expect him to have no hesitation about getting rid of Alejandro. On the other hand, from the rationale of expected behavior, Alejandro's response might seem more puzzling. Since he cold-bloodedly killed Fausto's wife and boys in the previous film, Alejandro's hesitation clearly has nothing to do with scruples about killing women or children. The moral shift that occurs in the second half of the film reaches toward a less objective code than the one that drove Kate. Alejandro cannot kill Isabel, in spite of the orders to do so, because several things that occur in this second half of the film move him out of the role of the vengeful killer and into the role of the protective father. Isabel clearly seems to evoke some of the feelings he had for his daughter, even if she is the daughter of his enemy Carlos Reyes. The change is underscored, for example, when he meets the deaf man Angel (Bruno Bichir) in Mexico and, communicating in sign language, seems to develop a friendship. Shortly after this meeting, Isabel asks Alejandro why he knows sign language, and Alejandro briefly answers that his murdered daughter was also deaf.

In fact, one consistent motif in both films is the appearance of children who are connected in various ways with the adults and who seem to provide a somewhat muted critique of the action. The relationship between Alejandro and Isabel, daughter of his enemy, and now surrogate daughter is remarkable. In some ways Isabel continues a role that Kate had in *Sicario*, and in one of the closing scenes of that film Alejandro tells Kate that she "looks like a little girl" when she is scared and then adds, "You remind me of the daughter they took away from me." Isabel is, of course, central to the plot of the film. David Sims says that Matt's plan "is to foster a cartel civil war by kidnapping Isabela Reyes, the daughter of a kingpin, and pretending she was taken by a rival gang," but the girl goes through what Travers characterizes as a "growing awareness of her place in this larger world." She understands, for example, that Alejandro is not a DEA officer, although he initially tries to convey that impression. She escapes in the middle of a gunfight with the Mexican police, and when Matt and the rest return to the border, Alejandro stays to find her. When she is picked up by someone else, he rescues her. Eventually, she realizes that it was her father who ordered the deaths of Alejandro's family. When she and Alejandro try to get back to the US, she poses as a girl who hired him to act as her father. She witnesses Alejandro being shot. At the end, when Matt believes Alejandro is dead, he rescues Isabel, and, rather than eliminate her, as was ordered to do, he places her in witness protection.

Two young people who have received almost no attention are two young men, Officer Silvio's (Maximiliano Hernandez) son, Eliseo (Jesus Nevarez-Castillo), in *Sicario*, and Miguel in *Soldado*. John Trafton and Eileen Rositzka mention that *Sicario*'s director "Villeneuve reminds the viewer of the war's unfinished business, the son of a slain Mexican police officer . . . plays soccer . . . [and] reaches what he is certain is a clear shot at the goal," but, "The moment is interrupted by the sound of an automatic weapon firing off in the distance, and the ball misses its mark, sailing over the goal posts." Chris Lambert writes, "Silvio's story is nothing more than a method to make us care about the kid at the end, to make that scene more poignant than it would be if this were the first time we'd ever seen the son." Actually, the soccer scene is Eliseo's fourth appearance. Early in the film, Eliseo wakes his father, who drinks his morning coffee with a shot of whiskey. Only when he goes to his car wearing his uniform do we realize Silvio is a policeman. About an hour into the film, Eliseo sits alone at breakfast and asks his mother about Silvio, and in a third scene, Eliseo brings his father breakfast and asks if he wants to play *fútbol*. Certainly, Silvio is a failed father, but the interrupted soccer game at the very end of the film suggests at least a shadow of how the drug war interrupts life on the border. Eliseo's story offers a kind of counterbalance, an almost naive attempt at a normal life, and so it contrasts with the extravagance of the main storylines. Eliseo himself is both a neglected son and a surviving son as a result of drug violence.

The story of Miguel is similarly paced throughout *Soldado*, but response to his story varies. Anthony Lane notes the boy's "air of shyness and cunning" and calls him "a minor presence in the story, and yet without him it would not twist and turn as it does" (76). Michael Sragow, however, calls his story a "major subplot" when the boy becomes a novice handler of the cartel's human bounty" and, in what amounts to "a devil's deal," realizes "he must follow narco culture's homicidal code of machismo to earn the cash." As we see him develop, Miguel is a fourteen-year-old border-town boy, living almost literally in the shadow of a barrier fence between Texas and Mexico. He stands with other children on a corner when a "middle school" bus drives up in the morning, but he is still there when it drives away, and he is soon picked up by his cousin Hector (David Castañeda). In a few minutes, they are sitting by the side of the Rio Grande, with Hector telling Miguel how he would have it made because he has both languages and a passport, and he can come and go as he pleases, and, to top it off, "the Matamoros cartel pays well." To prove his point, Hector pulls out a roll of bills. Miguel soon becomes a coyote, but instead of dealing with hordes of immigrants and dangerous Middle Eastern terrorists, as we saw earlier in the film, he is told, "Hey, they're sheep. Treat them like it." The boss of the organization, Gallo (Manuel Garcia-Rulfo), sees Miguel as an up-and-coming star.

Toward the end of the film, Miguel recognizes Alejandro, who is trying to smuggle Isabela out of the country. The traffickers pull guns on Alejandro and take him to a stretch of desert surrounded by canyon walls. One young man, José (Tenzin Marco-Taylor), is given the opportunity to prove his manhood by killing Alejandro, but, when he cannot fire the pistol, Gallo instead shoots José in the head and hands the gun to his protégé, Miguel, who stands over the body for a minute and then fires. We see a splash of blood hit the sand.

Gallo cheers, "Today you became a man!" On the way back, however, the troubled Miguel jumps off the truck and thus escapes being killed by Matt and the American military. Meanwhile, Alejandro suddenly revives because the bullet only went through his cheek. The film jumps ahead several months. Miguel now has a sleeve of tattoos. He walks through a mall and goes into a room, where to Miguel's surprise, Alejandro is waiting. However incongruous it may seem, Alejandro is ready to mentor the young man who almost killed him and to develop him into a legitimate sicario.

Miguel's story is a variation of a kind of narrative about children caught up in violence that has appeared frequently in contemporary film and literature. The growing emphasis on the younger people in these films reflects larger global movements, which depict children who have been drawn into a violent and corrupt adult world, films about child soldiers in Africa (*Beasts of No Nation*, 2015) and Cambodia (*First They Killed My Father*, 2017) as well as gangs in Mexico (*Los Olvidados*, 1950, and *De la calle* (2003), Colombia (*Rodrigo D: No futuro*, 1990), Brazil (*Pixote*, 1981, and *City of God*, 2002), and Italy (*Gomorra*, 2008), and more specifically young people affected by drug cartel violence, especially along the border with Mexico. One set of films that specifically deals with these issues is the *niño sicario* films, in which, according to Maite Villoria, "youngsters excluded by the system" tend to see becoming a sicario as "an exhilarating route to enrichment and social recognition" (76–77). Certainly Miguel, at least at the beginning of *Soldado*, fits into that category. Ruy Alberto Valdés Benavides explains, "Thousands of youngsters have been recruited in Ciudad Juárez and other cities in Mexico to work as sicarios for organized crime, they are better known as niños-sicarios (*kid-sicarios*)," and he adds, "A lot of them do not survive" (1). The world of the Latin American niños sicarios is the world of victims, and their efforts to gain individuality and power must be weighed against the methods they have chosen. By contrast, American films about children who become assassins, such as *Leon: The Professional* (1994), *Kick-Ass* (2010), and *Colombiana* (2011), have very little to do with economic circumstances and instead present children who learn to kill because they are ultimately seeking revenge for past wrongs; hence, the training they receive tends to be the result of working with a specific mentor, usually someone they sought out, and what they learn becomes a more specific kind of empowerment. They are trying to right a wrong, and in this context, narrowly conceived, it is possible to argue that there is a moral purpose in their killings, a theme that occurs in other films and is clearly an element in the character of Alejandro. This interrogation of action seems particularly relevant in the niños sicarios films, at least partly because of our "veneration of childhood innocence," as Landon

Palmer describes it. Hence, innocence and the lack of it are more clearly the determining factors in these films than in other hitman films. In the case of Miguel, the boy does not seem to have any wrongs that he plans to right.

While it would be impossible to defend what these young people do, it is possible to understand the thinking that leads these niños sicarios to these measures. In the ethics of the "land of wolves," they are operating in a self-preservation mode. In *Sicario* and *Soldado*, adults justify abandoning legal and ethical norms to defeat the cartels. The niños sicarios are different in that they want to survive, and they want to succeed, and, given the world in which they live, this seems the only option available to them. In these films, it is often villainous circumstances, including the corrupt world of the adults, that set violence in motion. However, according to Aldona Bialowas Pobutsky, they make up the "world of the *sicariato*, a sub-culture of organized adolescent assassins" (23). They first appeared in Colombia with the Medellin cartel in the 1980s and developed, as Ioan Grillo explains, because unlike the old professional assassins, niños sicarios were less expensive than professional hitmen and essentially disposable (155). Dan Slater, in *Wolf Boys* (2016), describes the process by which American border-town teens, like Miguel in *Soldado*, are lured into becoming hitmen for cartels, and Martin Corona describes his life as an American teen who became head of a hitman crew for the Sinaloa cartel in Mexico in *Confessions of a Cartel Hit Man* (2017). The three best-known niños sicarios films are the Venezuelan film *Sicario, Assassin for Hire* (1994); the Colombian *Our Lady of the Assassins* (2000), based on the autobiographical novel by Colombian author Fernando Vallejo; and the Mexican Spanish film, *Rosario Tijeras* (2004), which presents a kind of femme fatale character, based on the novel by Colombian writer Jorge Franco.

Of these, *Sicario: Assassin for Hire* may offer the best understanding of both the despair conveyed by these stories and the fact of how cheap life is held. The boy Jairo (Laureano Olivares) seems initially mostly interested in ethical issues. It troubles him that he and his mother live in comparative poverty, and, more especially, that she sleeps with her boss to make sure she keeps her job. Jairo becomes a sicario with the goal of making money and changing her life, and his. That said, it is noteworthy that his first kill is nearly accidental. Some friends offer him weed and show him how to smoke. One of them baptizes him with liquor, and they hand him a knife and set him up to participate in a robbery. The intended victim pulls a gun as Jairo's friends jump out, and Jairo ends up stabbing the man. Shortly after, they take him to a brothel, where he is also sexually initiated. All of this happens in the first twenty minutes of the film. After an arrest and a short time in jail, where he is assaulted, he ends up in a training camp for sicarios. A similar camp appears in the film *Loving Pablo* (2017). Boys like Jairo, who do well, receive jobs, but the less talented ones are simply shot dead.

He partners with Aurelio (Herman Gil), and the two become motorcycle sicarios who perform drive-by shootings, with one as driver and the other sitting behind as shooter, a well-documented method in the Colombian "murder business" (Grillo 155). However, as he is dressing before leaving on a job to kill a politician, Jairo asks Aurelio if he himself might be killed. Aurelio explains that "after this job you'll get another," but Jairo says, "That's a lie. The job is not to kill. The job is to die. And you can only die once." Aurelio replies, "But they pay well." Shortly after the hit, Jairo realizes that Aurelio is about to shoot him, so he kills him first. At the end of the film, a similar incident occurs, when Jairo tells his driver, Tigre (Néstor Terán), that he wants to get out because he is going to have a son. As he turns to leave, Tigre pulls a pistol on him, and Jairo has to kill him. Later, Jairo is sitting at the back of a bus next to Rosa (Melissa Ponce), the girl with whom he hoped to begin his new life, when another boy gets on the bus, shoots him dead, and escapes. It is an endless succession of senseless deaths in the same pattern. However despairing and even amoral the niño sicario films seem, one significant quality is that they tend to build sympathy toward the young killers. Certainly, that is true of Jairo, who dies trying to get out with his pregnant girlfriend. The boy that kills them is mostly nameless and faceless, reinforcing the idea that it is an endless progression of young people in the same situation. The story of *Rosario Tijeras* (Flora Martínez), a young woman assassin who got her name (scissors) from castrating a man who violated her when she was a girl, begins with her being driven to a hospital with a fatal wound. As the narrator reflects on her life, she is dying throughout the story she inspires. Wilmar (Juan David Restrepo), one of the assassins in *Our Lady of the Assassins*, killed his predecessor, Alexis (Anderson Ballesteros), who had killed Wilmar's brother, and Wilmar himself dies at the end trying to get a refrigerator for his mother.

Does whatever sympathy we may feel for these complicated and doomed characters become the same as understanding? Does understanding imply permission? Certainly we can feel sympathy for Alejandro, for example. He begins as a damaged man, cold and filled with hate, animated only by his need for revenge and perhaps his need to help his country and punish those who are evil, but clearly he is developing into something different by the time we get to the end of *Soldado*. We could do the same for Toby in *Hell or High Water*. In the end of that film, Ranger Hamilton tells Toby that he knows what Toby has done, and we see him begin to understand that Toby did not do it for himself. He does not live at the house that the stolen money financed. He is fixing it up for his sons and his ex-wife. So, for Hamilton, that rules out the personal gain motive, although he does say, "The things we do for our kids." Toby tells him to come by his own place, "a little house in town," so they can talk more. He adds, "I'd like for this to be over." Hamilton says, "It won't be over. It's gonna haunt you the rest of your days." His assumption here has to do with conscience and the ability to see that the means were wrong no matter how well they might have served the ends. In this, Hamilton is most like Kate in the array of characters Sheridan creates. He has a clear idea of an external right and wrong to which he wants to adhere. For example, he is the one who shot and killed Toby's brother Tanner, a hot-headed ex-con who was killing policemen, including Hamilton's longtime partner.

If in the third film of the *Sicarios*, Alejandro trains Miguel to become an assassin, what ethic can he convey? Will Miguel become a kind of vigilante with a badge, as Alejandro seems to be, or more simply just another killer for hire who happens sometimes to work for the law? Alejandro's relationship with Isabel opened new avenues for him. Matt saved her from being killed, so she survives in the witness protection program, but what she witnessed, of course, was a crime in which Matt and the rest of his team are implicated. Based on the evidence of films such as *Hell or High Water* and the two *Sicario* movies, it is clear that Sheridan prefers endings that are both complicated and ambiguous. In terms of a more simplified right or wrong, it might be helpful to consider Jack Ryan's distinction between black and white versus right and wrong. In Sheridan's work everyone is implicated, even Kate, even Hamilton, because there is no black or white. Right and wrong are far more complicated. Nothing any of the characters has done can really be erased, so Alejandro accepts Miguel even after the boy shot him and left him for dead. What will Isabel be called to do? Whom will she forgive? Whatever the case, as Hamilton explained, in terms of moral issues, it won't be over.

Works Cited

Beachum, Chris. "Taylor Sheridan Q&A: 'Sicario' Writer." 11 March 2015. https://goldderby
.com/video/taylor-sheridan-qu-sicario-writer.

Bensman, Todd. "Middle Eastern Migrants Part of Caravan?" *Center for Immigration Studies*, 22 October 2018. cis.org/Bensman/Middle-Eastern-Migrants-Part-Caravan.

Bergman, Andrew. *We're in the Money: Depression America and Its Films*. New York: Harper & Row, 1971.

Bowen, Charles. "The Sicario: A Juárez Hit Man Speaks." *Harper's Magazine*, May 2009, 44–53.

Bunch, Sonny. "'Sicario: Day of the Soldado' Review." *Free Beacon*, 29 June 2018. freebeacon
.com/culture/sicario-day-soldado-review/.

Burridge, James, and John Kavanagh. "Sicario." Central Intelligence Agency. cia.gov/library/
    center-for-the-study-of-intelligence/csi-publications/csi-studies/studies/vol-60-no-2/
    sicario.html.
Cave, Anthony. "Is ISIS Crossing the U.S.-Mexico Border?" PolitiFact Arizona. 10 March 2016.
    politifact.com/arizona/statements/2016/mar/10/jeff-dewit/isis-crossing-us-mexico
    -border/.
Clancy, Tom. *A Clear and Present Danger*. New York: Putnam, 1989.
Corona, Martin. *Confessions of a Cartel Hit Man*. New York: Dutton, 2017.
Debruge, Peter. "Film Review: 'Sicario: Day of the Soldado.'" *Variety*, 20 June 2018. variety
    .com/2018/film/reviews/sicario-day-of-the-soldado-review-1202853135.
Estrin, Mark W., ed. *Orson Welles: Interviews*. Jackson: University Press of Mississippi, 2002.
Franco, Jorge. *Rosario Tijeras*. Translated by Gregory Rabassa. New York: Seven Stories
    Press, 2004.
Gallego, Carlos. "'Juarez, the Beast': States of Fantasy and the Transnational City in *Sicario*."
    Arizona Quarterly 74, no. 1 (2018): 45–70.
Grillo, Ioan. *El Narco: Inside Mexico's Criminal Insurgency*. New York: Bloomsbury Press, 2011.
Higgins, Tucker. "Trump Declares without Evidence That 'Unknown Middle Easterners
    Are Mixed In' with Migrant Caravan." CNBC, 22 October 2018. cnbc.com/2018/10/22/
    trump-says-unknown-middle-easterners-are-mixed-in-migrant-caravan.html.
Kermode, Mark. "Emily Blunt's Star Quality Lifts Mexican Drugs Thriller." *Guardian*, 11
    October 2015. theguardian.com/film/2015/oct/11/sicario-review-emily-blunt-star-quality
    -lifts-thriller.
Lambert, Chris. "In *Sicario*, What Was the Role of Silvio, the Mexican Police Officer? Why
    Did He Say 'Medellin'?" *Film Colossus*, 12 September 2016. https://filmcolossus.com/
    single-post/2016/09/12/In-Sicario-what-was-the-role-of-Silvio-the-Mexican-police
    -officer-Why-did-he-say-Medellin.
Lane, Anthony. "Dark Places." *New Yorker*, September 21, 2015, 110–11.
Lane, Anthony. "Save the Children." *New Yorker*, July 9 and 16, 2018, 76–77.
Leitch, Thomas. *Film Adaptation and Its Discontents*. Baltimore: Johns Hopkins University
    Press, 2007.
Miyamoto, Ken. "Screenwriting Wisdom from the Oscar-Nominated Taylor Sheridan."
    Screencraft, 13 August 2017. screencraft.org/2017/08/13/screenwriting-wisdom-from
    -oscar-nominated-screenwriter-taylor-sheridan/.
Morris, Neil. "The Corrosive Effects of an Immoral Border War on Drugs in *Sicario*." *Indy
    Week*, 20 September 2015. indyweek.com/culture/screen/corrosive-effects-immoral
    -border-war-drugs-sicario/.
Nolte, John. "'Sicario: Day of the Soldado' Review: Border Wars Turn to Border Snores."
    Breitbart. 29 June 2018. breitbart.com/entertainment/2018/06/29/sicario-day-of-the
    -soldado-review-border-wars-turn-to-border-snores/.
Orr, Christopher. "The Almost Greatness of *Sicario*." *Atlantic*, 25 September 2015. theatlantic
    .com/entertainment/archive/2015/09/the-almost-greatness-of-sicario/407296/.
Palmer, Landon. "Culture Warrior: 3 Rules of Child Assassin Movies." 12 April 2011. https://
    filmschoolrejects.com/culture-warrior-3-rules-of-child-assassin-movies-fa302fe71a62/ .
Pérez-Reverte. *The Queen of the South*. Translated by Andrew Hurley. New York: Plume, 2005.

Pobutsky, Aldona Bialowas. "Toward the Latin American Action Heroine: The Case of Jorge Franco Ramos' *Rosario Tijeras*." *Studies in Latin American Popular Culture* 24 (2005): 23–35.

Scott, A. O. "'Sicario' Digs into the Depths of Drug Cartel Violence." *New York Times*, 17 September 2015.

Sims, David. "*Sicario: Day of the Soldado* Is Dead behind the Eyes." *Atlantic*, 2 July 2018. the atlantic.com/entertainment/archive/2018/07/sicario-day-of-the-soldado-review/564257/.

Slater, Dan. *Wolf Boys*. New York: Simon & Schuster, 2016.

Sobczynski, Peter. "Hell or High Water Movie Review." RogerEbert.com. 12 August 2016. rogerebert.com/reviews/hell-or-high-water-2016.

Sragow, Michael. "Deep Focus: *Sicario: Day of the Soldado*." *Film Comment*. 28 June 2018. filmcomment.com/blog/deep-focus-sicario-day-soldado/.

Teodoro, Jóse. "Controlling Chaos." *Film Comment*, September/October 2015. filmcomment .com/issue/september-october-2015/.

Trafton, John, and Eileen Rositzka. "A Land of Wolves: *Sicario* and the New Drug War Film." *Bright Lights Film Journal*, 10 February 2008. brightlightsfilm.com/wp-content/cache/ all/land-wolves-sicario-new-drug-war-film/#.XESoH817nIU.

Travers, Peter. "'Sicario: Day of the Soldado' Review: Sequel Brings the Carnage, Fearmongering." *Rolling Stone*, 28 June 2018. rollingstone.com/movies/movie-reviews/ sicario-day-of-the-soldado-review-sequel-brings-the-carnage-fearmongering-628464/.

Valdés Benavides, Ruy Alberto. "Who Becomes a Sicario and Why? A Supply-Side Analysis of Mexican Hitmen." Master's thesis. Erasmus University, Rotterdam. International Institute of Social Studies. 2015. http://hdl.handle.net/2105/33202.

Vallejo, Fernando. *Our Lady of the Assassins*. Translated by Paul Hammond. London: Serpent's Tail, 2001.

Villoria, Maite. "Colombia's Drug Trafficking Subculture: Its Literary Representation in *La Virgin de los sicarios* and *Rosario Tijeras*. *Caribbean Quarterly* 57, no. 2, (2011): 75–91.

Whittaker, Richard. "*Sicario: Day of the Soldado* Director Finds International Themes to Tex-Mex Thriller: Stefano Sollima goes Border to Border." *Austin Chronicle*, 29 June 2018. austinchronicle.com/screens/2018–06–29/sicario-day-of-the-soldado-director-finds -international-themes-to-tex-mex-thriller/.

MEDIA PORTRAYALS OF THE WOMAN SUFFRAGE MOVEMENT

Reconstructing a Usable Past

TINA OLSIN LENT

THAT THE WRITERS OF HISTORY CONTROL THE DISCOURSE MOTIVATED THE PIONEER GENERA-tion of American women suffragists, Susan B. Anthony, Elizabeth Cady Stanton, and Matilda Joslyn Gage, to become their own historians. They un-derstood that their organized campaign for political change was insufficient without a written history of the movement that would secure its enduring legacy in the terms they defined, so they self-consciously turned "the writing of history into a programmatic act, a political gesture for women's rights in the public sphere" (Des Jardins 177). The first three volumes of *The History of Woman Suffrage*, published by Stanton, Anthony, and Gage between 1881 and 1886, were followed by histories written by other feminists, both before and after the ratification of the Nineteenth Amendment in 1920. All revised and reinterpreted the movement's history according to their own ideological perspectives, and congruent with contemporary concerns so that the cause would remain relevant.

Histories of the suffrage movement, and interest in the movement itself, waned during and immediately after World War II, but the rise of the second wave of the feminist movement in the 1960s revived interest in it and spurred new interpretations of its history. The suffrage movement fared less well in the visual media. Although suffragists appeared in newsreel footage of actual events up through 1920, there are relatively few examples of them in fiction films between the silent era and 1995, the seventy-fifth anniversary of the ratification of the Nineteenth Amendment. The few portrayals that do exist depict them as either sinister or comic minor characters, the lat-ter stereotype making possibly its last appearance in the character of Mrs.

Banks (Glynis Johns) in *Mary Poppins* (1964).[1] At the end of the twentieth century, however, filmmakers working in both documentaries and historical dramas turned their attention to the portrayal of the suffrage movement, reviving and reinterpreting its meaning as its story was tailored to, and by, contemporary issues. While historians have investigated the construction and reconstruction of the written histories of the suffrage movement, little has been written on its various portrayals in film. Since 1995, there have been four major productions that focused on woman suffrage: Ruth Pollak's 1995 episode of PBS's *American Experience, One Woman, One Vote*; Ken Burns's 1999 documentary, *Not for Ourselves Alone: The Story of Elizabeth Cady Stanton and Susan B. Anthony*; Katja von Garnier's 2004 HBO feature, *Iron Jawed Angels*; and Sarah Gavron's 2015 feature film, *Suffragette*. Together, these projects provide a vivid lesson in the representation of politics, the politics of representation, the revision of history, and its transformation into a story that is timely and accessible to contemporary viewers.

Several major cultural shifts can be seen as coalescing by the mid-1990s to reestablish the relevance of the suffrage movement as a subject of media production after seventy-five years of obscurity. One of these is the growth in the number of women employed behind the scenes in the film and television industries, in such roles as writer, producer, executive producer, director, and editor. Data comparing the percentages of women employed in these positions from 1980 to 2017 show the biggest jump in participation occurring between 1980 and 1990, while after 1998 the numbers flatten out and remain relatively stable through 2017 (Lauzen 4). It is not too surprising that of the four suffrage projects investigated here, three of them are produced, directed, and written by women. Coinciding with the increased numbers of women behind the scenes is the rise in the number of projects featuring stories of women's friendship, solidarity, and empowerment (all characteristics seen in the suffrage movement) that began to appear in movies in the mid-1980s, such as *Desperately Seeking Susan* (Susan Seidelman, 1985), *Beaches* (1988), *Mystic Pizza* (1988), *Fried Green Tomatoes* (1991), *Thelma & Louise* (1991), *This Is My Life* (Nora Ephron, 1992), *A League of Their Own* (Penny Marshall, 1992), *Waiting to Exhale* (1995), *How to Make an American Quilt* (Jocelyn Moorhouse, 1995), *Now and Then* (Lesli Linka Glatter, 1995), and *Walking and Talking* (Nicole Holofcener, 1996), all of which were written by women, and six of which (indicated by their names in parentheses), had women directors.[2] Alison Bechdel's comic strip, *Dykes to Watch Out For*, which established her three criteria for content constituting a woman's film (now known as the Bechdel Test), an explicit critique of male domination of Hollywood films, also dates from this period (1985).

During the same period, women's prominence in politics had reached an unprecedented level, giving concrete reality to suffrage dreams. By the early 1990s, more than twenty women served internationally as prime ministers and presidents of their countries, including Prime Ministers Margaret Thatcher (UK), Gro Harlem Brundtland (Norway), Benazir Bhutto (Pakistan), Violeta de Chamorro (Nicaragua), Mary Robinson (Ireland), Khaleda Zia (Bangladesh), Edith Cresson (France), Tansu Ciller (Turkey), and President Corazon Aquino of the Philippines. A record number of women had run for (and been elected to) the US Congress in the aftermath of the Anita Hill/Clarence Thomas hearings of 1991, their representation doubling in 1992 (Ball 33). In the Bill Clinton White House, First Lady Hillary Clinton was becoming a prominent player in Washington (Traister 131–32). In 1997 President Clinton named Madeleine Albright as the first woman to serve as US Secretary of State.

These real-world accomplishments seemingly led to new representations of women in the media. By the mid-2000s, numerous women had already ascended to the American presidency in the media. Geena Davis, who had played Thelma in *Thelma & Louise*, played President Mackenzie Allen in *Commander in Chief* in 2005–6. Her role was followed by other women chief executives, most notably, Patricia Wettig in *Prison Break* (2006), Cherry Jones in *24* (2008–10), Alfre Woodard in *State of Affairs* (2014–15), Julia Louis-Dreyfus in *Veep* (2014–16), Andrea Savage in *Veep* (2016–17), Sela Ward in *Independence Day: Resurgence* (2016), and Robin Wright in *House of Cards* (2017).[3] These roles had been anticipated by Polly Bergen as President Leslie McCloud in *Kisses for My President* in 1964 (the same year Mrs. Banks was still comically fighting for suffrage), the earliest media appearance of an American woman president, and Patty Duke, who played President Julia Mansfield in a short-lived 1985 sitcom, *Hail to the Chief* (Geier), but they have a new significance in the evolving political landscape. Among other things, they open a new level of interest in the woman suffrage movement in the United States.

Internationally, interest in the struggle for woman suffrage was also on the rise in the early 1990s. While the movement provided lessons in resisting a tyrannical status quo, which were relevant in the conservative backlash against the second wave, these lessons became even more pertinent in the 2000s. Sarah Gavron, director of *Suffragette*, wrote that the events of 2015 made the film she was planning ever more timely, with "the challenging of repression by a new generation of activists from Malala Yousafzai to Pussy Riot." Finally, international suffrage anniversaries were looming in the early twenty-first century, including the centennials of women's right to vote in

New York State (2017), the 1918 Representation of the People Act in the U.K. that enfranchised women over age 30 who met the property qualifications (2018), and most prominently, the ratification of the Nineteenth Amendment in the US (2020).

Since the suffrage movement lasted seventy-two years in the US, and longer in the UK (where enfranchisement for all women over age twenty-one passed in 1928), there is enough historical material to tell just about any story, so it isn't surprising that each of the four films being considered took very different approaches.[4] Of the four, the earliest production, Ruth Pollak's 1995 episode of PBS's *American Experience, One Woman, One Vote*, originally broadcast on Susan B. Anthony's birthday (February 15) in the year marking the seventy-fifth anniversary of the ratification of the Nineteenth Amendment. It presents the American movement in the most straightforward, contemporary documentary style, with heavy reliance on historical texts and images, aimed at a general audience, which was consistent with the approach of the series. Narrated by Susan Sarandon (who played Louise in *Thelma & Louise*), it opens with newsreel footage of the huge 1913 suffrage parade in Washington, DC, attended by eight thousand women on the day before Woodrow Wilson's presidential inauguration (making an interesting contrast to the more than five hundred thousand participants in the Women's March on Washington on the day after Donald Trump's presidential inauguration in 2017). The film then uses a well-marked flashback to show "how it all had begun sixty-five years earlier in Seneca Falls." From this point, the story unfolds chronologically in well-marked "chapters," clearly delineating the broad sweep of participants and events up to the ratification of the Nineteenth Amendment. This documentary provides the basic narrative of the suffrage movement, giving distilled biographical information of the main players, simplifying the complexity inherent in a seventy-two-year movement, clarifying conflicts between leaders and goals, and highlighting the most dramatic actions within the larger historical context.

The editing together of archival news footage, photographs, documents, and onsite footage, complemented by voice-overs reading letters and speeches, introduce the viewer to primary source material while allowing a coherent story to develop, which is an impressive feat when fitting a complex and convoluted history into an hour and forty-eight minutes. The film's resolution includes an explicit statement of its overarching theme, that the vote was the tool to end all discrimination against women and to make them free and equal citizens, a very optimistic, upbeat, and emotionally satisfying message. Enhanced and reinforced by the truth claim inherent in its documentary style, the film at least temporarily stills intellectual doubts that the suffrage victory actually fulfilled those goals, doubts that were shared by even those women who had fought for suffrage, in the aftermath of victory in the 1920s and beyond. This is attested to by the fact that the Equal Rights Amendment (ERA), written by Alice Paul, leader of the National Woman's Party, and Crystal Eastman (and based on many of the ideas propounded by Elizabeth Cady Stanton), addressing the lack of equal justice under the law for women in such areas as divorce, property ownership, and employment, was introduced in Congress in 1923, only a few years after the suffrage victory. On January 15, 2020, Virginia became the thirty-eighth state to ratify the ERA, giving the amendment the number of states needed for approval, but coming forty-three years after the already-extended deadline.

In the comprehensiveness of its coverage of the suffrage movement, *One Woman, One Vote* anticipates and lays the groundwork for all of the subsequent films being discussed. Specifically, it outlines the personal relationships among the earliest pioneers (two of whom will be Ken Burns's focus), it describes the dissension over tactics in the early twentieth century, and introduces the phrase "Iron Jawed Angels" (both of which will concern von Garnier), and it introduces the strategy of the militant British suffrage movement (which will be Gavron's topic).

To reinforce the lessons of the documentary and to provide further reading, a companion volume, *One Woman, One Vote: Rediscovering the Woman Suffrage Movement*, was published with a subtitle added to emphasize that both the film and book were recovering a lost history. The anthology, edited by Marjorie Spruill Wheeler, included newly written and revised older essays by prominent scholars in women's history, all intended to be accessible and inviting to a general audience, students, and teachers of woman suffrage (Wheeler 7). The essays include primary source documents, such as the account of the 1848 Seneca Falls Convention from the first volume of *The History of Woman Suffrage* (1881), and classic essays from the early second wave, such as Alice S. Rossi's "A Feminist Friendship: Elizabeth Cady Stanton and Susan B. Anthony," originally published in *The Feminist Papers: From Adams to de Beauvoir*, a collection of primary source documents by major feminist writers reaching back into the eighteenth century, edited by Rossi in 1973. In this essay Rossi relies on the extensive collection of extant letters between Stanton and Anthony to illustrate and interpret their relationship, a subject that Ken Burns explores in his documentary.

Ken Burns's *Not for Ourselves Alone: The Story of Elizabeth Cady Stanton and Susan B. Anthony* (1999) approaches the suffrage movement from the perspective that not only the events of the movement itself but, more importantly, the personalities involved in it were "utterly" forgotten by history, at least by the history that Burns, producer Paul Barnes, and writer Geoffrey Ward had learned when they were in school (PBS Interviews). It does appear a bit disconcerting, if not disingenuous, that a documentary being made for PBS in 1999 seems to be unaware that *One Woman, One Vote* had already "rediscovered" the suffrage movement in an episode of the *American Experience* broadcast a mere four years earlier. Burns's strategy for sharpening the suffrage narrative and creating a vivid, compelling story was to focus on the fifty-year friendship and close collaboration of Stanton and Anthony, who are constructed as the architects of the woman suffrage movement. In this way he transforms the political story into a personal one, giving an interesting twist to the second wave mantra that the personal is political. Burns states that his approach grew out of "a certain amount of outrage that this story has been so long withheld from popular view" (PBS Interviews). The key word may be "popular," implying, as it does, that the companion volume to *One Woman, One Vote*, which included Alice Rossi's twenty-six-year-old article establishing that very friendship, was not accessible to the audience Burns intended to reach.

Burns's decision to focus his documentary on Stanton and Anthony created a structural and dramatic problem for his film from the outset, as both women had died before the best-known, most contentious, and ultimately victorious portion of the movement's history had even begun. Like almost all of the women who had participated in the American suffrage movement from its beginning in 1848, neither Stanton (d. 1902) nor Anthony (d. 1906) lived to see the successful outcome of their efforts. In addition, Burns made the decision (following Pollak) to open the documentary with the suffrage marches of 1912–13, comprising some of the most famous and dramatic suffrage images, but postdating his protagonists' deaths. While Pollak followed the footage of the suffrage march with a flashback to 1848 to start her story with the Seneca Falls Convention (considered to be the beginning of the movement), Burns's focus on the biographies of Stanton and Anthony forced him to use yet another flashback, to 1815 when Stanton was born. From this point his story cross-cuts chronologically between the lives of Stanton and Anthony until their deaths, effectively shifting the story thirty-three years earlier than Pollak's.

Since the film's story needed a satisfying climax that included the victorious ratification of the Nineteenth Amendment, which neither Stanton nor Anthony lived to see, Burns was forced to make a fourteen-year jump in a single cut at the end, going from Anthony's death in 1906 to the ratification of the Nineteenth Amendment in 1920, effectively eliminating the drama, characters, and conflict that would be the focus of the later films. Burns's story concludes with a contemporary interview with two elderly women, ninety-eight-year-old Ruth Dyk and one-hundred-year-old Edith Hall, who reminisce about having voted in 1920 (Burns ix). This is juxtaposed with the film's final shot, a photograph showing Stanton and Anthony as older women sitting together on the porch of Anthony's Rochester home, mirroring the previous two elderly women and seeming thereby to acknowledge the successful completion of their lives' work. A final monologue, in Burns's complacent voice, concludes that this documentary redresses an overlooked history and returns the forgotten Stanton and Anthony to their rightful place. The compositing of the interviews with his elderly subjects and the still photograph of Stanton and Anthony creates a denouement that while attempting to do justice to the competing interests of the historical record, the biographical facts, the demands of narrative closure, and the desire to appeal to a mass public, nevertheless feels forced and artificial. Historians have critiqued earlier Burns's projects for similarly labored, weak, and abrupt endings (Foner 190).

To enhance dramatic conflict throughout the film, Burns constructs Stanton's and Anthony's characters as polar opposites. Emphasizing their differences in every way—physical, emotional, marital, intellectual, vocational, organizational, and religious—the film creates heightened tension through their frequent disagreements (and even breakups) over the centrality of suffrage, the importance of other reform issues, and appropriate alliances and tactics. One cannot help thinking of Oscar (Walter Matthau) and Felix (Jack Lemmon) from *The Odd Couple* (a sequel to which had been released in 1998 as *The Odd Couple II*), where Stanton would be Oscar to Anthony's Felix. There is also the obvious reference to the squabbling banter of the love interests in the romantic comedy. This strategy aids the storytelling; by presenting the suffrage struggle as a story of the dedicated, yet conflicted, friendship of two women, Burns's documentary becomes a good, moving, and engaging story of women's empowerment through personal agency and belief in each other. Ironically, however, for a story focused on women and women's agency, it implicitly subscribes to the "Great Man" view of history, where historical agency is constructed as the result of the actions of a single great individual, who is most frequently a man. In doing this, the film belies the multiplicity of personalities, shifting ideologies, and evolving tactics that actually contributed to the complex project of winning the vote over almost three-quarters of a century. In this way, the film embraces and perpetuates a very traditional patriarchal approach to history, which contrasts sharply to the one that feminist historians had been taking for at least a decade by the time this film aired, which can be seen by the essays collected in *One*

Woman, One Vote, some of which dated back twenty years. Burns's *The Civil War* (1990) was also critiqued for its perpetuation of a nostalgic, traditional interpretation of historical events that is both parochial and simplistic by reducing the political to the personal (Foner 191, 193).

The companion volume that accompanied Burns's film, *Not for Ourselves Alone: The Story of Elizabeth Cady Stanton and Susan B. Anthony,* written by Geoffrey Ward and Ken Burns, compensates for some of the shortcomings in the film. In his preface Burns presents a more subtle understanding of the contemporary ideas about how history is written, who it is written by, and whose interests are presented. He acknowledges history's earlier perspective, focusing on Great Men and arrogantly told from the top down, as well as its newer effort to present a variety of perspectives from ordinary citizens, told from the bottom up (Burns vii). But he still subscribes to the ideology that historical events are the result of individual actors, even if they are women, and doesn't break away from that methodology as earlier feminist historians had done (Burns vii). Although he still maintains that Stanton's and Anthony's story is a hidden history, he also states that they are "responsible for the largest social transformation in American history," one that affected a majority of American citizens and served as a model for other twentieth-century reform movements (Burns viii). The main text of the book, like that of the film, follows the lives and work of Stanton and Anthony, but it fleshes out the historical context within which they worked and fills in some details from the panoramic sweep of the film. Interspersed within the lavishly illustrated chapters are primary source documents, such as the text of the "Declaration of Sentiments" (1848), and two pieces written by his protagonists, Anthony's "Homes of Single Women" (1887), and Stanton's "The Solitude of Self" (1892). In addition, in recognition of some of the feminist scholarship that had proliferated by 1999, three essays by contemporary scholars Martha Saxton, Ann D. Gordon, and Ellen Carol DuBois appear in the volume. Most interesting for this analysis is DuBois's "A Friendship through History," in which she traces the historiographic treatment of the Stanton/Anthony friendship after their deaths, as subsequent leaders of the movement reinterpreted their contributions in the context of changing times, with the result that Anthony's role was greatly elevated, while Stanton's was almost completely eclipsed (214). At the end DuBois gives a summary of the recovery of the history of the woman suffrage movement, seeing it as an effort to provide the legitimacy of tradition to the second wave of feminism developing in the 1960s (217).

By the beginning of the twenty-first century, the suffrage movement and its pioneer generation of activists had been rediscovered. But the subsequent second and third generations of suffragists, who brought the struggle to its successful conclusion, were still mostly unknown. Alice Paul and Lucy Burns, the founding leaders of the National Woman's Party, who named the Nineteenth Amendment the Susan B. Anthony Amendment, were far less familiar, even though Paul lived until 1977. This was redressed by Katja von Garnier's 2004 HBO feature, *Iron Jawed Angels*, which like Pollak's film debuted on television on Susan B. Anthony's birthday, and like Burns's focused on a pair of women protagonists. Unlike the previous two documentaries, this film is a historical drama that narrowed its focus to the action-filled eight years between 1912 and 1920 (that Ken Burns omitted from his film), so that the ratification of the Nineteenth Amendment truly functions as its narrative climax. As a fiction film based on historical events, it freely added fabricated characters and incidents to make the story more dramatic and engaging by interweaving fictional, personal stories into the historical, political story. Von Garnier and writers Jennifer Friedes, Sally Robinson, Eugenia Bostwick-Singer, and Raymond Singer argue for the indispensable role played by the radical suffragists led by Paul and Burns, who were united in their belief that taking extreme action was necessary for victory, and who were willing to direct that action against the movement's traditional allies: the mainstream suffrage organization (the National American Woman Suffrage Association or NAWSA), and the Democratic Party.

In the interest of telling a good and compelling story, *Iron Jawed Angels* modernizes and clarifies the characters, simplifies the conflicts, and untangles the complexities of history. The film constructs Alice Paul (Hilary Swank) and Lucy Burns (Frances O'Connor) as remarkably contemporary women who are more easily recognizable as modern third wave feminists than as women of their period, making them appealing central characters. Their youth and vivacious embrace of publicity-attracting action, and love of shopping, make them the epitome of modernity, particularly in contrast to the NAWSA leaders, Anna Howard Shaw, Harriot Stanton Blatch, and Carrie Chapman Catt, who are caricatured as staid, matronly, and out of touch with the times. Anjelica Huston's biting portrayal of Catt as older, conservative, and above all respectable, positions her as one of the villains of the story and turns her into the perfect dramatic foil for the youthful, energetic, and iconoclastic Alice Paul. This choice makes sense dramatically but ultimately distorts the complexity of the actual events, which will be discussed below. Other narrative choices also privilege dramatic invention over historical truth: Alice Paul was a Quaker who would not have spent time shopping for fashionable hats; her romance with Ben Weissman was completely fictional; the "conversion" of Senator Leighton's wife to the suffrage movement utilized a standard dramatic device involving completely fictional characters; and perhaps most critically, it was not the radical tactics of Paul and Burns that ultimately won the suffrage victory, but those of the mainstream NAWSA under the leadership of Carrie Chapman Catt (Fowler, *Feminist Politician* 153; Fowler and Spencer 180; Ford 236). It is this flattening out of the complexity of political action and the oversimplifying of the multiplicity of strategies needed for change that constitute the historical shortcomings of this dramatically successful story.

In the interest of crafting a clear narrative conflict, the writers of *Iron Jawed Angels* construct a sharp binary opposition between the conservative strategies of NAWSA and the radical ones followed by Paul and Burns, losing the fluidity, nuances, and connections between those factions and others, such as the labor movement. The film positions Paul and Burns as the sole conduits through which the radical tactics of Emmeline Pankhurst, her daughters, and the British suffragettes (as the radical faction in the UK was called) were introduced in the US when Paul and Burns returned from England in 1912. In reality members of the second generation of American suffragists had already introduced these ideas. In 1906 Alice Stone Blackwell (daughter of first-generation suffragists Lucy Stone and Henry Blackwell) published the Pankhursts' techniques and speeches in the *Woman's Journal* (Bolt 196). Harriot Stanton Blatch (daughter of Elizabeth Cady Stanton) invited Anne Cobden-Sanderson, one of the first members of the British Women's Social and Political Union (WSPU) to be arrested for suffrage protests, to the US in 1907 to tell about her experiences (DuBois, *Working Women* 237). In 1909 Blatch sponsored the Pankhursts' tour of the US (Bolt 189). She also embraced their publicity-attracting strategies and in 1912 organized a parade in New York City that drew more than ten thousand women into the demonstration (DuBois, *Next Generation* 208). In that same year, Carrie Chapman Catt, in the hiatus between her two terms as president of NAWSA, while serving as the president of the International Woman Suffrage Alliance (IWSA), attended meetings of both the moderate suffragists and the militant suffragettes of the WSPU in London; at the former she experienced a long parade of suffragists, including university women in their robes and workers in overalls, which she burned "with desire to reproduce . . . in New York," and at the latter witnessed the honor given to the 150 suffragettes who had been imprisoned for the cause (Van Voris 77). Although members of the mainstream American suffrage movement were familiar with the radical British tactics, Paul and Burns self-consciously and single-mindedly put them into practice in the final seven years of the suffrage campaign, advocating radical (but nonviolent) resistance and civil disobedience. Their actions brought them publicity and notoriety, and contrasted sharply with the more moderate and traditional organizational work of lobbying, petitioning, fundraising, and persuasion campaigns, being done by NAWSA (Fowler, *Strategist* 170). When Paul and Burns were expelled from NAWSA for their radical tactics and desire for faster action in 1913, they created their own organization, the Congressional Union, which became known as the National Woman's Party in 1917, and it is this organization that *Iron Jawed Angels* positions as the catalyst for the final victory as befitting their narrative focus.

In the crafting of this story, von Garnier and the writers pay implicit homage to Laurel Thatcher Ulrich's oft-repeated observation that well-behaved women seldom make history; they also tacitly acknowledge the film industry's predilection for narratives featuring protagonists who engage in physical action and conflict. The director and writers further understand the necessity for emotional intensity in a melodrama, so they ratcheted up all emotions in the situations involving the protagonists, including the antagonism between women in different factions of the suffrage movement and the violence instigated by the antisuffragists. As in any action-packed film, there is extreme physical conflict—love, violence, imprisonment, suffering, hunger strikes, and humiliation, all leading up to the thrilling climax—Woodrow Wilson's apparent capitulation to the radicals' demand in a 1918 speech before Congress endorsing woman suffrage as a war measure, and the amendment's ultimate approval by Congress. These actions are conflated in the film, as though in a direct cause-and-effect relationship (similar to the ending of Burns's film) occurring in an accelerated timeframe. While Wilson did give his speech to Congress supporting woman suffrage as a war measure in January 1918 (less than two months after Paul and other members of the Woman's Party were released from prison in late November 1917), it was at the behest of NAWSA president Carrie Chapman Catt, and while the House of Representatives did pass the amendment that month (on January 10, 1918), the Senate did not follow suit; as a result, the amendment had to be reintroduced in both chambers of Congress in 1919, where it passed in the House on May 21 and finally passed in the Senate on June 4 1919, seventeen months after Wilson's speech of support, and seven months after the armistice ending World War I (Sims 333; History). It took another fourteen months before it was ratified, on August 26, 1920.

With all of that said, it is undeniable that *Iron Jawed Angels* makes a vivid impression on viewers. The story is engaging and its argument for direct political action compelling. Of all four films being considered, this is unquestionably the best stimulus to political involvement. The relatability of the characters and the pace of the action make it appealing to contemporary viewers, as does its political message. In espousing the political ideology of nonviolent militancy (as Martin Luther King Jr. would later do), Alice Paul's well-organized, aggressive defiance of, and resistance to, authority points to an effective means of social protest that is particularly valid and meaningful today (Ford 222). The film's continued popularity on college campuses attests to the relevance of its political message to young women.

In contrast, Sarah Gavron's 2015 feature film, *Suffragette*, advocates violent action to foment social change. Gavron was motivated to make this film by the upcoming centenary of the British 1918 Representation of the People Act, by the relevance of the story to contemporary concerns worldwide, and by the question of what drove ordinary women into going this far (par. #5, 7, 11). Set in London in 1912 and 1913 (the narrowest time frame of all four films), this historical drama focuses on a fictional protagonist, Maud Watts (Carey Mulligan), who is accidentally and slowly pulled into the radical, militant suffragette movement led by the Pankhursts. Maud is converted to the cause by encountering public demonstrations demanding women's rights and by personally experiencing humiliation and losses due to the lack of those rights. Like *Iron Jawed Angels*, this film glorifies the radical faction of the suffrage movement that advocates "deeds not words." Even Carrie Chapman Catt recognized the different feel of the radical movement in London, writing in 1913, "The suffrage campaign in the United States is a dull and commonplace affair when compared with the sizzling white heat of the British struggle" (Somervill 82).

The English suffragettes embraced violent action that destroyed property (but never persons), and Gavron's film focuses on the effectiveness of this strategy, ranging from smashing windows, throwing rocks, cutting telegraph wires, bombing letter boxes, and blowing up Lloyd George's country home, for winning victory. The destruction was carefully orchestrated so that no men were seriously injured or killed by militants (Bolt 188). However, in 1913 Emily Wilding Davison ran out in front of the king's horse at the Epsom Derby and was killed, a historical incident that serves as the climax of *Suffragette*, which cuts from the fictional film to newsreel footage of her funeral. It also positions her as a martyr to the cause. The protagonists of *Suffragette*, as did those in *Iron Jawed Angels*, advocate for direct action. But they differ in what constitutes, and what limits, that direct action, thereby constituting a major ideological divergence between the two films. While the nonviolent militancy and civil disobedience depicted in the American radical suffrage movement evoke images of the later American Civil Rights Movement, particularly as portrayed in films such as *Selma* (2014), the violence in Gavron's films conjures up other recent violent acts of radicalism. Viewed from the perspective of 2020, the violent militant acts performed by the suffragettes appear as acts of domestic terrorism. After seeing footage of the June 2017 terrorist attack in London and those in other cities, these actions seem harder to condone and identify with, even when situated in a positive historical and narrative context.

All four films focusing on the suffrage movement do more than illuminate and elucidate the historical events upon which they are based—they also illustrate the contradictory demands imposed on history by the requirements of being represented in a different aesthetic medium. The basic formula for a successful film centers on an engaging protagonist who confronts a physical conflict to fulfill a personal goal or desire, whose story follows a narrative trajectory that ultimately changes them and evokes an emotional impact in viewers. Both of the suffrage documentaries, *One Woman, One Vote* and *Not for Ourselves Alone*, aimed to stay true to the historical accounts of the movement while simultaneously interpreting the events in a narrative fashion, by highlighting the continuity between events for clarity, emphasizing specific historical characters to create identification and empathy, and bringing the story to an emotionally satisfying conclusion. The fiction films had to struggle further with the inherent contradiction between recounting history and telling a story. Ultimately, *Suffragette* and *Iron Jawed Angels* needed to confront the paradox that the actions required to make a good movie story are not the same as those that constitute a viable political strategy for fomenting social change—and further, that while movies can function to motivate viewers into becoming more politically active, their primary function is entertainment, not to serve as educational treatises on political theory or social activism.

Direct political action plays well on the screen, but it is the end product of a process that is based on tedious, time-consuming labor that is not easily translated to the compressed, action-oriented narrative demands of a fiction film. Articulating a political theory, transforming it into discrete goals, enumerating strategies, developing tactics, building an organization that can operate over an extended time frame and geographical reach, and attracting dedicated leadership are the *sine qua non* of a political movement. But not of a movie. Yet this was the successful strategy followed by NAWSA in winning woman suffrage in the US, the final stages of which were engineered by Carrie Chapman Catt. The work is decidedly routine, monotonous, and dramatically dull, requiring painstaking attention to detail in order to coordinate all of the parts of an organized mass movement on the local, state, and federal levels. According to Catt, "agitation for a cause is excellent; education is better; but organization is the only assurance of final triumph of any cause in a self-governing nation" (Huxman 313). Organization was Catt's strength, and when she became president of NAWSA for a second time, in 1916, she insisted upon being given control over the implementation of her "Winning Plan," in which she declared that the "Woman's Hour has struck . . . the time of victory is here" (Croy and Catt 61). She called for a "mobilization of spirit" to organize, lobby, agitate, educate, and appeal to the voters to get a federal suffrage amendment passed by Congress (Croy and Catt, 61, 62, 71). She believed that lobbying efforts had to be aggressive and nonpartisan, and that they should occur simultaneously at the federal, state, and local precinct levels, aimed at winning strategic victories to increase the number of prosuffrage representatives in the US Congress (Fowler and Jones 174). Ever the pragmatist, the politically savvy, methodical Catt developed a hierarchical, military-like organization, produced efficient publicity to sway public opinion, developed "suffrage schools" to teach women how to organize and, above all, remained dignified, diplomatic, nonpartisan, nonthreatening, and willing to compromise (Fowler, *Strategist* 296). Although Catt did not share the antagonism that some in NAWSA felt toward Alice Paul, she disagreed with the tactics of the National Woman's Party, particularly the partisanship and picketing, believing they were a destructive influence on the cause (Fowler, *Feminist Politician* 147–48). Catt questioned whether the radicals had a realistic understanding of practical politics, because their actions, blaming the party in power and picketing the White House, were alienating the very Democrats in Congress (all of whom were men) whose votes were needed to give the woman suffrage amendment the two-thirds majority required to pass (Fowler, *Strategist* 307–8). She was also concerned that their tactics were bound to alienate President Wilson, whose "support was needed, especially to persuade reluctant southern Democrats in Congress [also exclusively male] to give their support" (Fowler, *Feminist Politician* 149). Catt personally worked the White House, convinced that "dignified lobbying was the way to get results," and quietly notified the White House of planned embarrassments to Wilson, which were leaked to her by friends in the Woman's Party (Fowler, *Feminist Politician* 149, 151). Catt also publicly appealed to Alice Paul in 1917 to stop the aggressive picketing of the White House, on the grounds that the national scandal they provoked hurt, rather than helped, their cause. Catt's greatest concern was that the radicals were not politically effective, not that they were young, brash, and unfeminine (Fowler, *Feminist Politician* 151).

But it is difficult to make a compelling and engaging fiction film featuring dignified and respectable middle-aged women, with gray hair and large hats, canvassing their local precincts for signatures on state referenda or buttonholing reluctant congressmen in Washington, DC. Obtaining thousands of names on a petition doesn't create the kind of emotional reaction that being arrested while picketing does, and in movies, as in real life, radical action draws attention and makes viewers empathize with the characters. This is perhaps the actual function of militant factions of social movements, as Malcolm X (Nigel Thatch) explains to Martin Luther King Jr. (David Oyelowo) in *Selma*—their extreme demands and tactics make those of the centrists look moderate, reasonable, and downright respectable, so that by contrast they become acceptable to the general public. Even Carrie Chapman Catt finally admitted that Alice Paul's radical tactics may have legitimated NAWSA and assisted the overall cause (Fowler, *Strategist* 312).

Catt was also "acutely aware of the power dynamics connected to memory" and wanted to ensure that the centrality of NAWSA's role in winning woman suffrage would not be forgotten. When she took over NAWSA's leadership for the second time, she also assumed control of its history, editing volumes 5 and 6 of *The History of Woman Suffrage* (1922), in which Alice Paul's National Woman's Party is barely mentioned—necessitating its leaders to write their own history (Delahaye; Des Jardins 185, 188).[5] Furthermore, Catt wrote her own account, *Woman Suffrage and Politics: The Inner Story of the Suffrage Movement*, in 1923 (with NAWSA secretary Nettie Shuler); then in 1939 she donated her library, comprising NAWSA's reference collection (that included volumes from the libraries of the movement's pioneers), to the Library of Congress to ensure it entered the official archive of American history. Finally, Catt joined with other veterans of the movement to write *Victory: How Women Won It: 1840–1940* (1940), continuing the tradition of making, writing, and controlling women's history begun by Anthony, Stanton, and Gage in the 1880s, showing that well-behaved women do, in fact, make history, as both actors and the interpreters of those actions.

Works Cited

Ball, Molly. "The Women Are Winning." *Time* June 25, 2018, pp. 30–33.

Bolt, Christine. "America and the Pankhursts." *Votes for Women: The Struggle for Suffrage Revisited*, edited by Jean H. Baker, Oxford UP, 2002, pp. 184–200.

Burns, Ken. "Preface: Our Big Time." Geoffrey C. Ward and Ken Burns, *Not For Ourselves Alone: The Story of Elizabeth Cady Stanton and Susan B. Anthony*. Knopf, 1999, pp. vii–ix.

Croy, Terry Desch, and Carrie Chapman Catt. "The Crisis: A Complete Critical Edition of Carrie Chapman Catt's 1916 Presidential Address to the National American Woman Suffrage Association." *Rhetoric Society Quarterly* vol. 28, no. 3 (Summer 1998): 49–73.

Delahaye, Claire. "The Perfect Library: Carrie Chapman Catt and the Authoritative Historiography." *Nuevo Mundo Mundos Nuevos* (online) 26 November 2014. Accessed 25 July 2017.

Des Jardins, Julie. *Women and the Historical Enterprise in America: Gender, Race, and the Politics of Memory, 1880–1945*. U of North Carolina P, 2003.

DuBois, Ellen Carol. "A Friendship through History." Geoffrey C. Ward and Ken Burns, *Not For Ourselves Alone: The Story of Elizabeth Cady Stanton and Susan B. Anthony*. Knopf, 1999, pp. 213–17.

DuBois, Ellen Carol. "The Next Generation: Harriot Stanton Blatch and Grassroots Politics." *Votes for Women: The Struggle for Suffrage Revisited*, edited by Jean H. Baker, Oxford UP, 2002, pp. 202–19.

DuBois, Ellen Carol. "Working Women, Class Relations, and Suffrage Militance: Harriot Stanton Blatch and the New York Woman Suffrage Movement, 1894–1909." *One Woman, One Vote: Rediscovering the Woman Suffrage Movement*, edited by Marjorie Spruill Wheeler, NewSage Press, 1995, pp. 221–44.

Equal Rights Amendment: Unfinished Business for the Constitution, equalrightsamendment .org/. Accessed 25 August 2018.

Foner, Eric. "Ken Burns and the Romance of Reunion." *Who Owns History: Rethinking the Past in a Changing World*. Hill and Wang, 2002.

Ford, Linda. "Alice Paul and the Politics of Nonviolent Protest." *Votes for Women: The Struggle for Suffrage Revisited*, edited by Jean H. Baker, Oxford UP, 2002, pp. 221–36.

Fowler, Robert Booth. *Carrie Catt: Feminist Politician*. Northeastern UP, 1986.

Fowler, Robert Booth. "Carrie Chapman Catt, Strategist." *One Woman, One Vote: Rediscovering the Woman Suffrage Movement*, edited by Marjorie Spruill Wheeler, NewSage Press, 1995, pp. 295–314.

Fowler, Robert Booth, and Spencer Jones. "Carrie Chapman Catt and the Last Years of the Struggle for Woman Suffrage: "The Winning Plan." *Votes for Women: The Struggle for Suffrage Revisited*, edited by Jean H. Baker, Oxford UP, 2002, pp. 167–82.

Gavron, Sarah. "The Making of the Feature Film Suffragette." *Woman's History Review* 24:6 (2015): 985–95, published online.

Geier, Thom. "11 Woman Presidents in Movies and TV before Hillary Clinton," *The Wrap*. thewrap.com/female-us-president-movies-tv-actress-woman-hillary-clinton/. Accessed 25 August 2018.

History, Art & Archives United States House of Representatives. "Historical Highlights: The House's 1918 Passage of a Constitutional Amendment Granting Women the Right to Vote," history.house.gov/HistoricalHighlight/Detail/35873?ret=True. Accessed 11 June 2018.

Huxman, Susan Schultz. "Perfecting the Rhetorical Vision of Woman's Rights: Elizabeth Cady Stanton, Anna Howard Shaw, and Carrie Chapman Catt." *Women's Studies in Communication* vol. 23, no. 3 (Fall 2000): 307–36.

Lauzen, Martha M. *The Celluloid Ceiling: Behind-the-Scenes Employment of Women on the Top 100, 250, and 500 Films of 2017*. Center for the Study of Women in Television and Film. San Diego State University, womenintvfilm.sdsu.edu. Accessed 11 June 2018.

PBS Interviews with Ken Burns and Paul Barnes. "Not For Ourselves Alone: The Story of Elizabeth Cady Stanton and Susan B. Anthony." June 16, July 13, and August 17, 1999. pbs. org/stantonanthonyfilmmakers/index.html. Accessed 25 July 2017.

Sims, Anastatia. "Armageddon in Tennessee: The Final Battle over the Nineteenth Amendment." *One Woman, One Vote: Rediscovering the Woman Suffrage Movement*, edited by Marjorie Spruill Wheeler, NewSage Press, 1995, pp. 333–52.

Somervill, Barbara A. *Votes for Women! The Story of Carrie Chapman Catt*. Morgan Reynolds, 2003.

Traister, Rebecca. "Citizen Clinton: The Surreal Postelection Life of the Woman Who Would Have Been President." *New York* (May 29–June 11, 2017): 26–33, 131–32.

Van Voris, Jacqueline. *Carrie Chapman Catt: A Public Life*. Feminist Press, 1987.

Wheeler, Marjorie Spruill. "Acknowledgments." *One Woman, One Vote: Rediscovering the Woman Suffrage Movement*, edited by Marjorie Spruill Wheeler, NewSage Press, 1995, p. 7.

Notes

1. Suffragists appear in some early short silent films before the ratification of the Nineteenth Amendment, often as sinister or comic minor characters, in a vein similar to the political cartoons of the period. Examples include *The Lady Barber* (1898) and Chaplin's *A Busy Day* (1914). The comic portrayal reappears in the 1960s, with Glynis Johns's character of Mrs. Banks in *Mary Poppins* (1964).

2. *Desperately Seeking Susan* was directed by Susan Seidelman and written by Leora Barish. *Fried Green Tomatoes* was written by Fannie Flagg and directed by John Avnet. *Thelma & Louise* was written by Callie Khouri and directed by Ridley Scott. A new book on *Thelma & Louise*, Becky Aikman's *Off the Cliff: How the Making of Thelma & Louise Drove Hollywood to the Edge* (Penguin, 2017), calls it the "feminist sensation." Other films featuring strong female friendships with women behind the scenes from this period include: *Beaches* (1988) directed by Garry Marshall, written by Iris Rainer and Mary Agnes Donoghue; *Mystic Pizza* (1988) directed by Donald Petrie, written by Amy Holden Jones; *This Is My Life* (1992) directed and written by Nora Ephron in her directorial debut; *A League of Their Own* (1992) directed by Penny Marshall, written by Kim Wilson and Kelly Candaele; *Now and Then* (1995) directed by Lesli Linka Glatter, written by I. Marlene King; *Waiting to Exhale* (1995) directed by Forest Whitaker, written by Terry McMillan; *How to Make an American Quilt* (1995) directed by Jocelyn Moorhouse, written by Whitney Otto and Jane Anderson; and *Walking and Talking* (1996) written and directed by Nicole Holofcener in her directorial debut.

3. Multiple websites provide lists of women presidents in the media, such as the Wrap and the *Hollywood Reporter*.

4. The suffrage movement lasted for more than one hundred years in the UK. Women were not explicitly banned from voting there until the 1832 Reform Act. In 1918 the Representation of the People Act enfranchised all men as well as women over the age of thirty who met the property qualifications. In 1928 the Representation of the People (Equal Franchise) Act passed, giving the vote to all women over the age of twenty-one.

5. There was an unwritten code that the mainstream suffrage movement would preserve a unified front to the outside world, so Lucy Stone, leader of the competing suffrage organization between 1869 and 1890, was conspicuously absent from the early volumes of *The History of Woman Suffrage* edited by Anthony, Stanton, and Gage (Des Jardins 183). Leaders of the National Woman's Party subsequently wrote their own histories.

#METOO AND THE FILMMAKER AS MONSTER

John Landis, Quentin Tarantino, and the Allegorically Confessional Horror Film

MARC DIPAOLO

FOR AS LONG AS THERE HAVE BEEN GOTHIC NARRATIVES—BE THEY BOOKS, SHORT STORIES, films, poems, comic books, or other forms—consumers of these narratives have found themselves equally attracted to and repelled by the figure of the monster. Two of the most iconic Gothic monsters are Count Dracula and Victor Frankenstein's motherless creation, two unnaturally alive figures who stand at opposite ends of the social class spectrum. Dracula is a charming, exotic aristocrat, possessed of enormous physical strength, eternal youth, immortality, vast wealth, a castle, and a harem of supernaturally gorgeous vampire brides. As the embodiment of toxic, patriarchal masculinity unleashed, Dracula is every evil impulse of the male id made flesh. To men who want to surrender to their basest desires, Dracula is endlessly appealing and fascinating. To men who wish to flee from these same desires and are ashamed of them, Dracula is a loathsome manifestation of imperial appetites and the will to rape who cannot be staked and beheaded soon enough.

In contrast, the Frankenstein monster is the patron saint of the unloved. Mary Shelley's novel links him symbolically to Lucifer, God's once-favored creation, now cast down to the abyss. Shelley also symbolically connects the monster to the oppressed proletarian, the unloved foundling, the aborted fetus, the leper, the physically disfigured and disabled, and the liberated woman turned social pariah. As the embodiment of all who are brutalized and maltreated, Frankenstein's monster is a romantic, revolutionary figure who is driven to hatred and murder by the father who abandoned him and the society that shunned him. Readers of the novel who find it difficult to acknowledge the very existence of members of disenfranchised communities in the real world, or who are disgusted by them, are likely to shrink from the Frankenstein monster with the same disgust the "Bride of Frankenstein" exhibited in the 1935 James Whale film of the same name. On the other hand, anyone who has been made to feel ugly, unloved, reprehensible, or irredeemable will see in the monster a kindred spirit and will love that monster precisely because no one else does.

Some of us are more repelled by these monsters than attracted to them. For some, it is the reverse. And then there are those who love and hate these creatures all at once, in equal measure. We love them and hate them because we see in them what we are and what we might be. They are at once "othered" figures and stand-ins for ourselves. Different monsters and different Gothic tales achieve widespread fame and recognition at different points in history, and the stories that are popular at given cultural moments are those most likely to speak to the social crisis of the day. The reason that zombies, for example, are so popular today is that they are a portent of the apocalypse, an event most of us fear is imminent, for one reason or another. Similarly, in many ways, the Hollywood filmmaker is the monster of the moment in modern America.

In the early months of the #MeToo movement that began in 2017, a series of Hollywood directors, actors, and producers were outed as unrepentant sexual predators who habitually preyed upon the career ambitions of would-be collaborators. Actresses were trapped into sexual relations they did not want in exchange for film roles. These women were subjected to repeated gropings and advances. In several cases, most infamously involving the producer Harvey Weinstein, actresses such as Rose McGowan and Asia Argento were allegedly raped. After McGowan helped open the floodgate of accusations against Weinstein, more victims came forward to name their tormentors (Sini). Corey Feldman reiterated his claims that child actors were often turned into prostitutes by Hollywood executives, and his conspiracy-theory-sounding exposé was granted more public credence in this suddenly new context than Barbara Walters, for one, had given it several years ago during his appearance on *The View* (Sager).

When the horrors of the real world depicted on the news seem infinitely more disturbing and world-shaking than those ever depicted in fiction, horror films sometimes seem quaint and in danger of losing their potency; however, some horror films are particularly worth revisiting during this particular moment. Since horror films are replete with sexual violence, any number of "monster and the girl," "final girl," or "rape-revenge" films would seem salient. Still more salient, though, would be several confessional, autobiographical horror films by filmmakers who have used and abused the actors in their power—men, women, and children—and destroyed lives in the pursuit of making art and furthering their careers. The directors who have made some of the most disturbing confessional films include Quentin Tarantino (*Death Proof*, 2007) and John Landis (*Masters of Horror*: "Deer Woman," 2005). The complicity they potentially embed in their films makes them fascinating figures, whether or not their films stand as sincere confessions, and whether or not they are deserving of the absolution they seek.

What the Hollywood #MeToo scandals have done is throw into relief the long-standing view of the film director as a monster. He is a figure to be both admired and disgusted by. Film connoisseurs and would-be filmmakers fantasize about being like the iconic director-tyrant, while being at least leery of ever having to work for such a person. In contrast, as much as actors are glamorous and are beloved and respected for their acting ability—when their private lives aren't being plastered over the supermarket tabloids—they are also, in a very real way, considered the proles and the workhorses of Hollywood. Yes, they act, but they did not write the script or direct the film. The director generates the real respect, while the actors and actresses are the cats he needs to herd—and herd cruelly—in the great enterprise of making art. For all their wealth and pomp, even successful actors often have come from humble roots, retain some of their working-class mannerisms, and—beauty notwithstanding—are still the proles of the film system who are more like the manufactured, publicly condemned, and abandoned Frankenstein monster than the aristocratic Dracula. Hollywood producers and directors are the true royalty, the Dracula figures that see their studios as their castle, and the attractive actresses who come to them looking for work and mentoring as an endless supply of potential vampire brides for their harems.

Hollywood film history is filled with stories of directors who made their actors' lives miserable in the effort to make their films as great and realistic as possible. The abuse that these actors suffer is not always strictly and narrowly sexual—it is often emotional and physical. There are even times when directors ask actors to risk their health and lives in the pursuit of a dangerous stunt or special effect. That kind of exploitation is not necessarily the same kind or order of exploitation as the "casting couch" but is a related evil in any instance when the filmmaker is endangering, blackmailing, and coercing the actor in the name of career advancement, financial profit, and the creation of film art. To that extent a discussion of tyrannical directors endangering the lives of their actors can justifiably go hand in hand with a discussion of the #MeToo scandals. Unfortunately, up until #MeToo, victimized members of a film's cast and crew have not often garnered much sympathy from critics and fans, who have tended to choose to relate instead to the bullying directors, especially if the end result of the production process is a beloved and respected cinematic work.

For example, film historians have gleefully told tales of one of the main reasons *The Exorcist* (1973) is such a terrifying film—the actors themselves were in a constant state of fear as they made the movie, because they never knew when director William Friedkin would startle them by firing blanks on the set. Friedkin's reputation for being a martinet director inspired *Guardian* reporter Charles Bramesco to ask him about how his use and abuse of his actors might be similar to or different from Harvey Weinstein's, or any other abusive Hollywood figure's. Friedkin refused to stand in judgment of Weinstein and had no time for criticism of his own treatment of actors on set, including the moment when he may have caused Ellen Burstyn to injure her tailbone during filming of *The Exorcist*: "She never lost a day's work, let's put it that way. There was no insurance claim, and she's worked steadily ever since. I'm sure she was hurt by the fall—you fall on your backside, it's gonna hurt—but she wasn't injured. And for that I say, thank God . . . I'm not here to talk about the #MeToo movement, as much as I'm sure you'd like me to" (Bramesco).

If there has been a paradigm shift in how directors are viewed who prioritize the making of art over the safety of their actors and crew, then Friedkin is not the only one who might be viewed in a less charitable light these days. Certainly, Freidkin's sophistry is deconstructed easily enough; even if Ellen Burstyn happened to be fortunate enough not to sustain lasting injuries, other actors have, indeed, lost many days of work, stopped working steadily after their accident, and been permanently scarred, crippled, or killed during a shoot. In one of the most famous film-set tragedies of all, camera assistant Sarah Jones was killed in a freight train collision on February 20, 2014, while filming a Gregg Allman biopic called *Midnight Rider*. CSX Transportation paid Jones's surviving family members $3.9 million in damages after being found liable for her death in civil court, and the film's director, Randall Miller, pleaded guilty to criminal trespassing and involuntary manslaughter charges and spent a year in jail ("CSX to Pay $3.9M"). In addition to this high-profile film-set death, there have been other cast and crew members killed and countless others who have almost died but were spared by a near miss. For example, Sylvester Stallone was almost decapitated by a helicopter while filming *Rambo III* on location in Israel in 1987. The blade was supposed to pass well over his head, but dust blown into the air confused the pilot, and he banked lower than he should have, resulting in the blade coming within a hair's breadth of Stallone's head (Labrecque 293).

Two of the most infamous film-set tragedies were Quentin Tarantino's crippling of Uma Thurman in a stunt car during the filming of *Kill Bill* (released in two parts in 2003 and 2004) and the helicopter accident that killed Vic Morrow and two child actors—Myca Dinh Le and Shin-Yi Chen—on the set of *Twilight Zone: The Movie* (1983), in a segment directed by John Landis. Evidence suggests that both Tarantino and Landis knew they were placing their actors in danger but have, arguably, not faced the punishment that they should have for their actions, despite their feelings of guilt, damage to their reputations, and difficult-to-quantify "lost work opportunities." While both directors have passionately denied their culpability in the accidents when speaking to the press and/or during courtroom appearances, both men made pseudo-confessional follow-up films ostensibly about these real-life experiences, in which they hint that they actually see themselves as more responsible for the "accidents" than they have tended to let on during interviews. Tarantino made *Death Proof* (2007) as a meditation on the Thurman accident, and Landis made *Masters of Horror: "Deer Woman"* (2005) as a veiled apology to those who died on his set.

Watching these films merely as genre films—with *Death Proof* serving as a rape-revenge, 1970s "grindhouse film" tribute, and "Deer Woman" acting as a satirical take on police procedurals, femme fatales, and transformational horror films—means acknowledging that they are artistic low points for the two directors, with Tarantino himself branding *Death Proof* his worst film, and "Deer Woman" being one of the least compelling films directed by Landis (that also happens to commit the sins of appropriating and lampooning Native American folklore). Viewing *Death Proof* and "Deer Woman" instead as pseudo-autobiographical pieces, or "ripped from real-life" tragedies adapted into confessional, allegorical horror films, makes them far more compelling—and far more morally problematic—works of art. The films become "better" when viewed in this way. They are also more emotionally fraught and "horrifying," far more chilling than the overt "horror" genre tropes would be on their own. And yet perhaps most horrifying of all is the idea that both *Kill Bill* and the Landis segment of *Twilight Zone: The Movie* were ostensibly subversive narratives written and directed by progressive filmmakers who crippled and killed members of their own cast in the process of trying to make art designed to make the world a more humane place.

Whether or not it was John Landis's intention to turn his own life into an allegorized fiction, viewers of "Deer Woman" who know anything at all of Landis's personal history will be extremely likely to make a mental connection between that film and the worst day of his life: the accidental deaths of three actors during the filming of Landis's horror segment in *Twilight Zone:*

The Movie. During the early 1980s, Landis wrote a segment of *Twilight Zone: The Movie* in which an unabashed racist played by Vic Morrow is magically placed on a train to Auschwitz, on a slave plantation, and in the midst of a battlefield of the Vietnam War as an unidentified supernatural force of justice coerces him into empathy with oppressed peoples. The story was close to Landis's heart, since he is Jewish and has condemned fascism in his other work, most notably *An American Werewolf in London* (1981). Landis explained, "I was attempting to recreate the spirit of the original TV series. One of the many aspects of Rod Serling was his great liberal point of view. He always did stories about racism and anti-Semitism and antiwar shows. So, I was attempting . . . to capture the Serling gestalt. [My segment in the anthology film] dealt in a harsh way with a hard subject. It used the fantastic to deal with racism and ignorance and had no feel-good ending or creepy creatures." In addition to wanting to be true to the spirit of the series without resorting to remaking a classic episode, Landis felt that the best antiwar film is the most realistic one and wanted to make the Vietnam battle scene in the *Twilight Zone* film as harrowing as possible to adequately depict the horrors of war. Landis had been firmly committed to realistic filmmaking throughout his career and was known for filming some of the most exciting action set pieces in cinema history, including the wild car chase from *The Blues Brothers*. If he would film a dangerous car chase for an escapist musical comedy like *The Blues Brothers*, it makes sense that he would push the safety envelope still further for a film that he felt dealt with a subject of great moral import.

The fatal helicopter crash that took three lives occurred on July 23, 1982, at a nighttime studio shoot. Landis was staging an iconic Vietnam War scene in which an American attack helicopter strafed a Vietnamese village. The story called for Morrow's reformed racist character to try to save Vietnamese children from being killed by an American attack copter. On the night of the filming, Morrow was with Le and Chen, racing them away from the chopper. When special effects technician James Camomile set off explosive charges designed to add to the battle scene's verisimilitude, the heat from the explosion melted the chopper's rear rotary blade, causing it to crash into the three actors and kill them. The deaths, the trial that followed, and the lasting controversy surrounding the tragedy were the inspiration for two 1988 books—*Special Effects: Disaster at Twilight Zone: The Tragedy and the Trial* by Ron Labrecque, and *Outrageous Conduct: Art, Ego, and the Twilight Zone Case* by Stephen Farber and Marc Green, as well as a number of other journalistic sources published at the time and since. These works would provide a fuller and fairer account of the tragedy than can be accomplished here, in brief.

In the wake of the three deaths, Landis and several other set supervisors were charged with criminal negligence and involuntary manslaughter. In the end, he was cleared of the manslaughter charges but reprimanded by the Director's Guild for unprofessional conduct. Landis and his defense attorney, Arnold Klein, maintained that the accident was unforeseeable but that the blame ultimately rests with Camomile, who had the final authority to abort the detonation if he felt that conditions were unsafe. In contrast, prosecutor Lea Purwin D'Agostino argued that, as director, Landis bore the full responsibility for the accident. Her case was built around the idea that Landis approved of the placement of the explosives and did not warn Camomile that the helicopter would be flying closer to the blast zone on this take than it had in previous shots. The prosecutor was also able to produce witnesses on set that testified that Landis was a tyrannical director who barked orders at them all evening, recklessly waived safety precautions, and assigned a night shoot using illegal child labor without adequately warning the parents how dangerous the set would be.

Rolling Stone published an article shortly after the accident that condemned Landis for behaving like a tyrant and a criminal and getting people killed. In response, a number of Hollywood directors wrote a letter of support for Landis and sent it to the magazine, citing the helicopter crash as a horrible, unavoidable accident. Cosigners included Frank Oz, Jim Henson, George Lucas, Francis Coppola, Costa-Gavras, Louis Malle, John Huston, Billy Wilder, Fred Zinnemann, and Ron Howard. Landis has claimed to have never recovered from the trauma. According to his son, Max, Landis thinks about the deaths every day when they are not mentioned to him, and if anyone *does* mention them, he becomes nearly catatonic with grief for at least a day. Naturally, Landis's grief comes as little comfort to the victims of the accident or their friends and families, or those on the crew whom he tried to blame for the accident. Also, his escaping punishment meant that, in some ways, Hollywood felt free to continue to stage reckless stunts and not learn anything at all from the tragedy, although some safety oversight was supposedly installed on each film set in its wake (Vallan 110).

Certainly, the prosecutor of the case had no desire to see Landis make any more films after *Twilight Zone*. According to Ron Labrecque, D'Agostino was one of several to cry during the trial after a screening of the footage taken of the helicopter accident. The prosecutor proclaimed with outrage after viewing the footage, "Mr. Landis' quest for realism exceeded all bounds of safety. And he got his effect. But at what cost?" In court, she told the jury, "He took a gamble with other people's lives and he lost. He lost" (Labrecque).

There are many possible reactions to this story, but perhaps the most obvious apologetic reading would be offered by fans of Landis who think of him first and foremost as the director of the best comedies and horror films of the 1970s and 1980s—*Animal House, Trading Places, The Blues Brothers, Three Amigos!, Coming to America, Beverly Hills Cop III,* and *An American Werewolf in London*. Such fans would likely feel sympathy for his remorse and regard his hubristic fall from grace as being in the tradition of the classic Greek tragic hero. A more skeptical, hostile, or deconstructionist approach to this scenario would be more to argue that Landis was guilty of criminal negligence and the second-degree murder of three people and was exonerated because of his fame and white privilege. A perpetrator of the same crimes who had not been an artist responsible for iconic film comedies or who had been poor or female or an ethnic minority would have been executed or jailed for life, not invited to direct *Coming to America* (1988). Skeptics would not be impressed by Landis's lifetime of remorse, whether or not it is genuine, because regret for committing a sin afterward is nothing compared to having the courage and conscience to not commit the sin in the first place.

Eddie Murphy's reaction was an interesting combination of the above. Murphy had affection for Landis because he enjoyed acting for the director in *Trading Places*, but he had been convinced enough of Landis's guilt that he did not attend the trial. Still, Murphy did hire Landis for *Coming to America* later on to help rescue the director's floundering career. Murphy was surprised to find that, instead of being grateful for being hired, Landis was angry with Murphy for not showing him public support during the trial. As Murphy revealed in a 1990 *Playboy* interview, "I don't want to say who was guilty or who was innocent. [Pauses] But if you're directing a movie and two kids get their heads chopped off at fucking twelve o'clock at night when there ain't supposed to be kids working, and you said, 'Action!' then you have some sort of responsibility. So, my principles wouldn't let me go down there and sit in court. That's just the way I am" (Rensin). For many, Murphy treated Landis with too much generosity by hiring him, and Landis's ungrateful attitude validates that view.

Looking back on the experience in 2003, Landis concluded, "Despite our acquittal, I do think the trial has affected my career. There was so much bad press and untruth repeatedly printed. It is ironic that I was punished partly because of how movie directors have been portrayed in the movies. They're always martinets like Otto Preminger or DeMille or Peter O'Toole in *The Stunt Man*. . . . There are countless movies depicting the director as a lunatic. . . . They are always these mad geniuses" (Vallan 110).

Landis has become enough of a pariah in the film community that he has found himself relating to other pariahs, and he even directed "In Sickness and in Health," a 2008 episode of the NBC horror anthology series *Fear Itself*, which was written by convicted child pornographer and molester Victor Salva, creator of the *Jeepers Creepers* franchise. The story is about a woman who receives on her wedding day a note warning her that the man she is rushing to marry is secretly a serial killer. When the bride seems about to call off the wedding thanks to a shocking allegation made out of the blue by an anonymous stranger, Landis and Salva seem to be suggesting that they, like the groom-to-be, face the prospect of having their new friends and potential loved ones turn on them after finding out about (or being reminded of) the scandals in their respective pasts. It is difficult to know what to make to Landis's collaboration with Salva, ethically, but the episode is artistically and narratively engrossing and nauseating, despite a last-minute plot twist that seems to derail a reading of the episode as wholly applicable to the personal lives of the storytellers bearing the mark of Cain.

In interviews such as the one he gave in 2003, Landis presents himself as wholly innocent of any wrongdoing on the night of the accident. And yet the guilt he has reportedly felt since the accident and the references to it that he has placed in the films he has made since tell a different story. In "The Devils (the Angels): Sympathy for John Landis"—a 2014 *Bright Lights Film Journal* article—Steve Johnson argues that there are two sides to John Landis's personality: the deeply moral liberal and the petulant and unrepentant survivalist. Johnson sees both Landis figures in each of his films, both before and after the accident, and he finds himself particularly drawn to moments in Landis's post-accident films that seem to morbidly reference the accident through staging decapitations and depicting accidental deaths. Johnson writes that "for the critical viewer (as well as one with his or her own less-than-spotless conscience) it can make the films themselves a fascinating and confounding exercise—though seldom less than an experience. What makes Landis the artist tolerable is the sense that on some level Landis the moralist sees what he has done and will not let himself off the hook, even if the world (and Landis the survivalist) have managed to do just that." Johnson is also interested in any moral reaction a given viewer of a Landis film would have in light of the accident. He argues that any viewer's determination of whether Landis is guilty or innocent reveals more about the viewer than it does about Landis. He writes, "Any who try to reconstruct the *Zone* incident without having been there are in effect fashioning their own Twilight Zone, with their own reasons for assigning guilt or responsibility. None who attempt such is entirely innocent, either."

While it is possible one might object to Johnson's article on the grounds that it violates the taboo against discussing authorial intent in literary and film criticism, the textual evidence he provides is compelling. Furthermore, John Farrell has published a compelling defense of "the authorial fallacy" in his 2017 monograph *The Varieties of Authorial Intention*, which has opened up some much-needed space for cultural critics to discuss authorial intention without being castigated unreasonably for "committing the authorial fallacy." Both Johnson's work and Farrell's justify an effort to see Landis's work as writer and director after the *Twilight Zone* tragedy as imbued with a sense of that tragedy.

Johnson is most concerned with how Landis sneaks a depiction of himself as tragic hero into his film *Burke and Hare* (2010) via dialogue about Shakespeare's morally ambiguous Macbeth. However, it is a 2005 *Masters of Horror* episode, "Deer Woman"—which Landis not only directed but cowrote with his son Max—that is even more illustrative of Landis's willingness to adapt his own real-life guilt into film. Arguably, Landis filmed an odd stealth apology in the form of that television episode. The short-film entry into the Showtime anthology series is about a grief-stricken, eternally listless police detective named Dwight Faraday (played by Brian Benben). When Faraday is assigned a new partner, Officer Jacob Reed (Anthony Griffith), Faraday warns Reed that he's a dangerous man to work with. He explains that he accidentally shot and killed his old partner, Ted Neiman, during a sting operation in which the two were trying to apprehend a dangerous killer. A believer in redemption, Reed harbors some hope that Faraday eventually recovered from the trauma of his partner's death. Faraday makes it clear he has not. As he explains:

> There was this big investigation and for a while a few people said that I planned it—that I'd meant to shoot Ted—but eventually the whole thing was dismissed as an accident. But people don't forget so easy. . . . So, I was pretty fucked up in the thick of it, you know, and I was always out of it and doped on antidepressants, my wife left me, and I lost most of my friends, and then I had this kind of realization . . . I just realized that we all have our time to make our mark on this planet. And all I'd done with my time was get a decent man killed. That's the mark I made on the earth.

It is not possible for anyone familiar with the *Twilight Zone* trial to view this scene and not see it as Landis's adaptation of his own, real-life experience of the helicopter accident into the experience of his fictional police officer protagonist. Viewing the scene in this vein, Faraday acts as a stand-in for Landis and speaks for Landis. What he reveals is that Landis simultaneously believes the accident was indeed a freak accident but that he nevertheless sees himself as the cause of the deaths of Morrow and the two children. While this confession seems shocking and unprecedented, it would not be the first time a storyteller adapted their own real-life experiences into a horror story, nor would it be the only time a storyteller confessed a dark secret in a horror story, or adapted their real lives into a Gothic, allegorical autobiography.

Literary critics have written extensively about how Dante wrote his own real-life experiences into the proto-Gothic epic poem *Inferno*, how Oscar Wilde's real life shaped *The Picture of Dorian Gray* (1890), how Charlotte Perkins Gilman transmuted a harrowing experience into 1892's "The Yellow Wallpaper," and how the premature deaths of the women in Edgar Allan Poe's life inspired any number of his short stories about hauntingly beautiful deceased women. As Stephen King himself revealed in his treatise *On Writing* (2000), three of his most autobiographical works include the coming-of-age novella *The Body* (1982), adapted as the film *Stand by Me* (1986); *Misery* (1987), which creates an allegorical story of King's efforts to rid himself of drug addiction; and *The Shining* (1977), which portrays King at his most destructively patriarchal, and his wife at her most heroic for standing against him.

Horror films have been similarly autobiographical. In the 2015 documentary *De Palma*, American *giallo* director Brian De Palma described how scenes from his suspense films *Dressed to Kill* (1980) and *Raising Cain* (1992) were pulled directly from his own life. Autobiographical divorce storylines are a notable feature of several classic horror films. David Cronenberg's *The Brood* (1979) is widely known to be made in the wake of his divorce and reflective of his state of mind at the time. As angry as *The Brood* is, *Possession* (1981), cowritten and directed by Andrzej Żuławski, is angrier still. *Possession* is about the dissolution of the marriage of characters played by Isabelle Adjani and Sam Neill, who are obvious stand-ins for Żuławski and his wife, since Żuławski was going through a traumatic divorce as he worked on the screenplay. In interviews, Żuławski was asked repeatedly whether he had any regrets demonizing his wife by proxy, or compelling Adjani to fuck a Carlo Rambaldi tentacle monster on screen, but he stated that he had a right as an artist to do anything he wanted and, besides, the film camera was created to "penetrate" women and he was only using the invention the way it was intended to be used (*Possession*).

In addition to being used to depict disintegrating marriages, the horror film has arguably been the medium by which accused and convicted sex offenders have either planned their crimes in advance or confessed to their guilt in retrospect. For example, Roger Gunson, the assistant district attorney who handled the Roman Polanski rape case, used Polanski's movies as evidence against the director—including 1968's *Rosemary's Baby*—because of a frequently recurring motif of women being sexually assaulted beside or immersed in a body of water. Polanski had been accused of raping thirteen-year-old Samantha Geimer inside a Jacuzzi.

Perhaps most disturbing of all, Victor Salva arguably "reenacted" his sexual molestation of twelve-year-old Nathan Forrest Winters—an actor in his first film, *Clownhouse* (1989)—in a movie he wrote and directed after serving fifteen months in prison for the crime. The main storyline of *Jeepers Creepers* (2001) involves a seemingly invincible and relentless predatory creature's pursuit of a teenage boy along a lonely stretch of Florida highway. The monster is a clear stand-in for Salva, especially when it picks up the boy's scent by sniffing his underwear. The teenage Justin Long is a clear proxy for Winters. The franchise is further problematized by a scene in the third installment, in which a man argues that a thirteen-year-old girl's stepfather can't be blamed for trying to molest her: "Can you blame him, though? I mean look at her. The heart wants what it wants, am I right?" The sympathetic portrayal of child molestation in the film series is salt in the wounds of those who would have thought that Salva should not have been allowed to continue making films even if he were truly repentant for what he'd done. Since the films indicated a lack of penitence, efforts have been made to prevent their theatrical and home video distribution and keep profits from their sales from going to Salva.

If there is a spectrum of self-awareness exhibited by the makers of stealth autobiographical horror films, then Salva appears to be on the extreme end of self-congratulatory and unrepentant, and David Cronenberg is one of the more self-critical auteurs. During the course of his long career, the Canadian director best known for making gory body-horror films directed *Scanners*, *Videodrome*, *Dead Ringers*, *A History of Violence*, *Eastern Promises*, the remake of *The Fly*, and the literary adaptations *Crash*, *The Dead Zone*, *Naked Lunch*, and *Cosmopolis*. Despite seemingly skewering his ex-wife in *The Brood*, in many of his films Cronenberg shows a self-awareness of his own darkness and questions the artist's right to make art at the expense of other people, especially of women. Scholar William Beard, author of *The Artist as Monster: The Cinema of David Cronenberg* (2006 revised edition), writes:

> Cronenberg's work is relentlessly self-prodding, one might almost say narcissistically so. Perhaps the first area it delved inward to explore was transgressive desire, what was desired but forbidden, or desired

because it was forbidden. But . . . the works themselves simultaneously have presented a counter-narrative that showed the human cost of transgression—the cost to others, the ethical cost. . . . Transgression in these works eventually comes to coalesce in some crucial way around the area of male heterosexual sadistic desire. The cost of this desire is that it hurts another (female) human being, or simply that it *wants* to hurt one; it is this cost which finally rebounds upon the (male) subject himself to such an extent that it renders him an ethical monster in his own eyes and a biological monster as a physical metaphorization of his condition; the last stage of this monster-male is one of profound, suicidal melancholy. I see this process as a growth in the films' self-understanding, and as really coming into focus in *Videodrome* (1982) and the films that followed it. During this period of what is visually a kind of self-accusation, there is also a strong shift towards depicting the central male's project as something like artistic creation. . . . Hence this book's title, *The Artist as Monster.*

Where does John Landis fit into this tradition of confessional, autobiographical horror? He inhabits a world somewhere between the wholly unrepentant Salva's and the wholly self-aware Cronenberg's, which means that his "confessional" horror film "Deer Woman" is only partially successful as an apology—it strives toward authenticity but falls short of full believability. The fact that "Deer Woman" is an obscure short film makes the "shit happens"-style statement made by Faraday seem far too removed from the more public, less mediated forum of the trial itself. Also, the police officer's angry and self-pitying dialogue comes off as too self-justifying by half. And yet the monologue's highly evocative and explosive coda ("all I'd done with my time was get a decent man killed") slightly salvages what appears to be a non-apology apology, granting it enormous emotional power and psychological weight. The combined effect of all of the above is that Landis and his police officer proxy character emerge as more monstrous and terrifying to any viewer familiar with the *Twilight Zone* tragedy than the titular folk creature, "Deer Woman," does within the context of the horror-comedy short.

This observation, of course, raises the question of what an authentic apology or conversion narrative would look like, whether made through a fictionalized, allegorized autobiographical narrative or a more straightforward, literal autobiographical narrative. The classic template for the autobiography is Augustine's *Confessions*, which is a conversion narrative that is at once an autobiographical and a theological document. The intertwined conventions of autobiography and conversion narrative inform the aesthetics of the confessional, autobiographical horror narrative as a form of "real-life story" adapted into fiction. Consider Vincent Pollina's discussion of confessional autobiography in his 2009 *MLN* essay "Syntax, Confession, and Creation: Reflections on Dante, Augustine, and Saussure":

> Confessional autobiography plays on the sequential aspects of nar-ration. Works belonging to the genre are written by the subject, who underwent the experiences related therein. The end-point of the con-fession cannot therefore coincide with the close of the story itself, which is, by definition, the end of the life recounted. . . . Christian autobiography may lead gradually to the moment of conversion: the turning-from-self-and-turning to God that introduces a decisive rup-ture in the chain of events. The incorporation of this striking para-digmatic element may shed new light on all that went before it, while illuminating that which follows. The perspective from which such a story is told is frequently that of the "death" of a moral crisis occur-ring prior to the moment of conversion. This crucial circumstance, necessarily arising before the syntactic end-point, will constitute, in the midst of life, the occasion of re-birth.

In the case of works of "confessional autobiography" by horror genre sto-rytellers, the trajectory of the narrative is not usually toward conversion to Christianity per se, but instead to a realization that the confessor committed a form of life-marring, life-ending, or life-destroying sin against another person that needs acknowledging and confessing. Better still, the confessing storyteller knows that penance must be paid and reparations made—provid-ing the victim either wants or is in a position to accept apologies and repara-tions. Since Gothic horror is frequently concerned with the dark underbelly of noble people, institutions, and intentions, it would stand to reason that a Gothic confession or a Gothic conversion narrative is interesting not only for the way it depicts a subject striving to escape from the chains of a sinful past, but for the way in which such a confession comes off as insincere, presented by a Poe- or Nabokov-style unreliable narrator, or fails to fully redeem the penitent telling the story, despite (possibly/partially) good intentions.

   One question that remains fraught for contemporary film aficionados is whether or not Quentin Tarantino has sufficiently made amends to Uma Thurman for the wrongs he did her. The two met in late 2019 to discuss the possibility of reteaming to make a third installment of the *Kill Bill* franchise, suggesting that Thurman herself is at least open to the possibility of absolv-ing him of some of his guilt in permanently damaging her body. And yet there remains the possibility that she may be being too generous to him in contemplating or granting that forgiveness.

On February 3, 2018, Uma Thurman told *New York Times* reporter Maureen Dowd that "she has been raped [by Harvey Weinstein]. She has been sexually assaulted. She has been mangled in hot steel. She has been betrayed and gaslighted by those she trusted." In that same article, Dowd relates Thurman's story of how she was crippled driving a stunt car during the filming of *Kill Bill*—a stunt car she had begged Tarantino not to be forced to drive. While filming *Kill Bill*, Thurman learned from members of the film crew that the car in question was not safe and would be best driven by a stunt person, not herself. When she passed her fears on to Tarantino and begged off driving the car herself, he bullied her into doing it anyway. As Thurman explained, "Quentin came in my trailer and didn't like to hear no, like any director. He was furious because I'd cost them a lot of time. But I was scared. He said: 'I promise you the car is fine. It's a straight piece of road.'" Tarantino ordered her: "'Hit 40 miles per hour or your hair won't blow the right way and I'll make you do it again.' But that was a deathbox that I was in. The seat wasn't screwed down properly. It was a sand road and it was not a straight road." The car crashed and caused her a concussion and a lifetime of neck and knee damage and pain ever since.

Tarantino has denied brow-beating Thurman into doing the stunt herself, has emphasized that he test-drove the car himself to see that it was safe beforehand, and has questioned Thurman's skill as a driver. Despite these denials and obfuscations, he has said he has regretted that day his whole life. He regrets how the day's events hurt Thurman and permanently damaged their friendship. After the publication of the Dowd piece, Tarantino told *Deadline*'s Mike Fleming Jr., "Me and Uma had our issues about the crash. She blamed me for the crash and she had a right to blame me for the crash. I didn't mean to do it. I talked her into getting in the car, I assured her the road was safe. And it wasn't. The car might even have been dubious too even if I didn't know that then. We had our issues about it."

Several of Tarantino's statements seem designed to exonerate himself from criminal prosecution, lawsuits, and public opprobrium. Those attempts to blame the road for being worse than he thought or to accuse the crew of not informing him adequately of the unreliability of the stunt car seem especially deflective. The worst offense might be his claim that Uma has the right to blame him. If Tarantino does, indeed, feel that he is innocent of any real wrongdoing, it is somewhat surprising that he adds to these statements, "It's the biggest regret of my life, getting her to do that stunt." Tarantino walks a tightrope between "responsible" and "culpable," on the one hand, and "legally" and "morally" guilty, on the other. It is not clear based on his statement in the interview if his self-assessment is in constant flux, if he is sure of what he did and why, or if what he told *Deadline* at that particular moment, following the release of the explosive Dowd article, is what he would say today.

Since the interview Thurman has praised Tarantino for releasing the footage of the accident and condemned Weinstein for suppressing that same footage for years. Thurman wrote, "Quentin Tarantino was deeply regretful and remains remorseful about this sorry event, and gave me the footage years later so I could expose it and let it see the light of day, regardless of it most likely being an event for which justice will never be possible. He also did so with full knowledge it could cause him personal harm, and I am proud of him for doing the right thing and for his courage." By Thurman's reasoning, Tarantino's feelings of remorse are genuine; his desire to make amends and do penance motivated him in helping her make the story of her personal tragedy public. If her instincts are correct, then her assessment of his sustained emotional state and behavior to her over time matters more than the perhaps questionable word choice Tarantino employed during one *Deadline* interview given at one moment in time.

Furthermore, while Tarantino's direct, real-life "apology" to Thurman in the *Deadline* article seemed qualified, defensive, and deeply inadequate, the allegorical confession he made in film in *Death Proof* years earlier was notably sincerer and more melodramatic. If that film is to be read as the art he made in response to Thurman's accident, then it indicates that Tarantino privately accepts more of the blame for the accident than he was willing to own up to overtly in his *Deadline* interview. *Death Proof*, the very next film Tarantino made after *Kill Bill*, was marketed as a mindless tribute to the exploitation cinema of the 1960s and 1970s that Tarantino grew up watching on video and in grindhouse cinemas, but it was, in actual fact, a bizarre and pseudo-allegorical retelling of Thurman's accident. The film is about a serial killer called Stuntman Mike (Kurt Russell) who picks up beautiful women in his armored sports car and crashes it on purpose at high speeds, knowing that his driver's seat is well insulated and that his passengers will be killed on impact. Eventually he crosses paths with a group of women who turn the tables on him and avenge all those he's butchered by killing him. Among the women who bring him to vigilante justice is Uma Thurman's real-life stunt double Zoë Bell, playing herself. The film is grotesque and makes Stuntman Mike a little too "cool," but it suggests that Tarantino himself is represented by Mike, and that Zoë Bell is fighting Mike on behalf of Thurman. Read in this way, the movie ends with "Thurman" killing "Tarantino" in the car he forced her to drive. As veiled public apologies go, it is compelling.

In *Rape-Revenge Films: A Critical Study* (2011), Alexandra Heller-Nicholas observes that *Death Proof* operates as a rape-revenge film by quoting the tropes of famous films in the genre, such as the Australian film *Fair Game* (1986) but also by depicting the murders perpetrated by Stuntman Mike as symbolic rapes: "*Death Proof* is unambiguous in its linkage of sexual violence with vehicular homicide (both attempted and otherwise). In the first part of the film, Sheriff McGraw makes it clear that he views Stuntman Mike's behavior as 'a sex thing.'" Heller-Nicholas concludes that the "relationship between Stuntman Mike and these female protagonists is . . . more than a case of the latter seeking revenge for thinly disguised metaphorical sexual violence. It is about them reconfiguring the entire symbolic language of gender in relation to car culture, so commonly ascribed as a masculine domain."

If one were to pair Heller-Nicholas's interpretation of *Death Proof* with the contention that it is Tarantino's stealth apology to Uma Thurman, then—in the terms of the film—Tarantino is apologizing for not only critically injuring Thurman but symbolically raping her in the process, justifying his condemnation and punishment as a rapist by Stuntman Mike proxy through the narrative conventions of the rape-revenge film. Furthermore, if one were to interpret the "car culture" depicted in *Death Proof* as a proxy for Hollywood culture writ large, then the film expresses Tarantino's (subconscious?) wish that women will finally take over Hollywood and rewrite their role as dominant figures in the industry from this time forth. Tarantino might be saying, "I'm sorry that I raped my feminist friend" when he is hiding behind a horror film narrative of *Death Proof*, but he seems to be far cagier about his level of culpability when discussing the actual accident with an actual news reporter for *Deadline*.

Thurman's revelation of the covered-up car accident during *Kill Bill* tarred Tarantino's reputation in 2018 but did not derail his efforts to complete production of *Once Upon a Time . . . in Hollywood*—a film about the murder of Polanski's wife, Sharon Tate, by members of the Manson family—or completely halt the on-again, off-again negotiations between Tarantino and Paramount concerning his desire to direct a future *Star Trek* film. Nevertheless, the luster has faded from Tarantino's star. "Melissa Silverstein, founder and publisher of *Women in Hollywood*, a gender equality initiative and film news site [said this appeared to be] a watershed moment for the director that could have lasting impact on his career. 'This feels epic. I think people are really disgusted,' she told the *Guardian*. . . . 'There are a lot of men in our culture who are put up to us as visionaries and auteurs. . . . The stories that we've been told about them are stories that are based on a culture that is now no longer acceptable. We all want to ask the question, why are these people and why are these films the narrative of our culture? We are saying we want different kinds of narratives, and we want different kinds of stories."

It is a salient question. If the winning side writes history, then the perpetrators of crimes against women, working-class men, ethnic minorities, and even nature get to depict themselves as unabashedly heroic, or as tragic heroes or charismatic villains, while the stories of their victims go untold, or are granted far less dramatic weight. As much as *Death Proof* and "Deer Woman" have an undertone of self-flagellation, they are ultimately about the perpetrators, not the victims. Uma Thurman has not yet made her film turning her experience into art, and Vic Morrow's daughter, Jennifer Jason Leigh, has not made a film about the *Twilight Zone* accident. Furthermore, Morrow and the children are no longer alive to simply live their lives or to appear in more films. For her part, Uma Thurman appeared poised to become a major action star after *Kill Bill*, but the aftermath of the accident and her feud with Tarantino and Weinstein helped derail her career, making one wonder, rightfully, where Uma Thurman's *Inglorious Basterds* and *Django Unchained* are. It is hard to quantify lost work and lost opportunities, but there is a real human and artistic cost to the damage done to Thurman's acting career by the car accident.

Tarantino and Landis are more famous than their victims, and perhaps it is their fame that is part and parcel of the impulse to exonerate them. The extent to which they feel remorse (or don't) is notable. Tarantino has apologized to Thurman and the female victims of Harvey Weinstein after he consistently failed to grant adequate credence to their stories as victims. Sorry as he might be, Tarantino has not, possibly, paid as many reparations as he should. Kevin Smith, in contrast, has promised to donate all future dividends of the movies he made under Harvey Weinstein to the nonprofit organization Women in Film. Smith couldn't reconcile the success he had as a filmmaker writing and directing *Clerks*, *Dogma*, and *Chasing Amy* under Harvey Weinstein with the wrecked lives and careers of women Weinstein left in his wake. As Smith observed, "No f*cking movie is worth all this. Like, my entire career, f*ck it, take it. It's wrapped up in something really f*cking horrible. I know it's not my fault, but I didn't f*cking help. I sat out there talking about this man like he was a hero, like he was my friend, like he was my father and shit like that."

Whatever sense of human decency or Catholic guilt that motivated the religious Kevin Smith's decision to act to make things better in the future has not motivated Tarantino to make reparations for the damage he has done to the same degree. Arguably, Tarantino has committed far greater sins against women than Smith has. Ultimately, it is up to Weinstein's victims, to

Thurman, and the families of those killed in the *Twilight Zone* accident to decide when Tarantino, Landis, Smith, and Weinstein have paid enough for what they have done. It is not up to these men to decide when they can stop atoning because they are weary of being asked to do so, because it was all so long ago anyway, and don't they deserve a chance to live the rest of their lives in peace? No, it is not up to them to decide when their penance is over. Indeed, if the victims just want to be left alone, and do not even want to have any contact with their victimizers whatsoever—even contact that may well involve a sincere attempt at making amends—then that is their right. These people who have truly suffered deserve agency over their own lives and have the right to live their lives without having to contend with the feelings and careers of their famous tormentors, as well as mass media coverage of all of their interactions.

One of the ironies of the *Kill Bill* tragedy is that Tarantino was making a film about empowering women while taking power away from Thurman. He operated from the assumption that he was a good man while he wrote male villains in his films who were monstrous in their sexism. It seems as if, during the time he was making the film, and in the period that followed, Tarantino was willing to dramatically depict certain men as evil in his films but was willing to doubt or deflect accusations leveled against his financier, Harvey Weinstein—even not giving adequate credence to those made by his girlfriend Mira Sorvino and friend Uma Thurman—and even fail to recognize his own worst patriarchal and self-aggrandizing tendencies. In this manner he exhibits a classic "good guy" and #MeToo ally flaw.

At the *Hollywood Reporter*'s 2018 Women in Entertainment gala, comedian Hannah Gadsby critiqued supposedly liberal male stand-up comedians like Jimmy Kimmel and Jimmy Fallon, who are fair-weather allies of victimized women. Certainly, they are capable of condemning serial rapists like Weinstein and Bill Cosby as monstrous—so monstrous that they are not of the same species as Kimmel and Fallon and cannot, in any way, reflect their actual or potential behaviors and attitudes as men, she said. However, they sometimes use cutesy and euphemistic terms when discussing Weinstein and Cosby by dubbing them "creepy" men. In contrast, when any celebrity that they know personally commits an act of sexual violence that is anything short of serial rapist behavior, the two Jimmys redraw the line of moral acceptability and defend their friends as having committed a worse-than-usual faux-pas. That kind of male ally is not of much use, if any, Gadsby explained, especially since the line of acceptable behavior should be drawn by actual women, not male nighttime talk show hosts (Steiner). Tarantino's behavior on the set of *Kill Bill* suggests that he saw himself as a "Good Man" in the same way that "the Jimmys" do. Tarantino regarded himself as an ally to women, who knows full well when men are being evil, as he was able to pit his feminist heroine, Beatrix Kiddo, against a slew of loathsome males capable of committing an array of patriarchial sins. Unfortunately, as aware of male evil as he was, Tarantino did not realize that he was treating Thurman much the same way his male villains treated Kiddo. He may have been too convinced of his own brilliance as a director and righteousness as a morally correct male-feminist to notice that he was betraying his friendship with Thurman, undercutting her agency, and endangering her life. This is something he appears to recognize in retrospect. The part of him that made *Death Proof* does, anyway. Consequently, *Death Proof* is a more self-aware, self-critical allegorical apology than "Deer Woman." Tarantino's art dramatizes that he is more emotionally and psychologically capable of accepting responsibility for what happened on the set of *Kill Bill* than Landis has been of accepting responsibility for the deaths that occurred during the shooting of *Twilight Zone*. Of the two films, *Death Proof* seems to be the more authentic and successful apology. And yet the problematic nature of Landis's more ambivalent "Deer Woman" dialogue makes Landis's horror film more challenging for the audience to interpret and contemplate.

In the final analysis, what is to be made of the pseudo-confessions of Landis and Tarantino—confessions offered up so allegorically that it isn't clear their intended audiences were even aware that apologies were made? Is an apology, made in such a manner, even "worth" anything, morally speaking? Should fans of these directors take these confessions at face value, as authentic expressions of remorse, and weigh those in the director's favor? In some ways these films do demonstrate more remorse and thoughtfulness than public statements made by either Landis or Tarantino. The filmmakers might not have even written those public apologies. It is quite likely that those statements were at least partly drafted by lawyers and publicists. They sound as though they are looking to deflect blame, prevent fines and jail time, and argue that the resultant film was great at least as much as they want to offer an apology. Like the other #MeToo pseudo apologies of Louis C. K. and Dustin Hoffman, there is always an "I'm sorry you were offended" quality to the apologies that shifts blame to the victim and exonerates the perpetrator. Rhetoric scholars such as Ferdinand de Saussure, I. A. Richards, J. L. Austin, and Mary Daly would be familiar with the narrative technique, obfuscation, and performative nature of the self-exonerating, non-apology "apology." It is a classic, long-standing form of what Plato would consider "sophistry." In contrast to Landis's and Tarantino's non-apology apologies to the courts and the court of public opinion, the satirical and confessional horror narratives "Deer Woman" and *Death Proof* do not let these men off the hook to the same degree, though Landis's work is certainly not as self-flagellating as Tarantino's. Perhaps in a work of fictional horror allegory, these men are freer to be more honest? Horror is designed both to condemn and exonerate, to celebrate and disgust.

On some level, Tarantino and Landis both know they are Dracula. They are the tortured artist and the fascist filmmaker all at once. Tarantino tried to make a feminist revenge film that crippled his feminist best friend. Landis tried to make an antiwar film that killed two Vietnamese children. These men took risks on behalf of their own cast and crew, gambling with the lives of others, because they thought they were invincible and could place a cloak of invincibility over their whole set. After all, the industry itself, its folklore, and its history of stories of Hitchcock making *The Birds* and Friedkin making *The Exorcist* all stand behind the director's right as an artist to push the envelope of safety in the name of their art. It was an act of hubris. Landis and Tarantino experienced a tragic fall not unlike so many tragic heroes.

Or is it an insult to the victims of the accidents to consider these men tragic heroes? Perhaps we should ask Uma Thurman and the friends and family of those killed on the set of *Twilight Zone* if they appreciate the term "hero" being applied to either director, even with the word "tragic" appended to it. Certainly, a "tragic hero" title does not wash the guilt and the blood off the hands of all of those Hollywood executives and artists who fed upon starstruck would-be movie stars who had the temerity to want to have a career in film without having to allow themselves to be molested as a form of universally accepted hazing.

In "I Want a Twenty-Four-Hour Truce during Which There Is No Rape" (1983), Andrea Dworkin asserted that women no longer have time or sympathy for any man who spends his life regretting raping a woman, beating a woman, murdering a woman, sexually harassing a woman, whoremongering, or consuming endless quantities of porn. What women want from men is that they not do any of these things in the first place. In fact, if men even refrained from doing these, as a gender, for one whole day, it would be an unprecedented miracle and the beginning of true freedom and peace on Earth. Such a ceasefire has never happened; instead, feminists are greeted by an endless stream of "good men" who do not commit these crimes (#NotAll-Men) but also do not do enough to speak out against such atrocities. Worse, there are those who commit these crimes and see those moments as some sort of character-building exercise, or as giving their life a romantically tragic gloss. Dworkin explains, "Hiding behind guilt. That's my favorite. I love that one. Oh, it's horrible, yes, and I'm so sorry. You have the time to feel guilty. We don't have the time for you to feel guilty. Your guilt is a form of acquiescence in what continues to occur. Your guilt helps keep things the way they are."

Dworkin's argument is the most compelling one on the side of the victims of Hollywood's #MeToo. Stack against Dworkin's argument the reverse—that the pain caused by Friedkin, Hitchcock, Polanski, Tarantino, and Landis is morally justifiable because that pain was part of the alchemy that created the great films *The Exorcist, The Birds, Rosemary's Baby, Kill Bill Vol. 1* and *2,* and *Twilight Zone: The Movie*—and suddenly those films don't seem worth the high cost of their creation, no matter how many of them are among "the best films ever made." Yes, these movies are great. Who cares? Rose McGowan has been driven to the edge of sanity by being raped and abused her entire career, Uma Thurman has a lifetime of pain from a permanent car accident injury, and Vic Morrow and Myca Dinh Le and Shin-Yi Chen are dead. None of the resulting films are great enough to justify these people's losses. They really are not.

The Hollywood filmmaker is one of the premier monsters of our time—a time replete with monsters. During the modern era, we have seen America enter a new Gilded Age on the path to becoming a real-world Gilead. We are living in a time of industrial capitalism unchained, the climate crisis, and the war on women. All of these evils are linked in an ascendant global fascism's assault on the values of ecofeminism. Providing films—the bread and circuses of a cruel society—Hollywood filmmakers and producers place profit and artistic standards above the safety and happiness of the cast and crew members who make the films. Such attitudes and reckless decision-making renders filmmakers as monstrous. These filmmakers—Landis and Tarantino among them—are monsters. Perhaps redeemable and forgivable. Perhaps not. But they are monsters, nonetheless. They are monsters in that they are both appealing and repellent at the same time; in that we see ourselves in both them and their victims; and in that they represent a portent of a wider set of social ills. There is much we can learn from them about how not to act, so that we, in our own way, can do our part to not join them in their monstrousness or in mirroring and duplicating their tragic mistakes.

Works Cited

Beard, William. *The Artist as Monster: The Cinema of David Cronenberg.* Toronto: U of Toronto P, 2006, x–xi.

Bramesco, Charles. "William Friedkin: 'You Don't Know a Damn Thing, and Neither Do I.'" *Guardian.* 24 April 2018. Accessed 23 August 2020. https://www.theguardian.com/ film/2018/apr/24/william-friedkin-interview-exorcist-director-you-dont-know-a-damn -thing-and-neither-do-i.

Carroll, Rory. "'I Think People Are Really Disgusted'—Quentin Tarantino Faces Hollywood Backlash." *Guardian*, 7 February 2018. theguardian.com/film/2018/feb/07/quentin-taran tino-hollywood-baclkash-uma-thurman-roman-polanski. Accessed 7 December 2018.

"CSX to Pay $3.9M for Train Crash That Killed Movie Crew Member Sarah Jones." *USA Today*, 18 July 2017. usatoday.com/story/life/movies/2017/07/18/jury-railroad-to-pay-39m-for -train-death-of-film-worker/103790804/. Accessed 9 December 2018.

D'Alessandro, Anthony. "Kevin Smith to Donate Dividends from Weinstein-Made Movies to Women in Film." *Deadline*, 18 October 2017. deadline.com/2017/10/harvey-weintein -kevin-smith-wif-donation-1202190654/. Accessed 9 December 2018.

Davies, Caroline. "Harvey Weinstein: The Women Who Have Accused Him." *Guardian*, 13 October 2017. web.archive.org/web/20171014073346/https://www.theguardian.com/ film/2017/oct/11/the-allegations-against-harvey-weinstein-what-we-know-so-far. Accessed 7 December 2018.

De Palma. Directed by Noah Baumbach and Jake Paltrow. Empire Ward Pictures, 2015.

Dowd, Maureen. "This Is Why Uma Thurman Is Angry: The Actress Is Finally Ready to Talk about Harvey Weinstein." *New York Times*, 3 February 2018. nytimes.com/2018/02/03/ opinion/sunday/this-is-why-uma-thurman-is-angry.html. Accessed 7 December 2018.

Dworkin, Andrea. "I Want a Twenty-Four-Hour Truce during Which There Is No Rape." *Available Means: An Anthology of Women's Rhetoric(s)*, edited by Joy Ritchie and Kate Ronald, Pittsburgh: University of Pittsburgh Press, 2001, 333.

Farber, Stephen, and Marc Green. *Outrageous Conduct: Art, Ego, and the* Twilight Zone *Case*. Maryland: Arbor House, 1988.

Farrell, John. *The Varieties of Authorial Intention*. London: Palgrave Macmillan, 2017.

Fleming, Mike Jr. "Quentin Tarantino Explains Everything: Uma Thurman, The *Kill Bill* Crash & Harvey Weinstein." *Deadline*, 5 February 2018. deadline.com/2018/02/quentin-taran tino-uma-thurman-harvey-weinstein-kill-bill-car-crash-new-york-times-1202278988/. Accessed 7 December 2018.

Heller-Nicholas, Alexandra. *Rape-Revenge Films: A Critical Study*. Jefferson: McFarland, 2011, 158–59.

Johnson, Steve. "The Devils (the Angels): Sympathy for John Landis." *Bright Lights Film Journal*, 9 July 2014. brightlightsfilm.com/wp-content/cache/all/devils-angels-sympathy -john-landis/#.XA2hp2hKhPY. Accessed 9 December 2018.

King, Stephen. *On Writing: A Memoir of the Craft*. New York: Scribner, 2010.

Kreps, Daniel. "Quentin Tarantino Clarifies Role in Uma Thurman's *Kill Bill* Car Crash." *Rolling Stone*, 6 February 2018. rollingstone.com/movies/movie-news/quentin-tarantino -clarifies-role-in-uma-thurmans-kill-bill-car-crash-203753/. Accessed 7 December 2018.

Labrecque, Ron. *Special Effects: Disaster at Twilight Zone: The Tragedy and the Trial*. New York: Scribner. 1988.

Pollina, Vincent. "Syntax, Confession, and Creation: Reflections on Dante, Augustine, and Saussure." *MLN*, Comparative Literature Issue Supplement: Special Issue in Honor of J. Freccero: Fifty Years with Dante and Italian Literature, vol. 124, no. 5 (December 2009), p. S98.

Possession. Directed by Andrzej Żuławski. Performances by Sam Neill and Isabelle Adjani. DVD commentary. Anchor Bay/Starz, 2000

Rensin, David. "Playboy Interview: Eddie Murphy." *Playboy*, February 1990.

Rife, Katie. "An Incomplete, Depressingly Long List of Celebrities' Sexual Assault And Harassment Stories [UPDATED]." *AV Club*, 22 November 2017. avclub.com/an-incomplete-depressingly-long-list-of-celebrities-se-1819628519. Accessed 7 December 2018.

Sager, Jessica. "Corey Feldman Titles Sex Abuse Film 'Truth: The Rape of 2 Coreys.'" *Page Six*, 23 October 2018. pagesix.com/2018/10/23/corey-feldman-titles-sex-abuse-film-truth-the-rape-of-2-coreys/. Accessed 7 December 2018.

Sini, Rozina. "How 'MeToo' Is Exposing the Scale of Sexual Abuse." *BBC News*, 16 October 2017. bbc.com/news/blogs-trending-41633857. Accessed 7 December 2018.

Skal, David J. *The Monster Show: A Cultural History of Horror*. New York: Farrar, Straus and Giroux, 2001.

Steiner, Chelsea. "Hannah Gadsby Delivers an Emotional Speech Calling Out 'Good Men.'" *Mary Sue*. 6 December 2018. themarysue.com/hannah-gadsby-good-men/?utm_source=web&gutm_medium=bitch&utm_campaign=linkswap. Accessed 10 December 2018.

"The Technician Whose Special Effects Explosions Caused a Fatal . . ." *UPI Archives*. 2 December 1986. upi.com/Archives/1986/12/02/The-technician-whose-special-effects-explosions-caused-a-fatal/2300383665428/#ixzz5ZBgqF6Ta. Accessed 9 December 2018.

Thurman, Uma. "I post this clip to memorialize . . ." *Instagram*, 5 Feb. 2018. https://www.instagram.com/p/Beox6OCFRwQ/?utm_source=ig_embed.

Vallan, Giulia D'Agnolo. *John Landis*. Milwaukie, OR: M Press, 2003.

CONTRIBUTORS

ZOE BURSZTAJN-ILLINGWORTH is a doctoral candidate in the department of English at the University of Texas at Austin. She received her bachelor's degree from Reed College in Portland, Oregon. Her research focuses on the intersection of modern and contemporary American poetry, contemporary narrative film, poetic theory, and film theory.

MARC DIPAOLO is associate professor of English at Southwestern Oklahoma State University and treasurer of the Working-Class Studies Association. He is the author of *Fire and Snow: Climate Fiction from the Inklings to* Game of Thrones (2018), *War, Politics, and Superheroes* (2011), and *Emma Adapted: Jane Austen's Heroine from Book to Film* (2007). He is the editor of anthologies on Mike Leigh, Ozu, and working-class comic book characters. He has published autobiographical comics on *Okie Comics* online.

EMINE AKKÜLAH DOĞAN is a research assistant and PhD candidate in the English language and literature department at Hacettepe University. She holds an MA degree from the same department, having written a thesis entitled *The Picture in Dorian Gray: Object Agency and Oscar Wilde's Decadent Ideas in* The Picture of Dorian Gray *and Its Screen Adaptations* (2018). Her research interests include the nineteenth-century novel, adaptation studies, cultural studies, and "thing theory."

CAROLINE EADES is associate professor of French, film, and comparative studies at the University of Maryland. Her research interests include European cinema, postcolonial studies, film, and mythology. She is the coeditor of *The Essay Film: Dialogue, Politics, Utopia* (2016). She is the author of *Le Cinéma post-colonial français* (2006), as well as more than thirty book chapters and scholarly articles.

NOELLE HEDGCOCK holds a master's in English from Syracuse University. Her scholarly interests include nineteenth-century British literature and culture,

Victorian popular culture, afterlives and adaptation, and reception studies. She is the recipient of the 2017 Literature/Film Association Conference
Outstanding Graduate Student Paper Award.

TINA OLSIN LENT is professor of visual culture and director of the Museum
Studies Program at the Rochester Institute of Technology. Her research is
situated at the intersection of film studies, museum studies, and women's
and gender studies and is disseminated through traditional scholarly sources
and exhibitions.

RASHMILA MAITI holds a doctorate in comparative literature and cultural studies
from the University of Arkansas, Fayetteville. Originally from India, she is an
independent scholar who lives in Oregon. When not writing about books or
films, she volunteers as an editor and a social media coordinator for various
nonprofit organizations.

ALLEN H. REDMON is professor of English and film studies at Texas A&M University Central Texas. He is president of the Literature/Film Association. He
is the author of *Constructing the Coens: From* Blood Simple *to* Inside LLewyn
Davis (2015), and coeditor (with Charles R. Hamilton) of *Clint Eastwood's
Cinema of Trauma: Essays on PTSD in the Director's Films* (2017).

JACK RYAN is vice provost and dean of arts and humanities at Gettysburg
College. He has been a faculty member at the college for more than twenty-
five years in the Department of English. He is the author of *John Sayles:
Filmmaker,* and he contributes to *Aethlon: The Journal of Sport Literature.*

LARRY T. SHILLOCK is professor of English and college marshal at Wilson College.
He teaches in the areas of composition studies, critical theory, literary history,
and visual media. His recent work has appeared in the *Journal of Cultural and
Religious Theory, Interdisciplinary Humanities,* and *Moveable Type.* In the field
of adaptation studies, his interests span cognitive psychology and film noir,
especially with respect to the narrative contributions of the femme fatale.

RICHARD VELA is professor of English at the University of North Carolina at
Pembroke, where he teaches courses in Shakespeare, Latino literature, film,
and contemporary literature. He is area chair for Shakespeare on Film and
Television for the national PCA/ACA. He coauthored *Shakespeare into Film*
(2002). He is the author of the Shakespeare articles for *The Encyclopedia
of Orson Welles* (2003), and "Post-Apocalyptic Spaces in Baz Luhrmann's

Romeo + Juliet" in *Apocalyptic Shakespeare: Essays on Chaos and Revelation in Recent Film Adaptations* (2009). He also authored "Huston's Mexico" in *John Huston, Essays on a Restless Director* (2010).

GEOFFREY WILSON is an instructor in the School of Creative and Performing Arts at the University of Calgary. His research interests focus on representation and meaning in music from the art and popular music traditions and the intersection of music, language, and philosophy.

INDEX